雅思全攻略（基础版）

雅思考试必备，详尽知识梳理，实用策略指导，开启留学逐梦之路！

IELTS

All-in-One Guide (Basic Edition)

主　编：徐　坚　唐雪虹
主　审：杨　光
副主编：（按姓氏笔画排序）
　　　　卢　蕊　李　丹　张若碧　袁　曦

图书在版编目（CIP）数据

雅思全攻略：基础版 / 徐坚，唐雪虹主编.
成都：四川大学出版社，2025.3. -- ISBN 978-7-5690-7760-5

Ⅰ．H310.41

中国国家版本馆CIP数据核字第2025KB0526号

书　　名：	雅思全攻略（基础版）
	Yasi Quangonglüe （Jichu Ban）
主　　编：	徐　坚　唐雪虹
选题策划：	刘　畅　余　芳
责任编辑：	余　芳
责任校对：	刘　畅
装帧设计：	墨创文化
责任印制：	李金兰
出版发行：	四川大学出版社有限责任公司
	地址：成都市一环路南一段24号（610065）
	电话：（028）85408311（发行部）、85400276（总编室）
	电子邮箱：scupress@vip.163.com
	网址：https://press.scu.edu.cn
印前制作：	成都墨之创文化传播有限公司
印刷装订：	成都市新都华兴印务有限公司
成品尺寸：	210mm×285mm
印　　张：	17.25
字　　数：	601千字
版　　次：	2025年5月 第1版
印　　次：	2025年5月 第1次印刷
定　　价：	98.00元

扫码获取数字资源

四川大学出版社
微信公众号

本社图书如有印装质量问题，请联系发行部调换

版权所有　◆　侵权必究

前言

在全球化日益加深的今天，英语作为国际交流的通用语言，其重要性不言而喻。无论是求学深造、职业晋升，还是国际交流，良好的英语能力都是开启无限可能的钥匙。而雅思（IELTS）作为评估非母语者英语能力的权威考试之一，更是众多国内外高校、移民机构及职业认证认可的重要标准。

雅思考试，全称 International English Language Testing System，由英国文化教育协会、剑桥大学考试委员会外语考试部和澳大利亚教育国际开发署（IDP）共同管理，是全球范围内接受最广泛的英语语言能力测试之一。它不仅评估考生在听、说、读、写四个方面的英语能力，还注重考生在实际语境中运用语言的能力，确保考试成绩能够真实反映考生的英语水平。雅思考试分为学术类（Academic）和培训类（General Training）两种，前者主要针对申请国外大学或研究生课程的考生，后者则更侧重对移民、工作等非学术类需求的评估。考试内容涵盖了从日常生活到学术研究的广泛话题，确保考生能够全面展示自己的英语能力。

随着中国经济的快速发展和国际地位的提升，越来越多的中国学子选择走出国门，追求更多元的教育资源和更广阔的发展空间。因此，雅思考试在中国也迎来了前所未有的热潮。无论是高中生申请海外本科，还是大学生及职场人士寻求海外深造或工作机会，雅思成绩都成为他们不可或缺的"敲门砖"。同时，雅思考试因其公平性、科学性和广泛认可，赢得了众多考生和家长的信赖。

鉴于雅思考试在中国英语语言能力测试中的重要性和广泛影响力，我们精心编写了这本《雅思全攻略（基础版）》。本书旨在为准备参加雅思考试的考生提供全面而系统的基础阶段学习材料，帮助考生逐步建立扎实的语言基础，进一步提高雅思成绩。在内容编排上，本书紧扣雅思考试的四大板块——听力、阅读、写作和口语，通过丰富的例句、实用的技巧和详细的解析，帮助考生理解考试要求，掌握应试技巧。同时，我们还特别注重培养考生的英语思维能力和实际应用能力，让考生不仅能够提升考试成绩，更能够真正提升英语水平。

我们相信，通过本书的学习，广大考生一定能够在雅思考试中取得更好的成绩，开启自己精彩的人生旅程。让我们一起努力，向着梦想迈进！

在本教材的编写过程中四川大学教育培训部领导及同事们都给予了我们无私的指导和大力的支持。同时，教材能够出版也离不开四川大学出版社编审、校对、排版老师们的辛苦付出。在此向他们致以最诚挚的谢意。

目 录 CONTENTS

第一部分 雅思听力 ·· 01

1 雅思听力概述 ·· 02

1.1 雅思听力考试结构解析 ··· 02

1.2 雅思听力考试评分标准（A 类 /G 类）·· 02

1.3 雅思听力考试题型综述 ··· 03

    1.3.1 选择题 ··· 03

    1.3.2 匹配题 ··· 03

    1.3.3 标注题 ··· 03

    1.3.4 填空题 ··· 03

    1.3.5 句子完成题 ··· 04

    1.3.6 简答题 ··· 04

1.4 雅思听力基础能力提升及难点解析 ·· 04

    1.4.1 发音和辨音 ··· 04

    1.4.2 记录信息 ·· 06

    1.4.3 定位和捕捉信息 ··· 09

    1.4.4 理解文本大意和逻辑 ··· 09

2 雅思听力解题技巧与策略 ··· 11

2.1 雅思听力场景对话题 ·· 11

2.2 雅思听力标注题 ·· 13

    2.2.1 地图题 ··· 13

    2.2.2 物品标注题 ··· 14

2.3 雅思听力填空题 ·· 15

    2.3.1 听力填空练习题（一）·· 16

    2.3.2 听力填空练习题（二）·· 17

    2.3.3 听力填空练习题（三）·· 17

    2.3.4 笔记填空练习题 ··· 18

    2.3.5 流程图填空练习题 ·· 19

    2.3.6 概要填空练习题 ··· 20

2.4 雅思听力匹配题 ·· 20
　　2.4.1 听力匹配练习题（一） ··· 21
　　2.4.2 听力匹配练习题（二） ··· 21
2.5 雅思听力选择题 ·· 22
　　2.5.1 雅思听力选择题答题技巧 ·· 22
　　2.5.2 雅思听力选择练习题 ··· 23
2.6 雅思听力简答题 ·· 24
　　2.6.1 雅思听力简答题答题技巧 ·· 24
　　2.6.2 听力简答练习题 ··· 24

3 雅思听力模拟试题 ·· **25**

第二部分　雅思阅读 **43**

1 雅思阅读概述 ·· **44**
1.1 雅思阅读考试结构解析 ·· 44
1.2 雅思阅读考试评分标准 ·· 44
1.3 文章介绍 ·· 45
1.4 雅思阅读考试题型综述 ·· 45
　　1.4.1 完成句子题 ··· 45
　　1.4.2 摘要／表格／笔记／示意图题 ·· 46
　　1.4.3 简答题 ·· 46
　　1.4.4 判断题 ·· 46
　　1.4.5 选择题 ·· 46
　　1.4.6 段落标题配对题 ·· 46
　　1.4.7 特征匹配题 ··· 46
　　1.4.8 段落细节配对题 ·· 46
　　1.4.9 句子和结尾配对题 ··· 46
1.5 雅思高效阅读方法与策略 ··· 46

2 雅思阅读解题技巧与策略 ·· **48**
2.1 雅思阅读填空题 ·· 48
　　2.1.1 完成句子题 ··· 48
　　2.1.2 摘要／表格／笔记／流程图题 ·· 51
　　2.1.3 简答题 ·· 53
2.2 雅思阅读判断题 ·· 55
　　2.2.1 题型介绍 ·· 55
　　2.2.2 解题策略 ·· 55
　　2.2.3 解题步骤 ·· 55
　　2.2.4 真题解析 ·· 55

目 录

2.3 雅思阅读选择题 ·· 57
    2.3.1 题型介绍 ·· 57
    2.3.2 解题策略 ·· 57
    2.3.3 解题步骤 ·· 58
    2.3.4 分析原则 ·· 58
    2.3.5 真题解析 ·· 58
2.4 雅思阅读匹配题 ·· 61
    2.4.1 特征匹配题 ·· 61
    2.4.2 句首句尾匹配题 ·· 66
    2.4.3 段落信息匹配题 ·· 69
    2.4.4 标题匹配题 ·· 73

3 雅思阅读模拟试题 ·· 78

第三部分　雅思写作 ·· 111

1 雅思写作概述 ·· 112
1.1 雅思写作考试结构解析 ·· 112
1.2 雅思写作考试评分标准 ·· 112
    1.2.1 写作任务完成情况/回应情况 ·· 112
    1.2.2 连贯与衔接 ·· 113
    1.2.3 词汇丰富程度 ·· 113
    1.2.4 语法多样性及准确性 ·· 113
1.3 雅思写作考试题型综述 ·· 114
    1.3.1 Task 1（小作文）·· 114
    1.3.2 Task 2（大作文）·· 117

2 雅思写作基本要素与技巧 ·· 119
2.1 基本要素 ·· 119
    2.1.1 语法准确性 ·· 119
    2.1.2 词汇的积累与运用 ··· 126
    2.1.3 句子结构 ·· 129
    2.1.4 逻辑连贯性 ·· 133
2.2 Task 1 写作技巧 ··· 137
    2.2.1 图表作文简介 ·· 137
    2.2.2 数据图表作文写作技巧 ··· 137
    2.2.3 其他图表作文题写作技巧 ··· 146
    2.2.4 Task 1 写作技巧练习 ·· 152
2.3 Task 2 写作技巧 ··· 153
    2.3.1 Task 2 题型分类及作文结构 ·· 153

2.3.2 Task 2 写作技巧 ··· 153
　　2.3.3 不同题型作文的写作要点 ·· 160
　　2.3.4 范文分析 ·· 165
　　2.3.5 Task 2 写作技巧练习 ·· 170
3 雅思写作模拟试题 ··· **174**

第四部分　雅思口语 ·· **179**

1 雅思口语概述 ··· **180**
　1.1 雅思口语考试构成及流程 ··· 180
　1.2 雅思口语考试评分标准 ·· 181
　　1.2.1 流利性与连贯性 ··· 182
　　1.2.2 词汇多样性 ··· 182
　　1.2.3 语法多样性及准确性 ··· 182
　　1.2.4 语音 ··· 183
　1.3 雅思口语考试评分标准解析 ·· 183
　　1.3.1 发音与词汇：准确发音 ·· 183
　　1.3.2 发音与语法：语块和节奏 ··· 188
　　1.3.3 基于"发音、词汇、语法"的流畅 ··· 189
2 雅思口语答题技巧与策略 ·· **193**
　2.1 第一部分策略：攻克重点句型 ··· 193
　　2.1.1 "主谓宾"句型 ··· 194
　　2.1.2 "主系表"句型 ··· 195
　　2.1.3 There be 句型 ·· 196
　　2.1.4 It 开头的典型句型 ··· 197
　　2.1.5 被动语态的使用 ··· 198
　2.2 第二部分策略：攻克典型主题 ··· 200
　　2.2.1 描述时间 ·· 200
　　2.2.2 描述地点 ·· 202
　　2.2.3 描述人物 ·· 203
　　2.2.4 描述经历 ·· 205
　　2.2.5 描述过程 ·· 206
　2.3 第三部分策略：攻克问题模式，按需作答 ······································· 207
　　2.3.1 表达观点 ·· 207
　　2.3.2 解释及给出理由 ··· 209
　　2.3.3 比较 ··· 210
　　2.3.4 谈论过去与现在 ··· 212
　　2.3.5 表达赞同或反对 ··· 213

  2.3.6 推测未来 ………………………………………………………………………… 214
3 雅思口语模拟试题 …………………………………………………………………… **216**
  3.1 考场实战小贴士 …………………………………………………………………… 216
  3.2 雅思口语模拟试题 ………………………………………………………………… 217

参考文献 ………………………………………………………………………………… **218**

听力文本 ………………………………………………………………………………… **221**

参考答案 ………………………………………………………………………………… **241**

IELTS
All-in-One Guide
(Basic Edition)

第一部分
雅思听力

1 雅思听力概述

1.1 雅思听力考试结构解析

听力考试分为四个部分，每部分有 10 道题，总共 40 道题。问题的顺序与录音中的信息一致，因此第一个问题的答案往往会在第二个问题的答案之前，以此类推。从听力考试内容形式来讲，考试的第一部分和第三部分多为对话，第二部分和第四部分多为独白。从内容主题来讲，第一部分和第二部分涉及如订酒店、租车、旅行安排等日常社交情境，第三部分和第四部分涉及教育和培训情境。第三部分为两人或三人组成的对话（例如，两名大学生的讨论，或由导师引导的三人交谈），内容涉及学校学习生活等方面。第四部分多为学术讲座，内容涉及历史、艺术、经济管理等学术科目。

听力考试各部分时长以录音时间为准，誊抄或检查答案的时间根据考试模式有所不同：纸笔考试模式下，听力部分录音结束后需要将答案填写在答题纸上，考生有 10 分钟的时间完成这一步；机考模式下，听力部分录音结束后无须将答案填写到答题纸上，因此只有 2 分钟检查答案的时间。在填写答题纸和检查答案时应当小心，因为拼写错误和语法错误会扣分。整个听力部分，考生将只能听到一次录音。录音使用不同的英语口音，包括英国口音、澳大利亚口音、新西兰口音和北美口音。听力考试由多种题型组成，一个部分可能出现多种题型。听力答案根据题目要求，也有不同的字数限制，考生应注意仔细审题。另外，学术类（Academic）和培训类（General Training）雅思考试的听力部分考题都是一样的。

1.2 雅思听力考试评分标准（A 类 /G 类）

正确题目数	分数	正确题目数	分数
39–40	9.0	16–19	5.0
37–38	8.5	13–15	4.5
35–36	8.0	10–12	4.0
33–34	7.5	6–9	3.5
30–32	7.0	4–5	3.0

续表

正确题目数	分数	正确题目数	分数
27-29	6.5	3	2.5
23-26	6.0	2	2.0
20-22	5.5	1	1.0
缺席			0.0

1.3 雅思听力考试题型综述

1.3.1 选择题

选择题可能是一个问题，提供三个选项，或者题目是一个句子的前半句，提供三个可能的句子结尾。考生需要从 A、B、C 中选择一个正确答案，然后在答题纸上写下正确的字母。有时考生需要从更多选项中选择多个答案。应仔细审题，确认需要选择答案的数量。

这类题型测试多种听力技能，例如对特定观点的详细理解，或者对录音主要内容的总体理解能力。

1.3.2 匹配题

在回答匹配题的时候，考生需要将录音中的一系列内容与试题纸上的选项列表进行匹配，然后在答题纸上写下正确的字母。这类题型考查考生听取详细信息的能力。例如，是否能理解日常对话中关于旅馆或客房住宿类型的信息，是否能够理解两个人之间的对话，或者是否能够识别录音中的事实如何相互关联。

1.3.3 标注题

标注题要求考生根据录音中听到的信息，为可视化信息进行标注。这些信息可能是一个物品（例如一件设备）、一组图片、一个平面图（例如一个建筑的平面图），或者一张地图（例如一个城镇部分区域的地图）。标注题考查考生是否能够理解对于一个地方、物品、图片等的描述以及该描述与可视化图表的关系。它还可能考查考生是否能理解对物品位置的解释以及考生遵循指示的能力（例如直走、上楼梯等）。题目可能会以填空题或匹配题的形式出现。

1.3.4 填空题

在这种类型的题目中，考生需要根据录音填补题目中的空白。考点侧重于录音中的主要观点或事实，可能包括以下几种类型。

- 完成句子：捕捉文本中的细节信息。
- 笔记：总结信息并显示不同点之间的关系。
- 表格：总结可以分为明确类别的信息，例如姓名、地点、时间、价格。
- 流程图：总结过程中的各个阶段，并通过箭头显示过程的方向。

考生需要从录音中选择适合填补题目中空白的词语，同时需要遵循指示中给出的词数限制，但大部分情况下不需要以任何方式改变录音中的词语，所听即所写。

考生要仔细阅读指示，因为填补空白所允许的单词或数字数量可能会有所变化。指示中会给出字数限制，例如"最多两词和 / 或一个数字"。超过字数限制会导致失分。缩写词如"they're"不会被考查。带有连字符的词如"check-in"算作一个单词。

本题型侧重于考查考生是否能记录下听力材料中的要点。

1.3.5 句子完成题

句子完成题要求考生阅读总结包含重要信息的句子，这些信息可能来自整个听力文本或其中的某一部分。考生需要根据录音中的信息填补每个句子的空白。

这类题型侧重于考查考生识别录音中重要信息的能力，以及理解观点、事实和事件之间的关系（例如因果关系）的能力。

1.3.6 简答题

简答题的题量在雅思听力中相对较少，但也不能忽视练习。该题型要求考生阅读问题后使用录音中的信息写一个简短的答案。

与填空题一样，简答题要求考生仔细地阅读指示，因为要求用于填补空白的单词或数字数量可能会有所变化。指示中会给出字数限制，例如"最多两词和 / 或一个数字"。超过字数限制会导致失分。缩写词如"they're"不会被考查。带有连字符的词如"check-in"算作一个单词。有时可能会遇到要求考生写两个或三个不同答案的问题。

这种类型的问题侧重于考查考生听取录音中事实信息的能力，例如地点、价格、时间等。

1.4 雅思听力基础能力提升及难点解析

1.4.1 发音和辨音

大部分学习者会认为英语发音的准确性只影响口语得分，但实际上，它也是备战雅思听力考试应注重的基础能力。首先，英语中有一些常见的易错发音，这些发音容易混淆或者被误读。其次，要注意英语中的重音和轻音，因为重音的不同会改变单词的意思和词性。比如，"record"作名词时重音在第一个音节，读作 /ˈrekɔːd/，而作动词时重音在第二个音节，读作 /rɪˈkɔːd/。重音的错误会影响我们对听力文本中已知词汇的辨音。大量的听力训练、模仿和口语练习，可以提高英语发音和辨音能力。这一部分的练习对听力和口语都是有帮助的。

1.4.1.1 常见的易错发音

（1）字母的发音。

B P T　　B V W　　L M N　　A E　　G J

（2）/ð/ 和 /θ/：这两个音很多学习者都容易混淆。

/ð/　there　　that　　mother　　though

/θ/　thank　　mouth　　three　　thought

（3）/ɪ/ 和 /i:/：这两个音在发音上很相似，但它们的长度不同。

/ɪ/　pig　　hit　　sit　　ship

/i:/　sheep　　please　　agree　　team

（4）/v/ 和 /w/：这两个辅音在一些语言中并没有明显区别，容易混淆。

/v/　very　　voice　　view　　vehicle

/w/　was　　water　　worry　　word

（5）辅音 /l/ 的发音在词首和词尾时略有不同。在词首的发音为齿龈边音，跟中文发音类似，较好掌握；但在词尾的发音为软腭化的齿龈边音，很多学习者会把这个音与 /ɔ:/ 和 /ɜ:(r)/ 混淆。

/l/ 位于词首：lake　　look　　listen　　love

/l/ 位于词尾：all　　file　　towel　　bubble

（注：此处只关注听力中易忽视或发错的音，更多的发音规则和练习请学习第四部分"雅思口语"。）

在雅思听力考试中，拼写能力直接关系到考生的听力成绩，很多考生能够准确找到答案，但誊写答案时出现拼写错误导致无法得分。而拼写准确度除了反映考生的单词量，也反映考生对字母组合和发音关系的掌握。掌握了常见字母或字母组合的发音，背单词也能做到事半功倍。

1.4.1.2 常见的字母组合发音

（1）除 er 外可以发作 /ɜ:/ 的常见字母组合。

① ir/ɜ:/　first　　skirt　　dirt　　girl

Write vowel pair "ir" and read the words.

b___d　　f___　　s___　　sh___t　　fl___t

② or/ɜ:/　work　　word　　worth　　world

Write the vowel pair "or" and read the words.

w___se　　w___st　　w___m　　w___ker

③ ur/ɜ:/　burn　　turn　　hurt　　murder

Write vowel pair "ur" and read the words.

t___key　　t___n　　t___tle　　p___ple

（2）元音 ou 组合常常发作 /aʊ/ 和 /əʊ/，但除 ou 外，ow 组合也可以发这两个音。

① ow/aʊ/   down   town

Write the vowel pair "ow"/"ou" and read the words.

t____er   cl____n   h____l   br____n

② ow/əʊ/   follow   slow   tomorrow   blow

Write the vowel pair "ow" and read the words.

sn____   thr____   sh____   kn____   wind____

（3）元音 ei 组合常发 /eɪ/ 音，但除 ei 外，以下几个组合也可以发 /eɪ/ 音。

① ai/eɪ/   straight   train   afraid   rain

Write the vowel pair "ai" and read the words.

w____t   p____n   g____n   p____d   tr____t   sn____l   t____l

② ay/eɪ/   subway   today   pay   stay

Write the vowel pair "ay" and read the words.

s____   pl____   h____   J____   r____   cl____   w____

③ eigh/eɪ/   eight   weight

Write the vowel pair "eigh" and read the words.

sl____   n____bour

（4）字母 or 组合在一起常常发 /ɔː/ 音，但除 or 外，aw 也可以发 /ɔː/ 音。

aw/ɔː/   awful   crawl   saw   straw

Write the vowel pair "aw" and read the words.

dr____   l____yer   str____berry   y____n   ____ful   p____

（5）字母组合 ai 常发 /aɪ/ 音，但除 ai 之外，字母组合 igh 也可以发 /aɪ/ 音。

igh /aɪ/   right   tonight   light

Write the pair "igh" and read the words.

h____   m____t   br____t   he____t

1.4.2 记录信息

（1）句子听写，录音重复三遍。

（2）段落听写，录音重复三遍。

1.4.3 定位和捕捉信息

在英语听力题中,选择定位词是非常重要的,因为定位词可以帮助考生准确地理解听力材料中的信息并定位关键内容。以下是一些常用的定位词和使用技巧。

(1)时间词:时间词可以帮助确定事件发生的时间,例如:yesterday, tomorrow, next week, last month 等。通过时间词,可以更好地理解对话或文章中的时间线索。

(2)数字:数字可以帮助理解事件中涉及的数量,例如:two, three, fifty, hundred 等。数字可以帮助考生理解价格和货币单位,例如:$10, €20, 50 cents 等。

(3)地点词:地点词可以帮助确定事件发生的地点,例如:in the park, at the store, on the street 等。通过地点词,可以更好地理解对话或文章中的场景。

(4)人物词:人物词可以帮助确定谁在对话或文章中发言或参与事件,例如:John, Mary, the teacher, the doctor 等。通过人物词,可以更好地理解对话或文章中的人物关系和角色分配。

(5)动作词:动作词可以帮助理解事件中发生的动作或活动,例如:running, eating, talking, studying 等。通过动作词,可以更好地理解对话或文章中的事件发展和行为表达。

(6)关系词:关系词可以帮助理解事件之间的关联或逻辑关系,例如:because, although, however, therefore 等。通过关系词,可以更好地理解对话或文章中的逻辑推理和信息连接。

在选择定位词时,要注意根据听力内容的语境和逻辑关系进行推断,并结合上下文理解整个句子或段落的含义。通过练习,考生会逐渐提高对定位词的敏感度和准确性。

1.4.4 理解文本大意和逻辑

1.4.4.1 理解文本大意

理解听力文本的大意也是关键,以下是一些技巧,可以帮助考生更好地理解听力文本的大意。

(1)预览题目:在录音开始之前,快速预览听力题目,了解主题和关键信息,如题目中出现的标题、小标题、专有名词、数字、时间等信息。这有助考生在听录音的过程中更有针对性地聚焦关键内容。

(2)留意开场白:通常,录音尤其是独白类录音,说话人在开始时会简要地介绍主题和内容,留意这部分内容可以帮助考生快速了解录音的主题。

(3)抓关键词和关键信息:在听录音的过程中,留意文本中的关键词和关键信息,尤其是文本中的数字、名词等。这些关键信息通常能够帮助考生理解该部分录音内容的主题和重点。

(4)理解上下文:注意听力材料中的上下文信息,周围的句子和段落通常会提供线索,帮助考生理解关键信息的含义和作用,也能帮助考生猜测题目中生词的意思。

(5)注意语气和语调:注意讲者的语气和语调变化,这可以帮助考生更准确地理解说话人的情感和态度。

(6)理解逻辑关系:注意听力材料中不同信息之间的逻辑关系,如因果关系、转折关系等,帮助考生理解内容的逻辑结构和思路发展。在下一个部分会具体讲解。

1.4.4.2 理解文本逻辑

对录音文本逻辑的理解贯穿雅思听力的四个部分。但在雅思听力的第四部分,理解逻辑显得尤其重要。第四部分主要是关于学术场景或讲座的内容，通常会包括一段长篇讲座或演讲的部分内容，涉及各种学术话题，如科学、历史、文化、社会学等。这一部分录音内容更具学术性，因此词汇和句型也更复杂，而这往往就给考生理解录音内容造成了障碍。理解讲座内容的逻辑，如因果、转折等，能够帮助考生在冗长且复杂的录音中找出演讲者的思路，并最终获得答案的线索。以下是理解录音的关键。

（1）主题思路：要抓住主题思路，了解讲座或演讲的主要内容和目的。考生常常会因为急于关注具体的题目而忽视录音的开头。演讲者通常会在讲座的开头或开场白中明确介绍主题和讲座内容安排，帮助考生迅速抓住讲座内容的逻辑结构。

（2）段落结构：要注意讲座或演讲的段落结构。讲座或演讲通常会有明确的段落划分，每个段落讨论一个特定的话题或论点。段落结构也可能会更直接地体现在笔记填空题等题目的小标题中。理解段落结构有助于考生更好地跟随演讲者的思路和逻辑去寻找答案。

（3）逻辑连接词：注意听力材料中的逻辑连接词，它们可以帮助考生理解不同观点或信息之间的关系。以下是一些雅思听力常见的逻辑连接词。

①转折词：

but, however, yet, while, whereas, by contrast, on the other hand, on the contrary

although, though, despite, in spite of

in fact, actually, instead

②因果关系词：

because, since, as, for, due to, the reason that, because of, result from

so, therefore, as a result of, result in, lead to

③并列、递进词：

and, or, another, the other, a second / third one, besides, moreover, furthermore, in addition

④顺序词：

firstly, secondly, thirdly...

to start with / begin with, at first, in / at the beginning, originally

then, next, after that, afterwards

finally, lastly, at the end of, in conclusion, to sum up

（4）阐述观点的逻辑：雅思录音材料中，尤其是第四部分的讲座中，演讲者可能会提出多个观点或论据。考生应具备迅速抓住文本主题句，分清主题句和论据的能力，要能根据上面所列举的顺序词等听出演讲者是否已经从某个观点过渡到另一个观点。同时，考生也应理解演讲者的态度，分析演讲者对这些观点是否持有积极或消极的态度。

2 雅思听力解题技巧与策略

2.1 雅思听力场景对话题

听力场景对话题多出现在雅思听力的第一部分，场景涉及日常生活的各个方面，旨在检测考生理解各类场景对话的能力。常见的雅思听力场景有租房、租车、求职、维修、就医、旅行安排、教育咨询、失物招领等。听力录音多为男女对话，以便考生分清录音中的说话人。此类题型多以各类填空题（如表格题等）的形式出现，但也可能出现选择题。

下面，我们以剑桥真题为例来分析雅思听力场景对话题的特点，解析答题技巧。

第一步：了解题干要求

SECTION 1   *Questions 1–10*

Complete the form below.

*Write **ONE WORD AND/OR A NUMBER** for each answer.*

（Cambridge ESOL，2007：55）

应首先注意如上题题干中的字数限制信息：Write ONE WORD AND/OR A NUMBER for each answer。考生拿到试卷，往往着急去看试题而忘记关注题干中的重要信息，并因此而丢分。此处题干要求为"每个答案填写一个单词和／或一个数字"，这表明答案有可能是一个单词或数字，也可能由一个单词加一个数字组成，同时也意味着数字并不包含在对字数的限制中。考生在审题时应细心谨慎，以免在一些不必要的地方丢分。

第二步：仔细审题，了解对话的主题

题干阅读完后，考生应关注对话的主题。雅思听力场景对话题的开头都会出现标题，而这也是考生容易忽略的部分。以下列剑桥真题听力第一部分场景对话标题为例。OPENING A BANK ACCOUNT 意为"开立一个银行账户"。阅读标题后就能了解本题的对话场景为银行，因此对话内容和词汇范围应与此相关。了解这一信息对接下来理解对话的逻辑和通过听到的发音辨别应该填入的答案都很有帮助。

```
         OPENING A BANK ACCOUNT

    Example                    Answer
    Application for a          Current bank account
```

（Cambridge ESOL，2007：55）

第三步：仔细审题，预测答案

这一部分涉及具体的每道考试题，考生应利用给出的看题时间迅速浏览题目，参加纸笔考试的考生应同时勾画出题目的关键词，以便听录音时能迅速地定位到题目的关键信息。

比如，下面的题目第 2 题和第 3 题中，Date of birth 和 Current address 都是核心词，考生应该能轻松判断出此处应填生日和地址，但却容易忽略核心词中的细节信息 Date 和 Current。其中，Date 表明此处除了能分析出要填时间，且应该细化到要填的是日期而不是星期几。Current 则表明应填写当前地址，暗示文本中多半会提及一个之前的地址来混淆视听，作为陷阱答案。因此，在看题的时候考生应认真仔细。

Date of birth: 2......................

Joint account holder(s):   No

Current address: 3...................... Exeter

（Cambridge ESOL，2007：55）

以下总结一些雅思听力场景对话题常考内容以及书写细节。

（1）姓名（Name）。

姓：Surname, Family name, Last name

名：First name, Given name

中间名：Middle name

姓名多为逐个字母念出，考查学生对字母准确发音的掌握，这在本部分 1.4 雅思基础能力提升及难点解析中已有练习。

（2）日期（Date）。

Date 的写法可以用完整形式，也可以用标准缩写，如：一月 January（Jan.），二月 February（Feb.）。但不能用简单的如 1.1 表示 1 月 1 日。举例来说，1 月 1 日可以有以下写法：

1st January（Jan.），January（Jan.）1st

（3）地址（Address）。

英文的地址与中文的书写规范不同，出现在地址最前面的通常是门牌号（门牌号可能是纯数字也可能是数字+字母），因此在审题时应观察所填信息在地址中的位置。以下为地址拼写中容易被忽视的有关"道路"的说法：

Avenue	大道，大街	Lane	小巷，小路
Alley	小街，小巷	Drive	车道

（4）货币（Currency）。

雅思听力考试中涉及货币拼写的部分多考查美金dollar（$），英镑pound（£）和欧元euro（€）。在书写答案时既可以写单词也可以使用货币符号，但由于dollar等单词前面加上数字可能需要使用复数形式，容易被遗忘，所以更推荐以符号代替。同时也应注意带小数点的货币值的读法，如：$8.50读作eight dollars fifty cents。

考查货币的信号词有pay，price，rate，salary，wage等。

第四步：检查答案

看似最简单的场景对话，其实也是最容易丢分的部分，因为轻敌所以容易粗心大意。检查答案尤其是拼写和单复数形式等语法细节是考生答题时应有的重要步骤。

2.2 雅思听力标注题

雅思听力标注题要求考生根据录音中听到的信息，为可视化信息进行标注。这些信息可能是一个物品（例如一件设备）、一组图片、一个平面图（例如一个建筑的平面图），或者一张地图（例如一个城镇部分区域的地图）。标注题考查考生是否能够理解关于地方、物品、图片等的描述以及该描述与可视化图表的关系。它还可能考查理解物品位置的解释以及遵循指示的能力（例如直走、上楼梯等）。

下面，我们以剑桥真题为例来分析雅思听力地图题、物品标注题的特点，解析答题技巧。

2.2.1 地图题

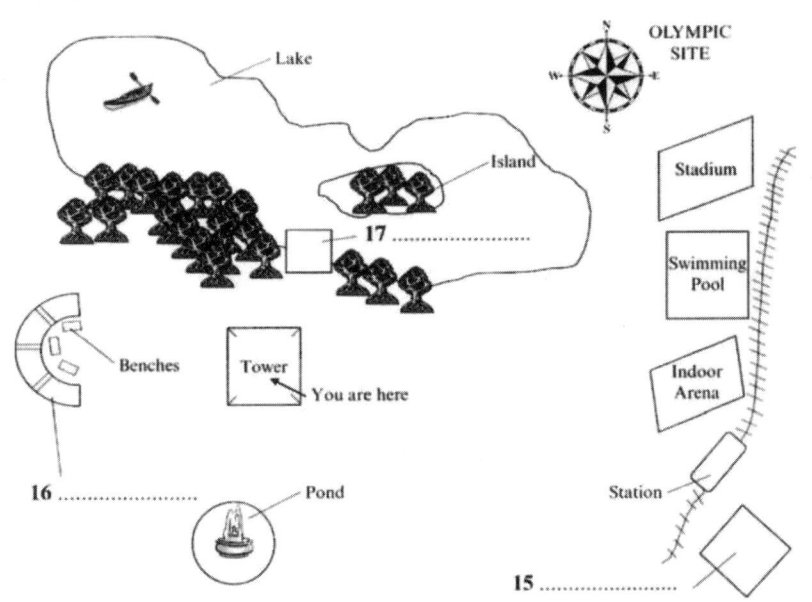

（Cambridge ESOL，2009：84）

第一步：预览地图

在录音开始之前，考生应仔细查看地图。注意已提供的标注以及它们所在的位置，如上图中的 Lake, Island, Stadium 等，或出现的建筑的形状（如长方形的建筑、环形的路等），比如本题中 Benches 后面环形的建筑、长方形的 Station 等，并尝试理解整体布局。同时，注意观察图上是否有指南针，如上题图中包含指南针，考生需要熟悉东、西、南、北等八个方向。

第二步：找到起始点

上图中的 You are here，或其他题目里面的 Entrance, Hotel 等地点都常常被用作起始点。应注意地图中的关键词，关键词可能包括方向（左、右、南、北）、具体地点、建筑等，如图中的 Lake, Island, Stadium 等。尤其需要关注角落里容易漏掉的点，如图中的 Station。

第三步：做笔记

听的过程中做简短的笔记或记下关键词。可以用画箭头的方式速记路线。这有助于考生记住关键细节，并在录音播放结束后将它们与地图匹配。

以图中的 16 题为例，根据录音文本内容可以做如下速记：

West—benches—rose garden

第四步：定位答案

通过大量练习标注题，熟悉常见的指示方位的单词和表达，培养迅速定位答案的能力。

以下是地图题的常见单词和表达：

road, avenue, street, path, track, corner, center, left, right, top, down, bottom, north, south, west, east

go through, go pass, go straight, go over, at the end of, at the far end, walk down to the back of, at the corner of, in the far left/right corner

A is across the road from B.

A is opposite B.

第五步：检查答案

查看听题时漏填或只记了笔记还未作答的题目，补填答案。检查答案尤其是填空题的拼写和单复数形式等语法细节，这是考生答题时应有的重要步骤。

2.2.2 物品标注题

物品标注题做法与地图题类似，尤其是对物品零部件位置的描述与地图题类似。

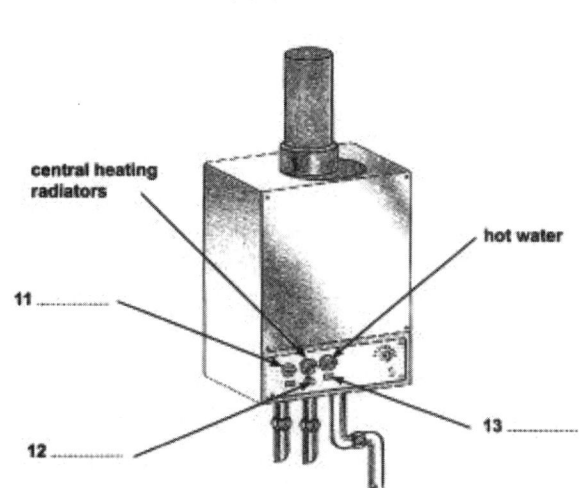

(Cambridge ESOL，2011：81）

物品标注题需要考生仔细观察箭头所指的位置，通常会用类似地图题的方位词来指示。如：本题中 12 题和 13 题所指的零部件分别在 central heating radiators 和 hot water 的下方，可能会用它们作为参照物，并用 under 或者 below 来描述。而 11 题所指示的零部件可能会以 central heating radiators 为参照物，并用用 next to 或者 to the left of 来指示。

下面是一些常见的方位指示词：

inside, outside, above, over, between, below, beside, at the top, on the left/right, in the middle, in front of, to the right/left (of), at the bottom, at the end of

物品标注题考查考生对物品整体和各部分形状的描述，以下是一些常见的表达：

square	square
rectangle	rectangular
triangle	triangular
semicircle	semicircular
circle	circular
cube	cubic
cylinder	cylindrical

n. is shaped like + *n.*

n. is + *adj.* + in shape.

n. is + *adj.*

be fixed to, be fitted over/to/into, be connected/linked to

2.3 雅思听力填空题

雅思官网将雅思听力的填空题分为两小类：第一类，信息表、笔记、表格、流程图和梗概题（form/note/table/flow chart/summary completion）。第二类，句子完成题（sentence completion）。

因为信息表题型多出现在 Part 1 的场景题中，而场景题又是雅思听力的重要题型，所以本书在听力 2.1 部分已经对场景题及信息表题型做了详细的讲解，此处不再赘述。其他题型完成方式有相似性，此处一起归纳讲解。

完成填空题需要先看题干中标出的答案字数要求，而这一点容易被考生忽略。如果题目中有图、标题、小标题、单词释义等，也需要耐心关注。之后，考生需要完成雅思听力填空题最重要的步骤：预测答案，即预测空格中应填词的词性，词的类型，如人或物、数字、动物等，以及关注语法细节，如名词的单复数等。录音开始播放后，在听题时应关注强调信号。在录音中会有些迹象表明重要信息即将出现，比如会有语音、语调信号，像短暂停顿、重读、音调等；同时，也会出现逻辑强调信号，比如因果、举例、列举等连接词；还有一些单词和句子本身就表示重要或是"重要"一词的替换表达，如 important, significant, above all, what makes it different is that… 等。在读题、听题时，考生要小心句序的前后颠倒，不要认为答案只会在某一个定位词的前或后出现，也建议不要仅依靠一个定位词来定位答案。当然，要做好填空题，考生还应具备同义转换的能力，这其实也是整个雅思考试的重点技能。

下面是填空题的技能训练。

2.3.1 听力填空练习题（一）

*Write **NO MORE THAN THREE WORDS AND/OR A NUMBER** for each answer.*

1 Black .... live throughout most of North America, including .... Mexico.

2 In fact the animal may travel .... miles a day to ....

3 When you arrive at the .... bay, you could see some ....

4 These rabbits often live on the .... of fields, farms, and other .... far from highly .... areas.

5 Your assignment should create a favorable .... to the examiner, this implies that your work should be orderly, utilize .... and ensure that your points are clearly spelt out and use .... referencing style.

2.3.2 听力填空练习题（二）

*Write **NO MORE THAN THREE WORDS AND/OR A NUMBER** for each answer.*

1. If you don't pass a course on your first try, you might have the option to take a ....

2. The cost covers a reef education lecture, a lunch buffet with .... options, and some water activities.

3. Students will be informed the ...., the necessary steps for successful completion, and the ....

4. There are materials available, but they are insufficient to support the .... goal. Additionally, in your presentation you provide some materials which are ....

5. We wanted to understand how blind individuals utilize .... to perceive moving objects. Our research revealed that individuals who became blind in ....showed superior abilities in tracking sounds compared to sighted individuals.

2.3.3 听力填空练习题（三）

请写出段落中的逻辑连接词。

表示递进	
表示对比	
表示原因/结果	
表示顺序	

2.3.4 笔记填空练习题

*Write **NO MORE THAN THREE WORDS AND/OR A NUMBER** for each answer.*

Artificial Intelligence（AI）

Definition: simulates human intelligence in machines programmed to think and imitate human 1 ....

Applications ranges from

- Virtual help: e.g. Siri

- 2 .... and money management

- Machine learning, as AI's key components can make 3 .... and predictions based on data analysis and learning.

AI functions:

- In healthcare: can analyse images and find patterns that 4 .... is unable to see.

- In finance: can tell market trends and find fraudulent transactions based on the analysis of large amounts of data.

Ethical concerns of AI

- Privacy

- In the job market, 5 .... among many people may occur because of the automation of AI.

2.3.5 流程图填空练习题

*Write **NO MORE THAN THREE WORDS AND/OR A NUMBER** for each answer.*

How coffee is processed?

Step 1: Harvesting the Coffee Beans

2 processes: strip picking and **1** .... picking

---

⬇

Step 2: Separation

Two methods: Wet and dry.

Wet: overripe and underdeveloped parts float

Dry: harvested cherries can be separated by **2** .... and also by machines

---

⬇

Step 3: Processing and Drying the Cherries

3 main methods

⬇

Step 4: Hulling and Polishing

Hullers: the outer covering of the bean are removed

Polishing: **3** .... are removed.

⬇

Step 5: Cleaning, Sorting, and Grading

Multiple methods are applied to sort and clean the **4** .... coffee.

⬇

Step 6: Roasting

Beans are roasted in large metal cylinders.

During the process: beans swell

darken in color

develop roasted **5** ....

And now you can brew and enjoy your coffee.

2.3.6 概要填空练习题

Write **NO MORE THAN THREE WORDS AND/OR A NUMBER** for each answer.

> The key to communicating effectively with your child is to use **1** .... in diverse scenarios. For instance, you can talk about an orange ball or cutting up an orange for lunch. When your child starts making communicating attempts such as cooing, gurgling, blowing raspberries or pointing, you should **2** .... to them promptly and appropriately. When the child starts using words, you can **3** .... them skillfully and encouragingly. Linking the content in the book to **4** .... actively and meaningfully helps the child talk. A significant and reliable source of books is **5** .... library.

2.4 雅思听力匹配题

雅思听力匹配题要求考生将一系列选项与给定的描述或问题进行匹配。这种题型通常会提供多个选项和多个描述，考生需要仔细聆听录音内容，理解其中的关键信息，并准确地将其与相应的选项进行匹配。

匹配题的一个特殊题型是分类匹配题。在这类题目中，考生的任务是根据听到的录音内容，将每个项目或描述准确地归类到相应的类别中。分类匹配题旨在考查考生对所听信息的综合理解、细节捕捉以及逻辑分类能力。它能够反映出考生在复杂听力语境中准确获取和处理关键信息的能力。

答题技巧：

第一步，注意看问题。匹配题在题目番号和题干要求之间有一个问题，容易被考生忽略。看完问题会对整个题目要求重点关注的信息有一个了解。

第二步，浏览选项。在录音开始播放之前，迅速浏览所有的选项，对其内容有一个大致的了解，注意关键词和关键信息。

第三步，抓关键信息。听录音的过程中，集中注意力抓取描述中的关键信息，如人名、地名、时间、数字、特定的名词等，这些往往是匹配的重要依据。

第四步，做笔记。对于听到的重要信息，可以简单做笔记，帮助记忆和后续的匹配。

第五步，注意同义替换。听力材料中的表述可能不会与选项完全一致，要留意同义替换和表达方式的转换。

第六步，排除法。如果听到某个描述明显与某些选项不匹配，可以先将其排除，缩小选择范围。

第七步，复查。完成匹配后，如有剩余时间，快速复查一遍，确保答案的准确性。

以下是听力匹配题的技能练习。

2.4.1 听力匹配练习题（一）

Which tourist groups are the following tourist destinations most suitable for respectively?

Write and correct letter A to G for each question.

Options:

A	Young people who are fond of shopping and urban art
B	Retired elders looking for a quiet environment
C	Families fond of sports and seafood
D	Tourists desiring life and joys in the countryside
E	Travelers interested in history and culture
F	Couples looking for places full of romance
G	Solo travelers seeking adventure and exploration

Questions:

1 Destination One ....
2 Destination Two ....
3 Destination Three ....
4 Destination Four ....
5 Destination Five ....

2.4.2 听力匹配练习题（二）

Match each project with the correct person.

Options:

A	Mary only
B	Tom only
C	Both Mary and Tom
D	Neither Mary nor Tom

1 Project One ....

2 Project Two ....

3 Project Three ....

4 Project Four ....

2.5 雅思听力选择题

2.5.1 雅思听力选择题答题技巧

雅思听力选择题是雅思听力考试中的常见题型之一。该题型分为单项选择题和多项选择题，答题技巧基本一致。选择题考查考生对细节、主旨、观点、态度等方面的理解，同时也是同义替换体现得最突出的题型。

答题技巧：

第一步，提前审题。

在听力开始前的看题时间，尽快浏览题目和选项，抓住关键词，对题目内容有一个大致的了解。参加纸笔考试的考生应勾画关键词，帮助定位信息，如：题目是关于学习生活主题的对话，关键词可能是人名，提示关注原因的词如 because、reason，提示关注态度的词如 feel、attitude，等等。

第二步，在听题过程中，应关注文本中的转折词。

but、however、yet 等词后面的内容往往是关键信息。比如，听力中说：The event was supposed to be held outdoors, but due to the bad weather, it was moved indoors. 这里的 but 就提示了重要的变化，极可能出现在考点中。

注意同义替换。听力原文中可能不会直接出现选项中的原词，而是用同义词或同义表达来表述。例如，选项是 increase，听力原文中可能会说 grow 或 rise。考前练习时应注意收集常见同义词，这些词汇在其他听力题型，甚至在阅读、写作、口语练习中也是用得上的。

第三步，排除干扰项。

有些选项可能会故意设置一些容易混淆的信息，要仔细分辨，根据听到的内容排除明显错误的选项。

比如，有以下三个选项：A. The project was completed on time. B. The project was delayed because of lack of funds. C. The project was ahead of schedule. 如果听到 The project was still not finished as planned. 就可以排除 A 和 C 选项。

第四步，做好笔记。

在听的过程中，可以简单记录一些关键信息，如时间、地点、人名等。尤其是对于无法立刻做出判定或者纠结于某两个答案的题，笔记可以帮助考生在检查或者誊抄答案的过程中回忆和分析题目。

以下是雅思听力选择题的技能练习。

2.5.2 雅思听力选择练习题

Questions 1–5

Choose the correct letter A, B or C.

1 The tourists are advised to bring

    A   warm clothes.

    B   raincoats.

    C   sunglasses.

2 The best way to explore the local area is

    A   by bike.

    B   on foot.

    C   by bus.

3 The local food is famous for

    A   spicy dishes.

    B   sweet desserts.

    C   fresh seafood.

4 The most popular tourist attraction in the city is

    A   an ancient palace.

    B   a modern museum.

    C   a beautiful park.

5 When is the peak tourist season in this place?

    A   Spring.

    B   Summer.

    C   Winter.

2.6 雅思听力简答题

2.6.1 雅思听力简答题答题技巧

雅思听力简答题可能出现在听力考试的任何一个部分。虽然是简答题，但仍然有对答案字数的要求，考生在答题时应关注答案的字数限制。简答题的题目多为特殊疑问句，需要考生根据文本给出包含具体含义的词作为答案。

答题技巧：

简答题的答题技巧与其他题型基本一致，唯一不同的是考生在审题时需要关注问题中的疑问词，对答案进行初步预测，这有助于考生在听题过程中更快地捕捉到相关信息。

比如，如果问题是How much does the ticket cost？，看题时应关注到疑问词是how much，那么在听题过程中，应集中注意力倾听与问题相关的数字和货币单位等重要信息。

另外，答题时需注意语法和格式，在检查答案或誊抄答案的过程中，应快速检查拼写错误和语法问题，确保答案的准确性。

以下是雅思听力简答题技能练习。

2.6.2 听力简答练习题

Answer the following questions 1-3.

*Write **NO MORE THAN THREE WORDS AND/OR A NUMBER** for each answer.*

Question 1: What is the name of the hotel the speaker stayed in?

....

Question 2: How long did the tour last?

....

Question 3: Who did the speaker travel with?

....

3 雅思听力模拟试题

Test 1

PART 1 Questions 1–10

Complete the notes below.

*Write **NO MORE THAN THREE WORDS AND/OR A NUMBER** for each answer.*

Job Interview

Work experience:	**1** More than ....
Qualifications of the Applicant:	Can type 100 words in one minute
	2 Proficient in ....
	3 Good .... skills
	Organised
	4 ....
Job responsibilities:	**5** .... office workers
	Handle correspondence
	6 Arrange ....
	Manage front desk
Office hours:	**7** 8.30 to ....
Work benefits:	**8** Covers medical and .... expense
	A pension plan
	9 .... holiday annually
Possible time to start working:	**10** .... of next month

PART 2   Questions 11–20

Question 11

Choose the correct letter A, B or C.

11   Where is Redang Island located?

   A   Summer Tea Island
   B   Malaysian Islands
   C   Redang Island Marine Park

Questions 12–14

Choose THREE letters, A–G.

12–14   What are the main attractions of Redang Island mentioned in the recording?

   A   Beautiful sunset
   B   Dense tropical rainforest
   C   Gorgeous mountain view
   D   Pebble beach
   E   Crystal-like waters
   F   Historic sites
   G   Diverse marine life

Questions 15–20

Complete the table below.

Time	Activities	Price
Day 1 afternoon	Visiting Langzhong Island	Total: **15** ....
Day 2 morning	**16** 1-hour .... session Observing and feeding fish	Discounted price: **17** ....
Day 2 afternoon	**18** .... Enjoying an afternoon tea	free
Day 3	Diving **19** .... Canoeing Boating	**20** .... for members

PART 3 Questions 21–30

Questions 21–27

Choose the correct letter A, B or C.

21 What can be inferred about the recent exams from Sam and Mohit's conversation?

    A   They found the re-exam to be more challenging than the initial exams.

    B   They both struggled with the board exams but found Economics particularly difficult.

    C   They are relieved that this year's exams were easier compared to last year.

22 What is Mohit's major career plan?

    A   He is determined to become a chemist.

    B   He will go into medicine.

    C   He plans to enroll only in a B.Sc course.

23 What is Sam uncertain about regarding his career plans?

    A   Whether he should pursue engineering like most of his classmates.

    B   Whether he should enroll in a B.Sc course after school.

    C   Whether he should switch to a career in medicine.

24 What is Gary's current occupation?

    A   Doctor.

    B   Engineer.

    C   Photographer.

Questions 25–27

Choose THREE letters, A–G.

25–27 As for Sam, compared with engineering, what are better for graduation?

    A   Business

    B   Photography

    C   Legal practice

    D   MBA

E   Science
F   Economics
G   Education

Questions 28–30

Complete the sentences below.

*Write **NO MORE THAN THREE WORDS AND/OR A NUMBER** for each answer.*

28 Mohit believed .... is a better choice than science for Sam. However, Sam worried this would disappoint his parents.

29 A .... workshop will be conducted via Internet by Pep education.

30 The workshop they agreed to go offers a .... discount for students.

PART 4   Questions 31–40

Complete the notes below.

*Write **NO MORE THAN TWO WORDS AND/OR A NUMBER** for each answer.*

Schools of psychology

Structuralists School

Major players:

● Wundt: regarded as the first true psychologist.

● Titcherner: one of Wundt's **31** ....

Players were especially influenced by scientific field: **32** ....

Introspection: A specific **33** .... is reflected and analyzed by an observer who has received training.

E.g. a person break a table down into basic elements.

Important things for the structuralists:

● Experience

● **34** .... mind

● Thoughts can be broken down into other simple thoughts

● Empiricism: information compiled through observation and **35** ....

Problems of the structuralism

E.g. Breaking down the concept of love

Different things are included in love: intimacy, **36** ...., compassion, etc.

Problems: no reliability, no validity, etc.

Gestalt School

Three major players were Kohler, Werner, and Kofka.

Contrary to structuralists, Gestaltists believe that the **37** .... is more significant than the sum of the components.

Functionalism School

There are several major players like: James, Hall, Cattell, and Angel.

The Functionalists focused on understanding the workings of the **38** ....

Behaviorist School

There are many players that will be involved in this school: Watson, Hull, etc.

Belief: Science can't study the mind, consciousness, images and things alike, because they are impossible to be **39** ....

Animals were used to discover fundamental laws, drawing from the concepts of **40** ....

Test 2

PART 1 Questions 1–10

Questions 1–6

Complete the notes below.

Write **NO MORE THAN TWO WORDS AND/OR A NUMBER** for each answer.

CHILDREN'S MUSIC WORKSHOPS

Workshops organised every Sunday

Adults must accompany children under **1** ....

Cost: £3.00

Workshops held in Spring Hall, **2** .... Street

Security device: must enter the **3** .... to open the door

Should leave customer's car in front of the **4** ....

Book workshops by phoning **5** ....

Name of the booking staff: **6** ....

Questions 7–10

Complete the table below.

*Write **NO MORE THAN TWO WORDS** for each answer.*

Next two workshops

Date	Workshop title	Children advised to wear	Bring (if possible)
December 18th	Playing 7	Comfortable clothes	8 ....
December 25th	9	(Nothing special)	10 ....

PART 2   Questions 11–20

Questions 11–13

Which department will handle each of the following tasks?

*Choose **THREE** answers from the box and write the correct letter, **A–G**, next to questions 11–13.*

Departments

- **A** Finance Department
- **B** Marketing Department
- **C** HR Department
- **D** IT Department
- **E** Legal Department
- **F** Customer Service Department
- **G** Research and Development Department

Tasks

11 Financial reports preparation ....

12 Product launch event ....

13 Employee training sessions ....

Questions 14–20

Complete the table below. Write **NO MORE THAN THREE WORDS AND/OR A NUMBER** *for each answer.*

Company Meeting: Temporary Staff Training Programme

Time Event Details

8.30 am   Talk by John: Information about benefits

                  Will hand out the **14** .... cards

9.00 am   Talk by Mary Smith: Will discuss office layout

                  Will explain about arrangements for **15** .... setups and air conditioning

9.30 am   Tea Break: Go to staff lounge on the **16** .... floor

10.00 am   Presentation: Go to **17** .... room

                  Presentation title: Prospects and **18** ....

11.00 am   Group Discussion in **19** .... hall

12.00   Buffet Lunch: Go to the **20** .... area

PART 3　　Questions 21–30

Questions 21–22

Complete the sentences below.

*Write **NO MORE THAN TWO WORDS** for each answer.*

The student has to finish a project on **21** ....

The professor suggested reading books written by **22** ....

Questions 23–25

Choose the correct letter, A, B or C.

23 Besides reading materials, the main difficulty the student is facing is

    A lack of time.

    B difficult research materials.

    C unclear assignment requirements.

24 The student plans to do extra research in the

    A library.

    B laboratory.

    C online database.

25 The best time for the student to meet the professor for feedback is

    A Monday morning.

    B Wednesday afternoon.

    C Friday evening.

Questions 26–28

Complete the table below.

*Write **NO MORE THAN THREE WORDS** for each answer.*

Tasks	Progress	Next Steps
Prepare presentation slides	Half done	Add more 26 ....
Write a summary	Not 27	Finish by next week
Revise the essay	In progress	Check 28 .... and citations

Questions 29–30

*Choose **TWO** letters, A–E.*

29–30 Which **TWO** benefits of group study are mentioned?

    A   Sharing thoughts

    B   Reducing conflicts

    C   Reducing stress

    D   Enhancing communicative abilities

    E   Easier to access resources

PART 4   *Questions 31–40*

Questions 31–35

*Complete the notes below. Write **NO MORE THAN TWO WORDS** for each answer.*

LECTURE ON NUTRITION

Preparation for discussion on healthy eating includes understanding **31** ....

Important elements of a healthy diet are:

● Fruits

● **32** ....

● Whole grains

Earliest understanding of healthy eating: It was mainly focused on **33** ....

But:

● Why are some people resistant to changing their diet?

    Possible reasons: habits, **34** .... preferences, etc.

● Why are certain diets not suitable for everyone?

People's unique bodies and metabolisms
- Why is it hard to stick to a healthy diet?
  Attractions to junk food, a lack of time or knowledge about proper nutrition, etc.

More recent approach:

Emphasizes personalized **35** ....

Questions 36–40

Complete the sentences below.

*Write **NO MORE THAN TWO WORDS** for each answer.*

A new study shows that diet can affect our **36** .... significantly.

People with certain health conditions need to be careful about their **37** ....

Excessive consumption of processed foods can lead to **38** ....

We should include more **39** .... in our diet for better health.

Combining a healthy diet with moderate training and **40** .... can lead to healthier bodies.

Test 3

PART 1   Questions 1–10

Questions 1–5

Complete the form below.

*Write **ONE WORD AND/OR A NUMBER** for each answer.*

Renting Apartment

Name: Sarah Taylor
No. of bedrooms: **1** ....
Purpose of renting: internship
Preferred location: **2** near the .... or city centre
Maximum monthly rent: **3** ....
Length of let required: nine months
Starting date: **4** ....
Proof of identity: **5** ....

Questions 6–10

Complete the table below.

*Write **ONE WORD AND/OR A NUMBER** for each answer.*

Address	Rooms	Rent	Problems
Oak Lane	living room, separate kitchen	£580	no **6** ....
7 .... Street	large living room and kitchen	£720	the kitchen is **8** .... expensive
Cedar Road	bathroom and a storage room	**9**	too far from public transport
Rose Square	living room, kitchen-diner, and a **10**	£700	next to a busy main road

PART 2 Questions 11–20

Questions 11–15

*Match the letters **A** to **G** in the diagram with the **Questions 11 to 15**.*

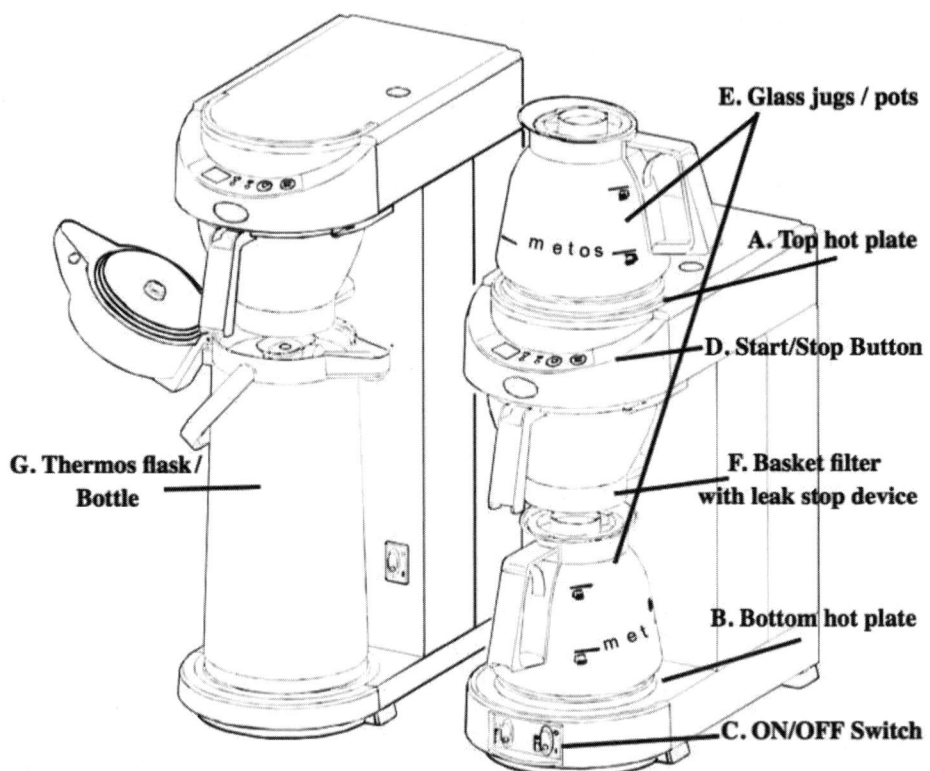

11 Used to start using the machine
12 Used to begin or pause the process when making the coffee
13 Used to contain coffee
14 Guarantee coffee will not be made without a jug under the filter
15 Keep the coffee warm

Questions 16–20

Choose the correct letter, A, B or C.

16 The landlord recommends going to the local beach in the morning because

    A It's less crowded.

    B The water is warmer.

    C The sun is not too strong.

17 For those interested in history, the landlord suggests visiting

    A The old castle.

    B The local museum.

    C The ancient market.

18 If you enjoy outdoor activities, the landlord advises trying

    A   Hiking in the mountains.

    B   Cycling around the town.

    C   Boating on the river.

19 The best time to explore the local park is

    A   Afternoon.

    B   Evening.

    C   Early morning.

20 To experience the local culture, the landlord recommends

    A   Attending a local festival.

    B   Visiting a traditional village.

    C   Trying the local cuisine.

PART 3   *Questions 21–30*

Questions 21–25

*Choose the correct letter, **A, B or C**.*

21 The exam is coming in

    A   two weeks.

    B   three weeks.

    C   one month.

22 They need to prepare

    A   a detailed report.

    B   an interactive presentation.

    C   a comprehensive analysis.

23 The main topic of their project is

    A   environmental protection.

    B   animal conservation.

C   modern technology.

24 Mary thinks it's best to do research at

  A   the school library.
  B   the city museum.
  C   the laboratory.

25 The best time for them to work on the project together is

  A   weekends.
  B   evenings.
  C   after class.

Questions 26–28

How did the students describe the following study methods?

*Choose **THREE** answers from the box and write the correct letter, A–E, next to **questions 26–28**.*

```
Descriptions:
A   Provides in-depth knowledge
B   Provides common sense
C   Helps to remember key points
D   Allow sharing of difficult parts
E   Allows sharing of different viewpoints
```

Study Methods

26 Making notes

27 Group discussion

28 Reading textbooks

Questions 29–30

*Choose **TWO** letters from **A** to **E**.*

29–30 Which **TWO** difficulties do they mention about the project?

  A   Limited resources
  B   Unclear concepts
  C   Time pressure

D Lack of teamwork

E Unclear instructions

PART 4   Questions 31–40

Questions 31–36

Complete the notes below.

*Write **NO MORE THAN TWO WORDS** for each answer.*

LECTURE ON EDUCATION INNOVATION

Education innovation is not just about applying **31** .... to classroom teaching and learning.

Examples of new educational methods:

- Project-based learning

    Activities:

    Building a car powered by renewable energy

    Constructing a **32** ....

    Running a business

- Personalized learning

    Based on the concept that students have distinct **33** ...., strengths, and weaknesses

    Advanced data analytical tool: AI

    CAN: Analyse academic performance data

    Help create a **34** ....

- STEAM

    Combining different subjects to help students develop a more **35** .... understanding so as to handle complicated issues

    Benefits:

    Help students make preparation for **36** ....

    Promotes creativity, innovation, and collaboration

Questions 37–40

Complete the summary below.

*Write **NO MORE THAN TWO WORDS** for each answer.*

Challenges of education innovation

The implementation of education innovation faces several challenges. Teachers need training and support to adapt to new methods and technologies as there is **37** .... from traditional educational systems and mindsets, often due to a lack of understanding or **38** .... Overcoming this requires extensive training for educators. Another challenge is the availability of resources as education innovation often needs technology but not all institutions have the necessary resources or **39** .... Additionally, **40** .... the effectiveness of education innovation is difficult and requires appropriate tools to measure its impact on student achievement.

雅思听力考试答题纸模版：

Listening Answer Sheet

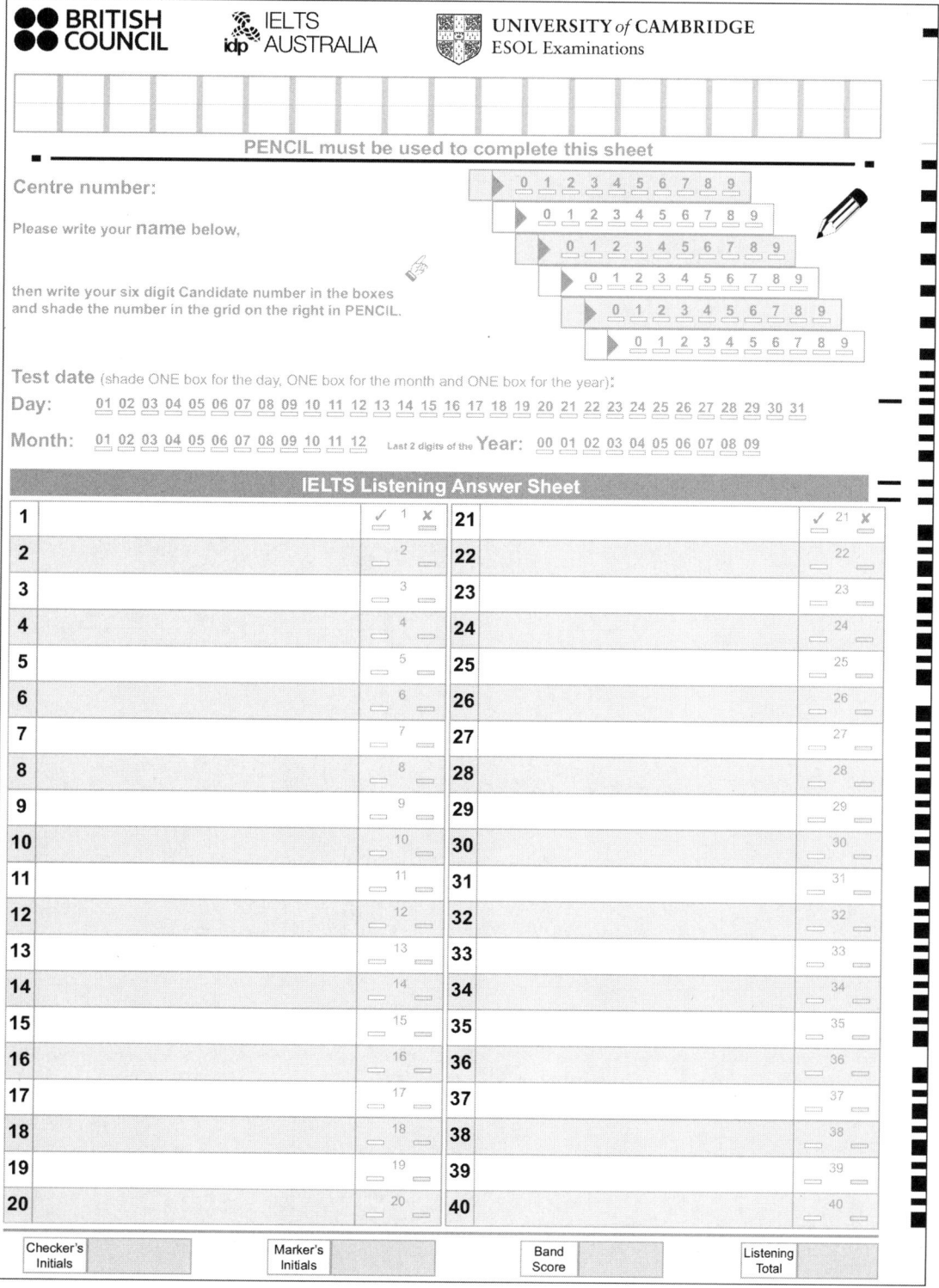

IELTS
All-in-One Guide
(Basic Edition)

第二部分
雅思阅读

1 雅思阅读概述

阅读是雅思考试中的一个重要组成部分，该部分旨在评估考生的阅读理解能力，主要测试考生对各种不同类型文章的理解能力，包括学术性文章、报纸文章、广告、说明文等。雅思阅读考试对于许多考生来说可能是颇具挑战性的，但通过有针对性的练习和备考，可以有效提高阅读理解能力，取得理想的成绩。当准备雅思阅读考试时，了解雅思阅读考试的结构，掌握高效的阅读方法，运用相应的解题技巧会帮助考生提高考试技能以及阅读技能。

1.1 雅思阅读考试结构解析

考试时长：60 分钟（含誊写答题卡时间）

文章数量：三篇文章；文章总计长度在 2000 词到 2750 词之间

题目数量：40 道题

1.2 雅思阅读考试评分标准

依据答对题的数量获取 1-9 的等级分数。具体对照如下：

阅读正确答题数（A类）	对应分数	阅读正确答题数（G类）	对应分数
39-40	9	40	9
37-38	8.5	39	8.5
35-36	8	38	8
33-34	7.5	36-37	7.5
30-32	7	34-35	7
27-29	6.5	32-33	6.5
23-26	6	30-31	6
20-22	5.5	26-29	5.5
16-19	5	23-25	5
13-15	4.5	19-22	4.5
10-12	4	15-18	4
6-9	3.5	12-14	3.5
4-5	3	8-11	3
3	2.5	5-7	2.5
2	2	2-4	2
1	1	1	1
缺席	0	缺席	0

1.3 文章介绍

阅读考试中所出现的文章是由真实的文章改写而成的。这些文章来源于期刊、书籍和报纸等，与考生未来在大学课程中将阅读到的文章极为相似。文章的内容包含与其认知水平相契合的常见话题。文章还包括了非文字性的内容，比如各类图表等。文章体裁多样，包括记叙文、说明文、议论文等文体。文章总计长度在 2000 词到 2750 词之间。

1.4 雅思阅读考试题型综述

雅思考试阅读（学术类）部分题型涵盖了上述多种题型，旨在全面评估考生的阅读理解能力，每种题型可根据具体情况有少许的变化。主要题型如下：

1.4.1 完成句子题

填空题型包括根据文章内容选择词或短语填空，考查语法和词汇知识，以及分析文本的能力。

1.4.2 摘要／表格／笔记／示意图题

摘要／表格／笔记／示意图题型要求考生使用文章中提供的信息填充图表中缺少的内容，考查对逻辑关系和细节的理解。

1.4.3 简答题

简答题要求考生根据文章内容回答题目，考查语法和定位的能力。

1.4.4 判断题

判断题考查考生对文章细节事实信息（TRUE/FALSE/NOT GIVEN）和作者观点（YES/NO/NOT GIVEN）的定位，以及替换表达的理解能力。

1.4.5 选择题

选择题包括单选和多选，考查对细节信息的理解和排除干扰信息的能力。

1.4.6 段落标题配对题

段落标题配对题要求考生从提供的选项中选出与文章中各段落内容相匹配的标题。每个选项只能用于一个段落。

1.4.7 特征匹配题

特征匹配题涉及文章中或部分段落中散布的多个平行信息的匹配，如人名观点配对、研究结果和历史时期配对等。

1.4.8 段落细节配对题

段落细节配对题考查全文细节匹配，要求考生在不对称的信息分布中找出匹配项，对阅读理解能力和阅读速度要求较高。

1.4.9 句子和结尾配对题

句子和结尾配对题是完成句子题的一种变体，考查同义转换的识别能力。考生应仔细阅读题目的指示和说明，并在规定时间内及时将答案誊抄在答题卡上。

1.5 雅思高效阅读方法与策略

雅思考试中的阅读不同于日常的英语阅读。一般来说，阅读是获取信息的途径之一，而雅思考试中的阅读则是通过阅读解决具体问题，找到问题对应的答案。在注重提高阅读能力的同时，也应掌握一些方法来提升获取信息的能力。以下方法在雅思阅读中是非常有帮助的。

（1）分析题目：在阅读文章之前先扫读题目，了解题型和考查内容，并从题目中找出关键词。

（2）定位信息：在阅读文章时，重点关注题目中的关键词以及相关信息在文章中的体现，通过扫读尽快地找到相关信息。

（3）略读：不必纠缠于细节，快速浏览文章，抓取段落结构及主旨信息的同时留意与题目内容有关的关键信息。

（4）做辅助笔记：在分析题目和浏览文章时，在题目和原文中标记关键信息有助于进行信息匹配。

（5）做好时间管理：每篇文章有一定的时间限制，确保能够在规定时间内完成阅读和解答问题。

上述做题方法可以帮助考生在做题时提升正确率，除这些方法外，考生还可以运用以下策略来全面提升阅读能力和信息获取能力。

（1）练习阅读不同类型的文本：雅思阅读涉及各种不同主题的文章，包括科学、历史、文化、商业等。确保练习阅读各种类型的文章，积累话题词和语料，以便在考试中更好地理解和应对不同的题材。

（2）提高阅读速度和强化信息提炼能力：在有限的时间内阅读三篇文章并回答相关问题需要较快的阅读速度。提高阅读速度的关键是获取与题目有关的主旨或细节信息，过滤掉无关或次要的信息。

（3）留意文章的结构和关键信息：在阅读文章时，注意文章的结构，如段落之间的逻辑关系、作者的论点和论据等。同时，留意关键信息，如人名、日期、地点等，这些信息可能在题目中涉及。

（4）掌握不同题型的解题技巧：雅思阅读考试包括多种题型，如多选题、填空题、判断题等。针对不同的题型，掌握相应的解题技巧，例如对比选项、预判答案等。

（5）积累词汇和阅读素材：扩大词汇量可以帮助考生更好地理解文章，同时也能提高答题的准确性。阅读更多的英语素材，包括书籍、文章、报纸等，有助于提高阅读理解能力。对一些常见话题，如科技、环境等，提前了解相关背景知识有助于更快地理解文章内容。

（6）注意时间分配：在考试中，合理分配时间是非常重要的。尽量在阅读和回答问题之间均匀分配时间，确保完成目标分数对应的题目数量。

（7）多做真题和练习题：通过做真题和练习题，可以更好地了解考试的难度和出题规律，同时也可以检验自己的备考效果并及时调整学习计划。

（8）模拟考试：在考试前进行多次模拟考试，以熟悉考试的时间限制和考题类型，评估自己的考试水平并找出需要提高的地方。

2 雅思阅读解题技巧与策略

2.1 雅思阅读填空题

雅思阅读填空题主要分为完成句子题（sentence completion）、摘要／表格／笔记／流程图题（summary/table/note/flow-chart completion）、简答题（short-answer）等几种类型。在雅思阅读所有题型中，填空题相对简单，容易定位到原文信息，考生在备考阶段可以通过练习填空题提升定位信息的能力。而在上述题型中，前两种题型往往都是针对单一的句子进行考查，所以这两种题型是填空题中较为基础的题型，而简答题在前两种题型的基础上涉及句子之间的逻辑关系和内容的推进，考查考生对段落主旨和细节理解、语言逻辑和语法运用的综合能力。

2.1.1 完成句子题

2.1.1.1 题型介绍

从原文中选词填写到空白处，使题目完整。该题型有字数要求，超出字数限制将不得分。含连字符的词算作一个词。该题型题目顺序与原文信息出现顺序一致，可以按顺序答题。

2.1.1.2 解题步骤

（1）审题（注意字数要求和题干提示）。
（2）画定位词（从题中找出考查对象和起到限定作用的表达作为定位的线索）。
（3）预判答案（根据语法确定词性／名词单复数／人／物）。
（4）回原文定位（注意定位词和限定信息常以同义替换的形式出现）。
（5）通过题文匹配，找出题目缺失的信息，确定答案。

2.1.1.3 真题解析

Questions 38–40 （from C16T3P3）

Complete the sentences below.

Choose **NO MORE THAN TWO WORDS** from the passage for each answer.

38 Daffodils are likely to flower early in response to .... weather.

39 If ash trees come into leaf before oak trees, the weather in .... will probably be wet.

40 The research was carried out using a particular species of ....

（Cambridge ESOL，2021：72）

提示：看到题目，先大致确定该题在原文中的位置，因为38-40题已经是该文的最后几道题了，可以尝试从文章靠后的位置定位（但要注意与其他题目相结合，避免因题目交叉而定位困难）。因为该阅读题是按顺序出题，可以利用38题中的daffodils确定该题相关内容从文章G部分第二句开始。

> G Some plants mainly use day length as an indicator of the season. Other species, such as daffodils, have considerable temperature sensitivity, and can flower months in advance during a warm winter. In fact, the discovery of the dual role of phytochromes provides the science behind a well-known rhyme long used to predict the coming season: oak before ash we'll have a splash, ash before oak we're in for a soak.
>
> Wigge explains: 'Oak trees rely much more on temperature, likely using phytochromes as thermometers to dictate development, whereas ash trees rely on measuring day length to determine their seasonal timing. A warmer spring, and consequently a higher likeliness of a hot summer, will result in oak leafing before ash. A cold spring will see the opposite. As the British know only too well, a colder summer is likely to be a rain-soaked one.'
>
> H The new findings are the culmination of twelve years of research involving scientists from Germany, Argentina and the US, as well as the Cambridge team. The work was done in a model system, using a mustard plant called Arabidopsis, but Wigge says the phytochrome genes necessary for temperature sensing are found in crop plants as well. 'Recent advances in plant genetics now mean that scientists are able to rapidly identify the genes controlling these processes in crop plants, and even alter their activity using precise molecular "scalpels",' adds Wigge. 'Cambridge is uniquely well-positioned to do this kind of research as we have outstanding collaborators nearby who work on more applied aspects of plant biology, and can help us transfer this new knowledge into the field.'

（Cambridge ESOL，2021：70）

解析 38 Daffodils are likely to flower early in response to .... weather.

审题：字数要求不超过两个词。

定位：38题的定位词daffodils（定位词尽量名词优先），限定线索 flower early。

预判词性：空格前有介词结构 in response to，空格后为名词，所以空格处应该填形容词或名词修饰空格后的 weather。

根据定位词回原文定位，可定位到G部分：Other species, such as daffodils, have considerable temperature sensitivity, and can flower months in advance during a warm winter.

匹配原文找出题目缺失的信息：daffodils 原词重现；flower months in advance 对应 flower early，during 对应 in response to，缺失内容为 warm/warm winter。

解析 39　If ash trees come into leaf before oak trees, the weather in .... will probably be wet.

定位：ash tree、oak tree、weather，限定线索 come into leaf、probably be wet。

预判词性：空格前有 in，此处应填名词，与空格前的 in 构成短语一起修饰 weather。

根据定位词回原文定位，定位到 G 部分：A warmer spring, and consequently a higher likeliness of a hot summer, will result in oak leafing before ash. A cold spring will see the opposite. As the British know only too well, a colder summer is likely to be a rain-soaked one.

匹配原文找到缺失信息：a warmer...hot summer will result in oak leafing before ash. A cold spring will see the opposite（即 ash tree come into leaf before oak tree），rain-soaked 对应 wet，one 代指 cold summer，所以此处缺失信息为 cold summer/summer。

解析 40　The research was carried out using a particular species of ....

虽然解题思路相同，但是 40 题有一处难点，即题中除了 research 以外，缺乏起到明确定位或限定作用的名词，所以此处既需要利用顺序出题的原则，又需要找到 using a particular species 在原文中对应的具体名词。

定位：research，限定线索 using a particular species。

预判词性：空格前是 of，此处应填名词，该名词体现 species 的名称或类别。

根据定位词定位到 H 部分：The new findings are the culmination of twelve years of research involving scientists from Germany, Argentina and the US, as well as the Cambridge team. The work was done in a model system, using a mustard plant called Arabidopsis.

匹配原文找到缺失信息：the work 代指前文中的 research，using a mustard plant 对应 a particular species，此处能确定缺失信息为 plant 的名称，即 Arabidopsis。

雅思阅读完成句子题的答题策略涉及一系列技能的结合，需要理解上下文、积累词汇和注意细节。以下是一些建议。

（1）仔细阅读说明：确保理解问题的要求，比如字数限制，或者是否需要使用文本中的确切词语。

（2）分析句子上下文：看看空白所在的句子，确定缺失词的词性（如名词、动词、形容词），考虑在语法和语义上符合的内容。

（3）使用上下文线索：空白周围的词语常常提供关于缺失信息的提示，注意连词、介词和关系代词有助于找到正确答案。

（4）预测同义词：雅思经常考查考生识别同义词的能力，预测题干中某些词在原文中可能出现的形式或表达，有助于提升定位速度。

（5）检查语法：确保选择的词在语法上正确，包括时态和数的一致性。

2.1.2 摘要／表格／笔记／流程图题

2.1.2.1 题型介绍

此类题型涉及原文中一部分内容的概括，考生需要用原文中的词将缺失的信息补充完整，并且对所填的词有字数要求。该类题型主要包括摘要题（题目说明中称之为 summary）、表格题（题目说明中称之为 table）、笔记补全题（题目说明中称之为 notes）、流程图题（题目说明中称之为 flow-chat）。该题型题目顺序并不一直与原文信息出现顺序一致，但是出题范围相对集中。

摘要题（summary）是雅思阅读中的常见题型，在阅读考试中占比较大。摘要题有两种出题形式。第一种是按照字数要求，从原文找出合适的原词来填空；第二种是从所给出的选项中选出合适的选项来填空。

本节将以摘要题为例，通过解析摘要题将填空题型融会贯通，从而提升考生对细节题的分析能力和理解能力。

2.1.2.2 解题步骤

（1）审题（注意字数要求以及是否有出题范围提示）。
（2）通过摘要标题和摘要开头句确定出题范围，根据空格所在单句画定位词，找限定线索。
（3）分析逻辑关系（注意题目中体现逻辑关系的信号词）。
（4）根据语法和线索预判答案（根据语法确定词性／名词单复数／人／物）。
（5）回原文定位（注意定位词和限定信息常以同义替换的形式出现）。
（6）通过题文匹配，找出题目缺失的信息，确定答案。

提示：虽然 summary 整体是按顺序原则出题，但是为了避免个别题目因为乱序而导致定位困难，切忌每看一道题就回到原文中找一道题，而是应先通读摘要了解大致内容和语义关系，分析语义间是否有逻辑关系的连接词。要注意先通过语法预判空格处所填词的词性，再根据顺序原则在空格前后找定位关键词定位回原文。

2.1.2.3 真题解析

Questions 20–22 （from C16T3P2）

Complete the summary below.

*Choose **ONE WORD ONLY** from the passage for each answer.*

*Write your answers in boxes **20–22** on your answer sheet.*

Interesting finds at an archaeological site

Organic materials such as animal skins and textiles are not discovered very often at archaeological sites. They have little protection against **20** ...., which means that they decay relatively quickly. But this is not always the case. If temperatures are low enough, fragile artefacts can be preserved for thousands of years.

> A team of archaeologists have been working in the mountains in Oppland in Norway to recover artefacts revealed by shrinking ice cover. In the past, there were trade routes through these mountains and **21** .... gathered there in the summer months to avoid being attacked by **22** .... on lower ground. The people who used these mountains left things behind and it is those objects that are of interest to archaeologists.

（Cambridge ESOL, 2021: 67）

提示：题目说明中虽然没有提示出题范围，但是本题可以通过摘要小标题中的 an archaeological site 和开头句中的 organic materials、animal skins and textiles 从原文 B 部分开始。

> **B** Organic materials like textiles and hides are relatively rare finds at archaeological sites. This is because unless they're protected from the microorganisms that cause decay, they tend not to last long. Extreme cold is one reliable way to keep artefacts relatively fresh for a few thousand years, but once thawed out, these materials experience degradation relatively swiftly.
>
> With climate change shrinking ice cover around the world, glacial archaeologists need to race the clock to find newly revealed artefacts, preserve them, and study them. If something fragile dries and is windblown it might very soon be lost to science, or an arrow might be exposed and then covered again by the next snow and remain well-preserved. The unpredictability means that glacial archaeologists have to be systematic in their approach to fieldwork.
>
> **C** Over a nine-year period, a team of archaeologists, which included Lars Pile of Oppland County Council, Norway, and James Barrett of the McDonald Institute for Archaeological Research, surveyed patches of ice in Oppland, an area of south-central Norway that is home to some of the country's highest mountains. Reindeer once congregated on these icy patches in the later summer months to escape biting insects, and from the late Stone Age**, hunters followed. In addition, trade routes threaded through the mountain passes of Oppland, linking settlements in Norway to the rest of Europe.

（Cambridge ESOL, 2021: 65）

解析 They have little protection against 20 ...., which means that they decay relatively quickly.

本句中的 They 代指前一句中的 animal skins and textiles。They have little protection against 后应该填名词，而后文中的 means that they decay relatively quickly 体现两个句子之间存在因果关联。根据定位词 animal skins and textiles 和 little protection 以及导致的结果定位到原文：Organic materials like textiles and hides are relatively rare finds at archaeological sites. This is because unless they're protected from the microorganisms that cause decay, they tend not to last long. 通过匹配对应信息得知，be protected from 对应 have protection against，而 microorganisms cause decay 则对应题中的因果逻辑，所以此处填 microorganisms。

解析 In the past, there were trade routes through these mountains and 21 ....gathered there in the summer months to avoid being attacked by 22 .... on lower ground.

因为 21 题和 22 题出现在同一个题干中，说明两题之间逻辑紧密，出题跨度小，应一起分析。通过 gathered 能确定 21 题空格处应该填名词充当主语。既然能做出 gathered 和 to avoid being attacked 的行为，那么 21 题和 22 题都应该是填跟生物有关的名词。通过 a team、Oppland 定位到 C 部分，然后通过 in the summer 确定到具体答案句：Reindeer once congregated on these icy patches in the later summer months to escape biting insects… 通过题文信息匹配确定 gathered 对应 congregated，to escape biting 对应 to avoid being attacked，所以 21 题和 22 题缺失的信息分别为 reindeer 和 insects。

2.1.3 简答题

简答题要求考生用原文中的信息进行回答，答案有字数要求，该题型题目出现的顺序与原文顺序一致，简答题的本质与完成句子题的本质相同，主要考查考生的定位能力和对细节信息的理解能力。

真题解析（C16T4P1）

PASSAGE

The Romans dug tunnels for their roads using the counter-excavation method, whenever they encountered obstacles such as hills or mountains that were too high for roads to pass over. An example is the 37-meter-long, 6-meter-high, Furlo Pass Tunnel built in Italy in 69–79 CE. Remarkably, a modern road still uses this tunnel today. Tunnels were also built for mineral extraction. Miners would locate a mineral vein and then pursue it with shafts and tunnels underground. Traces of such tunnels used to mine gold can still be found at the Dolaucothi mines in Wales. When the sole purpose of a tunnel was mineral extraction, construction required less planning, as the tunnel route was determined by the mineral vein.

Roman tunnel projects were carefully planned and carried out. The length of time it took to construct a tunnel depended on the method being used and the type of rock being excavated. The qanat construction method was usually faster than the counter-excavation method as it was more straightforward. This was because the mountain could be excavated not only from the tunnel mouths but also from shafts. The type of rock could also influence construction times. When the rock was hard, the Romans employed a technique called fire quenching which consisted of heating the rock with fire, and then suddenly cooling it with cold water so that it would crack. Progress through hard rock could be very slow, and it was not uncommon for tunnels to take years, if not decades, to be built. Construction marks left on a Roman tunnel in Bologna show that the rate of advance through solid rock was 30 centimeters per day. In contrast, the rate of advance of the Claudius tunnel can be calculated at 1.4 meters per day. Most tunnels had inscriptions showing the names of patrons who ordered construction and sometimes the name of the architect. For example, the 1.4-kilometer Çevlik tunnel in Turkey, built to divert the floodwater threatening the harbor of the ancient city of Seleuceia Pieria, had inscriptions on the entrance, still visible today, that also indicate that the tunnel was started in 69 CE and was completed in 81 CE.

（Cambridge ESOL，2021：83）

Questions 11–13

Answer the questions below.

*Choose **NO MORE THAN TWO WORDS** from the passage for each answer.*

11　What type of mineral were the Dolaucothi mines in Wales built to extract?

12　In addition to the patron, whose name might be carved onto a tunnel?

13　What part of Seleuceia Pieria was the Çevlik tunnel built to protect?

（Cambridge ESOL，2021：85）

解析 11　What type of mineral were the Dolaucothi mines in Wales built to extract?

根据题干中的 Dolaucothi mines in wales 定位到答案句：Traces of such tunnels used to mine gold can still be found at the Dolaucothi mines in Wales. 根据 what type of mineral 确定本题考查的是 mineral 的名称，应该填名词，通过与原文匹配，找到符合该条件的名词 mine。

解析 12　In addition to the patron, whose name might be carved onto a tunnel?

根据出题原则定位范围，确定 12 题应在 11 题之后，根据 patron 和 name be carved onto tunnel 定位答案句：Most tunnels had inscriptions showing the names of patrons who ordered construction and sometimes the name of the architect. 根据 in addition to 确定答案词应与 patron 为并列关系，inscription 对应 be carved onto tunnels，whose name 体现答案词应和 name 有所属关系，符合限定条件的内容只有 architect.

解析 13　What part of Seleuceia Pieria was the Çevlik tunnel built to protect?

根据 Seleuceia Pieria 和 Çevlik tunnel 定位到最后一段并确定答案句：the 1.4-kilometer Çevlik tunnel in Turkey, built to divert the floodwater threatening the harbor of the ancient city of Seleuceia Pieria…通过 what part 能确定答案是名词并与 Seleuceia Pieria 为所属关系，并作 protect 的宾语／对象；built to protect 对应原文 built to divert the floodwater，根据线索匹配，符合线索的信息为 harbour。

2.2 雅思阅读判断题

2.2.1 题型介绍

雅思阅读判断题考查考生对原文细节的理解能力，要求考生按照评判标准将题中的表述与原文内容进行比较然后做出判断。因此，考生首先需要明确每种情况的评判标准。

（1）**TRUE/YES**：题中表述的内容与原文信息一致，即原文有明确的信息来证实题中的内容。

（2）**FALSE/NO**：题中表述的内容与原文信息矛盾，即原文有明确的信息来驳斥题中的内容。

（3）**NOT GIVEN**：题中表述的内容无法从原文中得到证实，即原文没有明确的信息证实题中的内容，但是也没有明确的信息来驳斥题目中的内容。

考生在完成判断题时，应该从原文中寻找直接的证据来作答，而不是通过假设或者推理。值得注意的是，题中的信息往往都是对原文内容的改写，因此考生需要熟悉常规的同义表达或转述。

2.2.2 解题策略

仔细比对题目和段落，以准确判断信息是否匹配。

（1）注重细节：寻找精确的细节，而不是概括性的内容。

（2）寻找关键词：识别题目中的关键词，并在段落中找到它们，以验证信息的准确性。

（3）注意否定词：小心 not 或 never 这样的否定词，它们可以改变陈述的意思。

（4）考虑整体段落：有时候，信息可能是暗示而非明确陈述的。

（5）留意同义词：段落中可能会使用与题目中表述不同但意思相近的词语。

（6）检查上下文：确保段落中的信息与题目中的上下文相匹配。

2.2.3 解题步骤

（1）审题：确保充分理解题目中的信息，并找出定位词。

（2）判断考点：留意题中的细节信息，明确重点比较内容。

（3）回原文定位：注意同义表达或相关信息，虽然原文中的用词与题目中的信息并不完全一致，但是要留意题中词语的同义表达或者相关信息。

（4）定位到答案句后，将题目中的考点信息与原文相关内容进行比较，按照评判标准作答。

2.2.4 真题解析

下面以雅思真题（C15T3P1）为例，讲解阅读判断题。

PASSAGE

After the war, Moore enrolled at the Leeds School of Art, where he studied for two years. In his first year, he spent most of his time drawing. Although he wanted to study sculpture, no teacher was appointed until his second year. At the end of that year, he passed the sculpture examination and was awarded a scholarship to the Royal College of Art in

London. In September 1921, he moved to London and began three years of advanced study in sculpture.

Alongside the instruction he received at the Royal College, Moore visited many of the London museums, particularly the British Museum, which had a wide-ranging collection of ancient sculpture. During these visits, he discovered the power and beauty of ancient Egyptian and African sculpture. As he became increasingly interested in these 'primitive' forms of art, he turned away from European sculptural traditions.

(Cambridge ESOL, 2020: 58)

题目: Moore began studying sculpture in his first term at the Leeds School of Art.

答案: False

解析:

定位词: Leeds School of Art

考点信息: began studying sculpture in his first term. 题目中用 in first term 对动作发生情况进行限定,需要判断此处细节是否与原文一致。

通过定位词和考点信息定位到答案句: After the war, Moore enrolled at the Leeds School of Art, where he studied for two years. In his first year, he spent most of his time drawing. Although he wanted to study sculpture, no teacher was appointed until his second year.

原文中明确指出 In his first year, he spent most of his time drawing. Although he wanted to study sculpture, no teacher was appointed until his second year. 题目中的时间与原文的时间冲突,所以此题信息与原文信息矛盾。

题目: When Moore started at the Royal College of Art, its reputation for teaching sculpture was excellent.

答案: Not Given

解析:

定位词: The Royal College of Art

考点信息: its reputation...was excellent. 题目中用 excellent 对名词进行修饰限定,需要判断此处细节信息是否与原文一致。

通过定位词和考点信息定位到答案句: he passed the sculpture examination and was awarded a scholarship to the Royal College of Art in London. In September 1921, he moved to London and began three years of advanced study in sculpture.

原文中并没有与 reputation 相关的内容,也就没有与 excellent 有关的内容,所以原文既没有题目中所考查的主体,也没有证实或反驳题目中限定该主体的证据,所以此题结论在原文中不存在,也就无法证实或反驳。

题目: Moore became aware of ancient sculpture as a result of visiting London museums.

答案: True

解析：

定位词：ancient sculpture, London museums

考点信息：此题包含因果关系，即 became aware of ancient sculpture 是 visiting London museums 的结果。需判断此题中两个事件在原文中是否存在并且是否构成因果关系。

通过定位词和考点信息定位到答案句：Moore visited many of the London museums, particularly the British Museum, which had a wide-ranging collection of ancient sculpture. During these visits, he discovered the power and beauty of ancient Egyptian and African sculpture.

During these visits 代指前文提到的 visited many of the London museums。he discovered the power and beauty of ancient…sculpture 对应 became aware of ancient sculpture，并且是 visited many of the London museums 的结果或影响，能体现两个事件之间存在因果关系。所以此处信息与题目中结论一致。

2.3 雅思阅读选择题

2.3.1 题型介绍

雅思阅读选择题有单选题（四选一）和多选题（多选多）两种题型，两种题型的出题形式有以下两种：（1）题目是完整的问题，考生需要根据原文选出合适的选项回答问题；（2）题目是某个句子的前部分内容，考生需要根据原文选出合适的选项将句子补充完整。

所以考生需要仔细读题，确定每道题能选的数量，并在答题卡上作答。

选择题出题是按顺序出题，考生可以按照选择题的题号顺序作答。单选题基本上是一道题对应一个段落，每道题的选项在该题目出现的段落集中出现。选择题主要考查考生对某些特定细节信息的理解能力或者对某些主要内容的理解能力。

2.3.2 解题策略

雅思阅读多项选择题需要仔细阅读、批判性思维和策略性方法的结合。

（1）仔细阅读问题：确保在阅读文章之前理解问题的要求，专注于相关信息，忽略不相关细节。

（2）识别关键词：在问题中标出关键词，这将帮助考生在文本中找到答案。这些关键词可能是名词、动词、形容词，也可能是特定的数字或日期。

（3）扫读文章：不必逐字阅读整个段落，应通过扫读快速找到相关信息。寻找关键词，并注意包含它们的句子或段落。

（4）理解上下文：多项选择题通常要求考生理解语境或文章的更广泛含义，注意文本的整体主题和论点。

（5）排除错误答案：如果不确定正确答案，可尝试排除明显错误或没有原文论证的选项，这会增加选择正确答案的概率。

2.3.3 解题步骤

（1）审题：仔细读题，确定题目考查形式（根据原文作答／根据原文补充句子），找出定位词。

（2）分析选项：找出关键词，比较选项之间的区别。

（3）回原文定位：可利用题干中的定位词和选项中的关键词同时进行定位。

（4）从原文寻找证据：正确选项在原文中有相关的信息证实其成立；也可以通过排除与原文信息矛盾的选项或在原文中不存在的选项，缩小比较范围。

2.3.4 分析原则

（1）正确选项通常与原文是同义对应关系，相当于判断题中 YES/TRUE 的情况。

（2）非正确选项与原文矛盾或者无法判断，相当于判断题中 NO/FALSE 或 NOT GIVEN 的情况。

2.3.5 真题解析

2.3.5.1 单选题

（1）回答问题（C12T8P2Q15）。

PASSAGE

Rewilding means the mass restoration of damaged ecosystems. It involves letting trees return to places that have been denuded, allowing parts of the seabed to recover from trawling and dredging, permitting rivers to flow freely again. Above all, it means bringing back missing species. One of the most striking findings of modern ecology is that ecosystems without large predators behave in completely different ways from those that retain them. Some of them drive dynamic processes that resonate through the whole food chain, creating niches for hundreds of species that might other else struggle to survive. The killers turn out to be bringers of life.

（Cambridge ESOL，2017：83）

Question

What point does the writer make about large predators in the third paragraph?

A   Their presence can increase biodiversity.

B   They may cause damage to local ecosystems.

C   Their behaviour can alter according to the environment.

D   They should be reintroduced only to areas where they were native.

（Cambridge ESOL，2017：85）

解析：

按照解题步骤，可以通过 large predators in the third paragraph 定位到原文 One of the most striking findings of modern ecology is that ecosystems without large predators behave in completely different ways from those that retain them. Some of them drive dynamic processes that resonate through the whole food chain, creating niches for hundreds of species that might other else struggle to survive. The killers turn out to be bringers of life.

通过比较选项与原文的内容得知，A 选项是对原文 drive dynamic processes, creating niches for hundreds of species. The killers turn out to be bringers of life 的概括。而其余三个选项在原文中找不到对应信息。

（2）补全句子（C12T8P2Q17）。

PASSAGE

At sea the potential is even greater: by protecting large areas from commercial fishing, we could once more see what 18th-century literature describes: vast shoals of fish being chased by fin and sperm whales, within sight of the English shore. This policy would also greatly boost catches in the surrounding seas; the fishing industry's insistence on scouring every inch of seabed, leaving no breeding reserves, could not be more damaging to its own interests.

（Cambridge ESOL，2017：83）

Question

Protecting large areas of the sea from commercial fishing would result in

A practical benefits for the fishing industry.

B some short-term losses to the fishing industry.

C widespread opposition from the fishing industry.

D certain changes to techniques within the fishing industry.

（Cambridge ESOL，2017：85）

解析：

通过审题得知，此题干中包含因果关系，需要通过原文确定题干中描述的原因导致的结果。通过 Protecting large areas of the sea from commercial fishing 定位到原文 by protecting large areas from commercial fishing, we could once more see what 18th-century literature describes: vast shoals of fish being chased by fin and sperm whales, within sight of the English shore. This policy would also greatly boost catches in the surrounding seas。

通过上下文得知 this policy 指代 Protecting large areas of the sea from commercial fishing，那么带来的影响或结果就是 boost catches，与 A 选项中 practical benefits 一致。而其他三个选项在原

文中找不到相关表述。

2.3.5.2 多选题（C15T1P2 Q23–24）

> **PASSAGE**
>
> Another aim is to free the time people spend driving for other purposes. If the vehicle can do some or all of the driving, it may be possible to be productive, to socialise or simply to relax while automation systems have responsibility for safe control of the vehicle. If the vehicle can do the driving, those who are challenged by existing mobility models—such as older or disabled travellers—may be able to enjoy significantly greater travel autonomy.

（Cambridge ESOL，2020：20）

Question

Choose **TWO** letters, A–E.

23–24 Which **TWO** benefits of automated vehicles does the writer mention?

A   Car travellers could enjoy considerable cost savings.

B   It would be easier to find parking spaces in urban areas.

C   Travellers could spend journeys doing something other than driving.

D   People who find driving physically difficult could travel independently.

E   A reduction in the number of cars would mean a reduction in pollution.

（Cambridge ESOL，2020：23）

解析：

（1）审题：通过审题确定此题应从五个选项中选出两个答案。

（2）分析选项：每个选项都考查 automated vehicles 与不同名词之间的关联。A 选项强调 cost savings；B 选项强调 easier to find parking spaces in urban areas；C 选项用 other than 体现了并列关系，即 driving 的同时还能做其他的事情；D 选项强调身体不便的人可以独立出行；E 选项提到汽车数量减少使得污染减弱，该选项包含因果关系，需仔细跟原文比对。

（3）定位：利用题干中的 benefits of automated vehicles 定位到原文 If the vehicle can do some or all of the driving, 那么带来的结果有 to socialise or simply to relax while automation systems have responsibility for safe control of the vehicle, 该内容与 C 选项信息一致, socialise or simply to relax 与选项中 doing something 对应。

另一个好处是，原文中的 those who are challenged by existing mobility models—such as older or disabled travellers 对应 D 选项中 People who find driving physically difficult，而 may be able to enjoy significantly greater travel autonomy 对应 travel independently。

2.4 雅思阅读匹配题

雅思阅读匹配题可以按照考查形式分为特征匹配题、句首句尾匹配题、段落信息匹配题、标题匹配题等。但是这些题型的共同特点是题目的顺序与原文信息出现的顺序不同，题目中的信息也是对原文内容的同义改写。因此，这类题型要求考生具有良好的阅读理解能力和快速定位信息的能力，因此也是雅思阅读题型中难度较大的题型。多做练习并结合有效的解题策略是提高分数的关键。

2.4.1 特征匹配题

雅思阅读中的匹配题型考查考生对文章内容和表述的理解能力。这类题目要求考生将一组特征表述（通常是关于文章中具体内容或细节的描述，如观点、事件细节等）与另一组与特征有关的考查对象（通常是文章中的人物、时间、地点等专有名词）进行匹配，使用字母（A、B、C等）来标识它们。有可能某些选项不会被使用，而其他选项可能会被多次使用。当有可能多次使用选项时，题中介绍会说明：You may use any option more than once.

2.4.1.1 解题策略

（1）理解特征：在阅读文章之前，熟悉要匹配的特征或特点，包括具体的细节、描述或属性。

（2）识别关键词和短语：寻找代表匹配特征的关键词和短语，如名称、日期、地点等。

（3）扫读特定信息：一旦确定了相关部分，利用特征信息回原文定位。

（4）利用语境线索：注意特征周围的语境。有时，特征前后提供的信息可以帮助正确匹配或缩小匹配范围。

（5）排除无关信息：如果有特征与文章中的信息不匹配或矛盾，排除它们以缩小选择范围。

（6）注意相似特征：有时文章中可能有相似的表达，因此要小心，确保细节与题中的特征相符。

2.4.1.2 解题步骤

（1）确定考查对象（人名/事件/事物）：考查对象往往是专有名词，可以起到定位的作用。

（2）分析特征表述，并找出关键词：注意表述中的细节描述或者属性；注意限定条件和逻辑关系。

（3）定位：利用定位词和关键词回原文扫读，以找到与给定特征匹配的具体信息，标记与题目中的特征相关的部分。

（4）匹配原文：特征表述中的信息在原文中会有相关表述，但是有可能是以同义词的形式出现。注意考查对象与特征信息出现的前后文。

2.4.1.3 真题解析

下面以雅思真题 C11T2P1 Q5-8 为例，讲解特征匹配题。

Questions 5–8

Look at the following statements (*Questions 5–8*) and the list of dates below.

Match each statement with the correct date, **A–G**.

Write the correct letter, **A–G**, in boxes 5–8 on your answer sheet.

5　A search for the Mary Rose was launched.

6　One person's exploration of the Mary Rose site stopped.

7　It was agreed that the hull of the Mary Rose should be raised.

8　The site of the Mary Rose was found by chance.

A　1836　　B　1840　　C　1965　　D　1967　　E　1971　　F　1979　　G　1982

(Cambridge ESOL, 2016: 43)

PASSAGE

Then, on 16 June 1836, some fishermen in the Solent found that their equipment was caught on an underwater obstruction, which turned out to be the Mary Rose. Diver John Deane happened to be exploring another sunken ship nearby, and the fishermen approached him, asking him to free their gear. Deane dived down, and found the equipment caught on a timber protruding slightly from the seabed. Exploring further, he uncovered several other timbers and a bronze gun. Deane continued diving on the site intermittently until 1840, recovering several more guns, two bows, various timbers, part of a pump and various other small finds.

The Mary Rose then faded into obscurity for another hundred years. But in 1965, military historian and amateur diver Alexander McKee, in conjunction with the British Sub-Aqua Club, initiated a project called 'Solent Ships'. While on paper this was a plan to examine a number of known wrecks in the Solent, what McKee really hoped for was to find the Mary Rose. Ordinary search techniques proved unsatisfactory, so McKee entered into collaboration with Harold E. Edgerton, professor of electrical engineering at the Massachusetts Institute of Technology. In 1967, Edgerton's side-scan sonar systems revealed a large, unusually shaped object, which McKee believed was the Mary Rose.

Further excavations revealed stray pieces of timber and an iron gun. But the climax to the operation came when, on 5 May 1971, part of the ship's frame was uncovered. McKee and his team now knew for certain that they had found the wreck, but were as yet unaware that it also housed a treasure trove of beautifully preserved artefacts. Interest in the project grew, and in 1979, The Mary Rose Trust was formed, with Prince Charles as its President and Dr Margaret Rule its Archaeological Director. The decision whether or not to salvage the wreck was not an easy one, although an excavation in 1978 had shown that it might be possible to raise the hull. While the original aim was to raise the hull if at all feasible, the operation was not given the go-ahead until January 1982, when all the necessary information was available.

(Cambridge ESOL, 2016: 41-42)

解析：

（1）审题。通过阅读题目说明，得知需将表述中体现的事件与其发生时间进行配对。没有复选提示，所以不会出现选项被复选的情况。

（2）理解表述中的特征，并找出定位词和关键词。同时要注意题目之间的关联。

本文应该是按照时间顺序进行描述，所以根据选项中的最早时间 1836 和最晚时间 1982 可以确定题目在原文中的范围；但是由于该题型是乱序出题，为了避免定位困难而导致反复阅读，可以先集中分析题目，然后在回原文扫读的过程中按照题目在原文出现的先后顺序作答。

仔细分析题目，并对关键词的可能出现情况进行预判。

Q5：A search…was launched，原文中可能会出现 a search 对应的名词或具体名字，launched 体现的是人为规划或安排，在原文中可能会有与筹备工作相关的信息。

Q6：one person…of the Mary Rose site 在原文中会对应具体的人，stopped 体现终止，原文会出现否定信号词。

Q7：the hull of the Mary Rose 为本题的考查对象，比较具体，不易替换。

Q8：the site of the Mary Rose…by chance，体现的是地点或所在地。

在读题过程中可以大致对事件发生的顺序进行预判：第 8 题中的事件应该是这几道题里最先发生的，然后才会出现 6 题和 5 题中的情况。

（3）回原文扫读定位。

利用选项中最早的 1836 定位到 on 16 June 1836, some fishermen in the Solent found that their equipment was caught on an underwater obstruction, which turned out to be the Mary Rose，该句体现了第 8 题中表述的情况，in the Solent 对应 the site，所以 8 题表述的事件发生的时间为 1836，选 A。

紧接着文中提到 Deane dived down, and found the equipment caught on a timber protruding slightly from the seabed. Exploring further, he uncovered several other timbers and a bronze gun. Deane continued diving on the site intermittently until 1840，说明在 1840 年，Deane stopped diving the site，该句体现了第 6 题中的情况，Deane 对应 one person，explore、uncover、recover 等词体现 exploration，所以第 6 题选 B。

文中出现的下一个时间可定位到这两句：But in 1965, military historian and amateur diver Alexander McKee, in conjunction with the British Sub-Aqua Club, initiated a project called 'Solent Ships'. While on paper this was a plan to examine a number of known wrecks in the Solent, what McKee really hoped for was to find the Mary Rose.

提取主要信息：in 1965, Alexander McKee initiated a project called 'Solent Ships'…what McKee really hoped for was to find the Mary Rose. 该信息对应第 5 题中出现的事件，a search for the Mary Rose 对应 a project called 'Solent Ships'，initiated 对应 launched，所以第 5 题选 C。

后文中先后出现了 1967、1971、1979 三个时间，但是没有体现第 7 题中 the hull of the Mary Rose。直到 The decision whether or not to salvage the wreck was not an easy one, although an excavation in 1978 had shown that it might be possible to raise the hull 才出现关于 the hull 的信息，但是此时 decision was not an easy one 还没有体现 agreed。紧接着 While the original aim was to raise the hull if at all feasible, the operation was not given the go-ahead until January 1982, when all the necessary information was available 表明，the operation 直到1982年才开展，体现第7题的表述内容，所以第7题选G。

特征匹配题的典型代表为人名观点匹配题，接下来以C11T4P1 Q5-9为例进行分析。

Questions 5–9

Look at the following statements (**Questions 5–9**) and the list of researchers below.

Match each statement with the correct researcher, **A**, **B** or **C**.

Write the correct letter, **A**, **B** or **C**, in boxes 5–9 on your answer sheet.

NB　You may use any letter more than once.

5　invented a term used to distinguish two factors affecting human characteristics

6　expressed the view that the study of epigenetics will increase our knowledge

7　developed a mathematical method of measuring genetic influences

8　pioneered research into genetics using twins

9　carried out research into twins who had lived apart

A　Francis Galton

B　Thomas Bouchard

C　Danielle Reed

（Cambridge ESOL，2016：89）

解析：

（1）审题。通过阅读题目说明，得知本题要求将表述与其对应的研究人员进行配对。有复选提示，所以会有选项被复选。

（2）分析定位。由于该题型是乱序出题，为了避免定位困难而导致反复阅读，可以把题目集中分析，然后在回原文扫读的过程中，根据选项中的人名进行定位，按照人名及其观点或事件在原文中出现的顺序与对应的题目进行匹配。也就是说，此题只需要找到每个选项在原文中出现的位置，并仔细阅读其前后文即可。

（3）理解表述中的特征，并找出关键词。同时要注意题目之间的关联：第6题中有will increase our knowledge，此题的内容应该在其他题之后，甚至可能出现在文章结尾部分，体现对未来的展望。

（4）分析题目，并对其出现的情况进行预判。

Q5: invented a term...distinguish two factors affecting human characteristics，说明是专门创造一个词语或表达，原文中会有具体的名词。

Q6：the study of epigenetics will increase our knowledge，体现 epigenetics 的作用是 increase knowledge，原文中对应的观点也应该体现这两个名词之间的关联。

Q7：a mathematical method of measuring genetic influences，关键词为 mathematical method，其作用在于体现 measure genetic influence。

Q8：pioneered research into genetics using twins，关键词为 pioneered research, using twins，说明此人是 using twins 进行研究的先驱/第一人。

Q9：carried out research into twins who had lived apart，关键词为 twins who had lived apart，所以原文中此人的研究对象要对应 lived apart 的条件。

（5）带着选项中的人名回原文定位，按照人名在原文中出现的顺序，分别对应到句子。

Francis Galton

The idea of using twins to measure the influence of heredity dates back to 1875, when the English scientist Francis Galton first suggested the approach (and coined the phrase 'nature and nurture').

分析：Francis Galton first suggested the approach，此处 approach 代指前文 using twins to measure the influence of heredity，first suggested 和 approach 指代的前文信息则分别对应第 8 题 pioneered 和 using twins，括号中 coined the phrase 'nature and nurture' 则体现第 5 题 invented the term，所以第 5 题和第 8 题都与 Francis Galton 有关，都选 A。

Thomas Bouchard

Over two decades 137 sets of twins eventually visited Thomas Bouchard's lab in what became known as the Minnesota Study of Twins Reared Apart.

分析：Twins Reared Apart 对应第 9 题中 twins who had lived apart，说明第 9 题的行为发出者为 Thomas Bouchard，此题选 B。

Bouchard and his colleagues used this mountain of data to identify how far twins were affected by their genetic makeup. The key to their approach was a statistical concept called heritability.

分析：此句子中提及 The key to their approach was a statistical concept，其中 their 指代 Bouchard and his colleagues, approach 指代 used mountain of data to identify how far twins were affected by their genetic makeup；第 7 题提及 developed a mathematical method of measuring genetic influences，原文 statistical concept 对应 mathematical method，而 to identify how far twins were affected by genetic makeup 对应题中 measuring genetic influences, 故第 7 题也选 B。

Danielle Reed

Geneticist Danielle Reed has worked with many twins over the years and thought deeply about what twin studies have taught us. 'It's very clear when you look at twins that much of what they share is hardwired' she says. 'Many things about them are absolutely the same and unalterable. But it's also clear, when you get to know them, that other things about them are different. Epigenetics is the origin of a lot of those differences, in my view.

分析：此处是 Danielle Reed 第一次出现，但是没有体现与第 6 题 epigenetics will increase knowledge 有关的内容。

Reed credits Thomas Bouchard's work for today's surge in twin studies. 'He was the trailblazer,' she says. 'We forget that 50 years ago things like heart disease were thought to be caused entirely by lifestyle. Schizophrenia was thought to be due to poor mothering. Twin studies have allowed us to be more reflective about what people are actually born with and what's caused by experience.'

分析：此处是 Danielle Reed 第二次出现，但是也没有体现与第 6 题相关的关键词。

Having said that, Reed adds, the latest work in epigenetics promises to take our understanding even further.

分析：此处是 Danielle Reed 第三次出现，the latest work in epigenetics promises to take our understanding even further 体现了第 6 题中 epigenetics 与 knowledge 的关联，take our understanding even further 对应 increase our knowledge，所以此题选 C。

2.4.1.4 注意事项

（1）建立连接：将题目中每个特征与原文中的相应描述或内容匹配起来，如题目中的泛指或抽象内容在原文中会有具体对应。

（2）匹配细节：逐一对比题目和文章中的信息，确保题目中的修饰、限定等条件能够完全匹配而不仅仅是看起来相似。

（3）注意同义词和改写：文章中的描述可能不会完全重复选项中的词句，因此要注意同义词和改写形式。

2.4.2 句首句尾匹配题

句首句尾匹配题也称为句子补全题，在这一题型中，题干往往是一个句子的句首部分，考生需要基于原文中的信息，从一组选项中选出合适的选项作为句尾将句子补全。选项用字母（A、B、C等）标识。选项数量会比题干的数量多，因此不会全部用到。题干中句子开头部分出现的顺序与原文中出现的顺序相同，因此可以按顺序答题。句子配对题考的是考生扫读寻找信息的能力，以及对原文信息的理解能力，特别是当句首和句尾的信息与原文内容以同义替换的形式对应的时候，特别考查考生的细节理解能力。

2.4.2.1 解题步骤

（1）审题分析题干：分析题干缺失成分，缺什么补什么。如果是问原因的，就直接去原文中找表示原因的逻辑关系词。这类题型给出的选项数量通常比题干数量多，但是不会有选项复选。要先看题干，找出题干中的关键信息。不建议考生提前看选项，避免某些选项中的表达在原文中出现而干扰理解和匹配。

（2）画关键词：画出题干中的关键词，句首部分包含的主语是特定的考查对象，替换表达比较少，可以根据它进行定位。如果句首部分对主语有细节描述和其他限定，要注意这些线索并在原文中找到对应表达，才能精准定位。

（3）扫读原文并整合信息：利用题干中的定位词回原文定位，仔细阅读关键词或定位词前后的内容，包括上下文的句子，有时题干中的句首和其对应的选项并不是在原文中的同一个句子里出现，所以要注意原文信息内容和逻辑的完整性，要注意原文前后是否有否定词、转折词等。

（4）匹配同义词：将原文的内容与选项的内容进行匹配，匹配时必须应用逻辑推理，选择最适合句子的补充部分。选项的语法结构、具体用词可能与原文有所不同，考生需要选择与原文意思相同且逻辑对应的选项，去掉错误选项和已经选完的选项，减少对完成剩余题目的干扰。

（5）检查语法：在选完之后可以检查一下完整句子的语法，看看前后连起来是不是连贯且符合语法规范，从而进一步确定选择是否正确。

2.4.2.2 真题解析

下面以雅思真题 C13T4P2 Q18-21 为例，讲解完成句子题。

Questions 18–21

*Complete each sentence with the correct ending, **A–F**, below.*

*Write the correct letter, **A–F**, in boxes 18–21 on your answer sheet.*

18 Nutrients contained in the unused parts of harvested crops

19 Synthetic fertilisers produced with the Haber-Bosch process

20 Addition of a mixture developed by Pius Floris to the soil

21 The idea of zero net soil degradation

A may improve the number and quality of plants growing there.

B may contain data from up to nine countries.

C may not be put back into the soil.

D may help governments to be more aware of soil-related issues.

E may cause damage to different aspects of the environment

F may be better for use at a global level.

（Cambridge ESOL，2018：87）

解析：

该题型题文同序，可以按顺序做题，先分析 18 题，审题确定定位词和关键词。

18 Nutrients contained in the unused parts of harvested crops

利用考查对象 nutrients 和限定条件 unused parts of harvested crops 定位到原文以下句子：In the wild, when plants grow they remove nutrients from the soil, but then when the plants die and decay these nutrients are returned directly to the soil. Humans tend not to return unused parts of harvested crops directly to the soil to enrich it, meaning that the soil gradually becomes less fertile.

整合信息并分析：原文提到when the plants die and decay these nutrients are returned directly to the soil. Humans tend not to return unused parts of harvested crops directly to the soil。unused parts of harvested crops与题干中的Nutrients contained in the unused parts of harvested crops意思相符。根据原文信息tend not to return to soil这一否定逻辑和soil这个关键名词从选项中找对应信息和同义替换，C选项not to be put back into the soil与原文信息对应，此题选C。

19 Synthetic fertilisers produced with the Haber-Bosch process

本题可利用考查对象synthetic fertilisers和限定条件the Haber-Bosch process定位到原文以下句子：But these practices became inconvenient as populations grew and agriculture had to be run on more commercial lines. A solution came in the early 20th century with the Haber-Bosch process for manufacturing ammonium nitrate. Farmers have been putting this synthetic fertiliser on their fields ever since.

但是此处信息主要是对synthetic fertiliser出现的原因和应用的介绍，而题目中需要接续synthetic fertilisers产生的动作或结果，所以需要找出其带来的结果或影响，而此句话中并没有，所以要继续阅读后续信息：But over the past few decades, it has become clear this wasn't such a bright idea. Chemical fertilisers can release polluting nitrous oxide into the atmosphere and excess is often washed away with the rain, releasing nitrogen into rivers. More recently, we have found that indiscriminate use of fertilisers hurts the soil itself, turning it acidic and salty, and degrading the soil they are supposed to nourish.

此段落讲述的是chemical fertilisers对atmosphere, rivers, soil的负面影响，通过与剩余选项进行比较，E选项中cause damage to different aspects of the environment是对原文信息的概括和总结。damage to different aspects of the environment与原文release polluting nitrous oxide into the atmosphere, releasing nitrogen into rivers, hurts the soil itself都是讲这种负面影响，因此此题选E。

20 Addition of a mixture developed by Pius Floris to the soil

通过关键词mixture和Pius Floris定位到原文以下句子：When they applied Floris's mix to the desert-like test plots, a good crop of plants emerged that were not just healthy at the surface, but had roots strong enough to pierce dirt as hard as rock. The few plants that grew in the control plots, fed with traditional fertilisers, were small and weak.

句中，Floris's mix对应mixture developed by Pius Floris。原文通过将traditional fertilisers对plants的影响与Floris's mix对plants的影响做对比，发现Floris's mix给植物带来的是积极改变：a good crop of plants emerged that were not just healthy at the surface, but had roots strong。所以要在剩余选项中找到对plants带来的影响，A选项may improve the number and quality of plants growing there与原文a good crop, healthy, strong相对应，所以此题选A。

21 The idea of zero net soil degradation

通过关键词zero net soil degradation定位到原文以下句子：We need ways of presenting the problem that bring it home to governments and the wider public, says Pamela Chasek at the International Institute for Sustainable Development, in Winnipeg, Canada. 'Most scientists don't speak language that policy-makers can understand, and vice versa.' Chasek and her colleagues have proposed a goal of 'zero net land degradation'. Like the idea of carbon neutrality, it is an easily understood target that can help shape expectations and encourage action.

题干 the idea of zero net soil degradation 对应原文 a goal of 'zero net land degradation'。原文用 a goal of 'zero net land degradation' 与 the idea of carbon neutrality 进行类比，表明它们是 an easily understood target that can help shape expectations and encourage action，正好呼应了前文中的目标和作用：We need ways of presenting the problem that bring it home to governments and the wider public。easily understood 对应 bring it home to governments and the wider public，此句中的 it 指代前文中提及的 problem，说明题目中 the idea of zero net soil degradation 的功能和作用是使 government 更了解这个问题，而 D 选项 may help government to be more aware of soil-related issues 与原文意思相同，体现了 the idea of zero net soil degradation 的作用。故此题选 D。

2.4.2.3 注意事项

（1）注重逻辑：该题型考查考生对文意的理解以及对句子结构和逻辑关系的分析，原文的暗示和逻辑关系连接词都是解题的依据。考生要熟悉常见的句首句尾搭配形式，了解其关系，如因果关系、比较关系、转折关系等。

（2）注重整体：句首句尾有时候概括或总结了原文段落的主旨或重点，不能只通过个别单词匹配选项，而应通过原文用到的论证方法来确定段落结构，以及要论证的关键句。题干和正确选项连起来应该与原文关键句的意思相同或相似，并且逻辑相符。

2.4.3 段落信息匹配题

段落信息匹配题也被称为寻找信息题，顾名思义，此类题型要求考生在原文的段落（或部分）中找到特定的信息。段落（或部分）用字母（A、B、C等）进行标识。考生需要把正确的段落（或部分）的字母写在答题纸上的相应的题号里。不是每个段落（或部分）都一定会被使用，有些段落（或部分）可能会被多次使用。如果段落（或部分）会被多次使用，那么题目说明部分会给出 You may use any letter more than once 的指令。段落信息匹配题主要考查段落细节，如特定细节、例子、原因、描述、比较情况、解释等。该题型采用乱序出题模式，且题目与原文的同义替换形式灵活多样，考查考生在文章中定位和识别特定信息的能力，对考生的理解能力和同义匹配能力要求较高。但是值得注意的是，题目中的信息并不一定在原文的一个句子中体现，而有可能是对段落中几个句子的概括，所以匹配难度有可能增加，使该题型成为雅思阅读中难度较高的题型。

2.4.3.1 解题步骤

（1）审题：确定是否有复选提示，如果有复选提示，说明有两题来自同一个段落（或部分）。

（2）分析题目画关键词：明确题目考查的特定信息类别，如原因、解释、细节描述、例子等。确定题目中考查的对象和限定条件；可以将题目中的考查对象和限定条件作为关键线索与原文进行匹配。

（3）预判原文：根据题目内容预判关键词在原文里的功能及可能出现的形式，方便定位和同义匹配。

（4）定位关键词：逐段扫读，了解每个段落的大致内容和结构，仔细阅读段首或段落重点逻辑部分，判断段落主旨是否与题目有相关性，并在段落中找关键词或同义词。

（5）匹配信息：找到关键词后，仔细阅读上下文，确保其内容和逻辑与题目中的信息一致，即考查对象与限定条件等都能找到对应信息，确保语义和逻辑一致性。

2.4.3.2 真题解析

接下来以雅思真题 C14T4P2 Q14-17 为例来讲解该题型。

Questions 14–17

Which paragraph contains the following information?

*Write the correct letter, **A–F**, in boxes 14–17 on your answer sheet.*

14　a reference to how quickly animal species can die out

15　reasons why it is preferable to study animals in captivity rather than in the wild

16　mention of two ways of learning about animals other than visiting them in zoos

17　reasons why animals in zoos may be healthier than those in the wild

（Cambridge ESOL，2019：88）

解析：

由于该题型是乱序出题，不能通过题号确定题目在原文中出现的顺序，所以该题型需要一次性分析好所有题目，以便在扫读原文定位的时候解决遇到的题目。

14　a reference to how quickly animal species can die out

　　关键词：animal species；die out

　　分析：how quickly 体现 die out 的速度，原文会有与时间或速度有关的表达。

15　reasons why it is preferable to study animals in captivity rather than in the wild

　　关键词：study animals；in captivity；in the wild

　　分析：reasons 体现论证 it is preferable to study animals in captivity rather than in the wild 的方法是因果论证，答案句应该是 it is preferable to study animals in captivity rather than in the wild 的支撑信息，解释题中的结论产生的原因，要注意原文中因果关系的信号词。

16　mention of two ways of learning about animals other than visiting them in zoos

　　关键词：learning about animals；visiting them（animals）in zoos

　　分析：two ways 与 other than visiting them in zoos 作为支撑信息体现 learning about animals 的不同方式，三者之间既是并列的关系，也存在不同之处，所以原文会有表示对比和并列的信号词。

17　reasons why animals in zoos may be healthier than those in the wild

　　关键词：animal in zoos；healthier；in the wild

　　分析：reasons 体现原文会用因果方式论证 animals in zoos may be healthier than those in the wild，答案句要体现题中的结论产生的原因，所以要注意表示因果的信号词，另外 be healthier than 体现两者之间的比较关系，也要注意原文中表示比较的信号词。

　　分析完题目以后回原文逐段筛查，遇到体现以上相关信息的内容就仔细匹配找同义替换或对应的信息。

Why zoos are good
Scientist David Hone makes the case for zoos

A In my view, it is perfectly possible for many species of animals living in zoos or wildlife parks to have a quality of life as high as, or higher than, in the wild. Animals in good zoos get a varied and high-quality diet with all the supplements required, and any illnesses they might have will be treated. Their movement might be somewhat restricted, but they have a safe environment in which to live, and they are spared bullying and social ostracism by others of their kind. They do not suffer from the threat or stress of predators, or the irritation and pain of parasites or injuries. The average captive animal will have a greater life expectancy compared with its wild counterpart, and will not die of drought, of starvation or in the jaws of a predator. A lot of very nasty things happen to truly 'wild' animals that simply don't happen in good zoos, and to view a life that is 'free' as one that is automatically 'good' is, I think, an error. Furthermore, zoos serve several key purposes.

（Cambridge ESOL，2019：86）

解析：通过 A 段第一句话 it is perfectly possible for many species of animals living in zoos or wildlife parks to have a quality of life as high as, or higher than, in the wild 能确定此句包含 species of animals living in zoos 和 in the wild 的比较关系，as high as, or higher than 是比较关系和得出结论的信号词，后文进一步解释 many species of animals living in zoos or wildlife parks to have a quality of life as high as, or higher than, in the wild 的原因，any illness they might have will be treated 和 They do not suffer from...pain of parasites or injuries 体现 17 题 animals in zoos may be healthier than those in the wild，所以 17 题选 A。

B Firstly, zoos aid conservation. Colossal numbers of species are becoming extinct across the world, and many more are increasingly threatened and therefore risk extinction. Moreover, some of these collapses have been sudden, dramatic and unexpected, or were simply discovered very late in the day. A species protected in captivity can be bred up to provide a reservoir population against a population crash or extinction in the wild. A good number of species only exist in captivity, with many of these living in zoos. Still more only exist in the wild because they have been reintroduced from zoos, or have wild populations that have been boosted by captive bred animals. Without these efforts there would be fewer species alive today. Although reintroduction successes are few and far between, the numbers are increasing and the very fact that species have been saved or reintroduced as a result of captive breeding proves the value of such initiatives.

（Cambridge ESOL，2019：86）

解析：B 段第一句指出 zoos aid conservation。后文通过 species are becoming extinct, and many more are increasingly threatened and therefore risk extinction 和 Moreover, some of these collapses have been sudden, dramatic and unexpected 进一步突出说明 conservation 的重要性或原因。其中，extinct 与 14 题 die out 为同义表达，sudden, dramatic and unexpected 则对应 how quickly，体现 die out 的速度。所以 14 题的内容出自 B 段。

C　Zoos also provide education. Many children and adults, especially those in cities, will never see a wild animal beyond a fox or pigeon. While it is true that television documentaries are becoming ever more detailed and impressive, and many natural history specimens are on display in museums, there really is nothing to compare with seeing a living creature in the flesh, hearing it, smelling it, watching what it does and having the time to absorb details. That alone will bring a greater understanding and perspective to many, and hopefully give them a greater appreciation for wildlife, conservation efforts and how they can contribute.

（Cambridge ESOL，2019：86）

解析：本段第一句提到 zoos also provide education，后面进一步说明 zoo 是如何发挥 education 这一作用的。While it is true that television documentaries are becoming ever more detailed and impressive, and many natural history specimens are on display in museums, there really is nothing to compare with seeing a living creature in the flesh, hearing it, smelling it, watching what it does and having the time to absorb details 句中，While 引导的从句提到 television documentaries 以及 many natural history specimens are on display in museums 为两种 education 的形式或方法，与 seeing a living creature in the flesh, hearing it, smelling it, watching what it does and having the time to absorb details 这个方法进行比较。三种情况虽然都是 education 的方式，但 while 和 nothing to compare with 体现了方法之间的差异性，与 16 题 two ways of learning about animals other than visiting them in zoos 相对应，故 16 题的内容来自 C 段。

D　In addition to this, there is also the education that can take place in zoos through signs, talks and presentations which directly communicate information to visitors about the animals they are seeing and their place in the world. This was an area where zoos used to be lacking, but they are now increasingly sophisticated in their communication and outreach work. Many zoos also work directly to educate

> conservation workers in other countries, or send their animal keepers abroad to contribute their knowledge and skills to those working in zoos and reserves, thereby helping to improve conditions and reintroductions all over the world.

（Cambridge ESOL，2019：87）

解析：通过 D 段第一句能了解本段继续讲 education in zoos 的其他方式，与剩余题目即 15 题 reasons why it is preferable to study animals in captivity rather than in the wild 无关，可跳过本段。

> E　Zoos also play a key role in research. If we are to save wild species and restore and repair ecosystems, we need to know about how key species live, act and react. Being able to undertake research on animals in zoos where there is less risk and fewer variables means real changes can be effected on wild populations. Finding out about, for example, the oestrus cycle of an animal or its breeding rate helps us manage wild populations. Procedures such as capturing and moving at-risk or dangerous individuals are bolstered by knowledge gained in zoos about doses for anaesthetics, and by experience in handling and transporting animals. This can make a real difference to conservation efforts and to the reduction of human-animal conflicts, and can provide a knowledge base for helping with the increasing threats of habitat destruction and other problems.

（Cambridge ESOL，2019：87）

解析：本段第一句提到 zoos also play a key role in research，后文解释说明 zoos 是如何具有 research 的功能的。Being able to undertake research on animals in zoos where there is less risk and fewer variables 体现 research on animals in zoos 的好处。research 对应 15 题中的 study，there is less risk and fewer variables 对应 reasons，所以 15 题来自 E 段。

2.4.3.3 注意事项

（1）如果某段落明显不符合某个信息，可以将其排除，缩减选择范围。

（2）在找到关键词后，要确保题目中的内容和逻辑关系（如因果、比较）在相关段落里都能找到对应表达，才能确保准确性。

（3）合理分配时间给每个信息点的匹配过程，避免在某个题目上花费过多时间。

（4）注意同义替换的灵活性和逻辑对应的准确性。

2.4.4 标题匹配题

标题匹配题是一种给段落选标题的匹配题，此题型是由用罗马数字作为序号进行区分的一系列标题构成，标题概括了原文段落（或者部分）的主旨大意。考生需要将标题与段落进行匹配。原文中的段落用英文字母指代。考生要在答题卡对应的题号中填写罗马数字。标题数量往往比段落（或部分）的数量多，所以会有剩余的标题。有的时候有些段落（或部分）并没有被涵盖在此题型中。有时也会有范例。此题型中的每个标题只会被使用一次，所以不会有复选情况。该题型考查学生识别段落（或部分）主题和大意的能力，以及识别和区分主旨和细节的能力。

2.4.4.1 解题步骤

（1）审题：标题是唯一一种题目出现在文章前面的题型，可以先看一题目形式，如是否给出范例，如果有范例可以把对应的选项排除，避免再选；再看一看是否所有段落都被考查，可以划去未考查段落前的序号，避免匹配错误。

（2）先看段落，确定主旨和结构：与细节题不同，标题匹配题不需要通过定位词去原文中找定位来回答特定的问题，而是要在理解每个段落大意和结构的基础上，将段落与标题进行匹配。注意段落中能体现主题的句子，如段落中心句，以及包含重要逻辑关系的句子，如包含转折、递进、因果等逻辑信号词的部分，因为这些句子要么体现段落的重点，要么作为支撑句来突出主题。

（3）对比选项：将刚刚看到的段落重点与标题选项进行比对，找出与段落重点或中心对应的标题，或者能概括段落细节的标题。

（4）分析并匹配：确定选项能体现段落的重点或中心句，或者概括段落的支撑信息，与原文的内容和逻辑相符。

（5）选择并检查：每分析完一个段落，就可以分析选项并进行匹配和选择，边做边划掉选出的选项。这样一方面可以减少需要匹配的项目，另一方面也可以检查每个选项是否能够准确地概括相应段落的内容，避免出现遗漏或匹配错误。

2.4.4.2 真题解析

接下来以雅思真题 C12T7P1 Q1-4 为例进行分析。

Reading Passage 1 has seven paragraphs, **A–G**.

Choose the correct heading for each paragraph from the list of headings below.

*Write the correct number **i–viii**, in boxes **1–7** on your answer sheet.*

List of headings

i	The importance of getting the timing right
ii	Young meets old
iii	Developments to the disadvantage of tortoise populations
iv	Planning a bigger idea
v	Tortoises populate the islands
vi	Carrying out a carefully prepared operation
vii	Looking for a home for the islands' tortoises
viii	The start of the conservation project

Flying tortoises

An airborne reintroduction programme has helped conservationists take significant steps to protect the endangered Galapagos tortoise.

（Cambridge ESOL，2017：59）

解析：分析标题，预判文章结构和内容。通过文章标题能够确定文章主题词是 tortoises，而副标题体现文章重点说明 an airborne reintroduction programme has helped conservationists protect the tortoise 这个事件，那么文章会依次介绍 tortoises 的基本情况，endangered 的原因，通过什么样的方式来 protect，并且能让 tortoises 最终以 flying 的形式出现。

> A Forests of spiny cacti cover much of the uneven lava plains that separate the interior of the Galapagos island of Isabela from the Pacific Ocean. With its five distinct volcanoes, the island resembles a lunar landscape. Only the thick vegetation at the skirt of the often cloud-covered peak of Sierra Negra offers respite from the barren terrain below. This inhospitable environment is home to the giant Galapagos tortoise. Some time after the Galapagos's birth, around five million years ago, the islands were colonised by one or more tortoises from mainland South America. As these ancestral tortoises settled on the individual islands, the different populations adapted to their unique environments, giving rise to at least 14 different subspecies. Island life agreed with them. In the absence of significant predators, they grew to become the largest and longest-living tortoises on the planet, weighing more than 400 kilograms, occasionally exceeding 1.8 metres in length and living for more than a century.

（Cambridge ESOL，2017：60）

解析：先快速浏览段落，获取主旨大意。段落前三句属于环境描写，第四句通过 this environment 指代前文的环境，并引出是 Galapagos tortoise 的 home，并在后文进一步介绍了 Galapagos tortoise 在这个环境中的适应情况：As these ancestral tortoises settled on the individual islands, the different populations adapted to their unique environments, giving rise to at least 14 different subspecies. Island life agreed with them. In the absence of significant predators, they grew to become the largest and longest-living tortoises on the planet…数量增多，体型大，寿命长。

带着以上信息与选项进行匹配：第 5 个选项，也就是 **v** Tortoises populate the islands 符合本段主旨，the different populations adapted to their unique environments, giving rise to at least 14 different subspecies 体现了它们是如何 populate 的。

> B Before human arrival, the archipelago's tortoises numbered in the hundreds of thousands. From the 17th century onwards, pirates took a few on board for food, but the arrival of whaling ships in the 1790s saw this exploitation grow exponentially. Relatively immobile and capable of surviving for months without food or water, the tortoises were taken on board these ships to act as food supplies during long ocean passages. Sometimes, their bodies were processed into high-grade oil. In total, an estimated 200,000 animals were taken from the archipelago before the 20th century. This historical exploitation was then exacerbated when settlers came to the islands. They hunted the tortoises and destroyed their habitat to clear land for agriculture. They also introduced alien species—ranging from cattle, pigs, goats, rats and dogs to plants and ants—that either prey on the eggs and young tortoises or damage or destroy their habitat.

（Cambridge ESOL，2017：60）

解析：Before human arrival, the archipelago's tortoises numbered in the hundreds of thousands 这句话再次体现上文 Tortoises populate the islands 的情况，numbered in the hundreds of thousands 再一次验证标题，但是也暗示了随着 human arrival，tortoises 的数量会发生变化。后文描述了人类的行为，以及随着人类而来的外来物种如何对 tortoises 以及 their habit 造成负面影响，the tortoises were taken on board these ships to act as food supplies…their bodies were processed into high-grade oil…They hunted the tortoises and destroyed their habitat to clear land for agriculture. They also introduced alien species…that either prey on the eggs and young tortoises or damage or destroy their habitat.

文章列举了使得 number 变少的原因，即一些负面因素，体现了否定的色彩。**iii** Developments to the disadvantage of tortoise populations 中的 developments 概括了原文中描述的多个情况，disadvantage of tortoise populations 体现了 number 变少的情况，也体现了负面、否定的情感色彩。

> C Today, only 11 of the original subspecies survive and of these, several are highly endangered. In 1989, work began on a tortoise-breeding centre just outside the town of Puerto Villamil on Isabela, dedicated to protecting the island's tortoise populations. The centre's captive-breeding programme proved to be extremely successful, and it eventually had to deal with an overpopulation problem.

（Cambridge ESOL，2017：60）

解析：Today, only 11 of the original subspecies survive and of these, several are highly endangered 再一次体现 the disadvantage of tortoise populations。为了改善这一状况，In 1989, a tortoise-breeding centre dedicated to protecting the island's tortoise populations，而 The centre's captive-breeding programme proved to be extremely successful。**vii** Looking for a home for the islands' tortoises 此标题体现了 breeding centre 的作用 dedicated to protecting the populations。The centre's captive-breeding programme proved to be extremely successful, and it eventually had to deal with an overpopulation problem，说明 island's tortoise 在 breeding centre 的数量增多。标题中的 home 指代 breeding centre，a home for the islands' tortoises 体现了 the islands' tortoises 的数量在此处增加，缓解了本段开头提到的 endangered 的情况。

> D　The problem was also a pressing one. Captive-bred tortoises can't be reintroduced into the wild until they're at least five years old and weigh at least 4.5 kilograms, at which point their size and weight—and their hardened shells—are sufficient to protect them from predators. But if people wait too long after that point, the tortoises eventually become too large to transport.

（Cambridge ESOL，2017：60）

解析： The problem was also a pressing one 中的 the problem 指代上文的 overpopulation problem。不难发现，解决该问题的方法应该是 introducing captive-bred tortoises into the wild。但是本段提到了一个重要时间节点 at least five years old，早于此或者晚于此都会带来其他问题。带着此信息与选项比对，第一个选项 **i** The importance of getting the timing right 中，getting the timing right 概括体现了 at least five years old，而 the importance 概括了解释这个时间节点的原因，their size and weight—and their hardened shells—are sufficient to protect them from predators 以及 too large to transport。

2.4.4.3 注意事项

（1）避免细节干扰：标题是对原文的概括和总结，如果标题内容与原文细节用词一致，说明此标题没有起到概括作用。

（2）注意同义替换：标题的信息往往起到概括作用，标题用词能体现原文中的信息，但是不一定会用原文中的词语，所以要注重分析，联系原文的主旨、细节等进行判断。

（3）适当练习：通过适当的练习掌握分析和解题方法有助于提升分析能力和正确率。

3 雅思阅读模拟试题

Test 1

READING PASSAGE 1

*You should spend about 20 minutes on **Questions 1–13**, which are based on Reading Passage 1 below.*

Light Pollution

Most environmental pollution on Earth comes from humans and their inventions. Take, for example, the automobile or that miraculous human-made material, plastic. Today, automobile emissions are a major source of air pollution contributing to climate change, and plastics fill our ocean, creating a significant health hazard to marine animals.

And what about the electric lightbulb, thought to be one of the greatest human inventions of all time? Electric light can be a beautiful thing, guiding us home when the sun goes down, keeping us safe and making our homes cozy and bright. However, like carbon dioxide emissions and plastic, too much of a good thing has started to negatively impact the environment. Light pollution, the excessive or inappropriate use of outdoor artificial light, is affecting human health, wildlife behavior, and our ability to observe stars and other celestial objects.

Light pollution is a global issue. This became glaringly obvious when the World Atlas of Night Sky Brightness, a computer-generated map based on thousands of satellite photos, was published in 2016. Available online for viewing, the atlas shows how and where our globe is lit up at night. Vast areas of North America, Europe, the Middle East, and Asia are glowing with light, while only the most remote regions on Earth (Siberia, the Sahara, and the Amazon) are in total darkness. Some of the most light-polluted countries in the world are Singapore, Qatar, and Kuwait.

Sky glow is the brightening of the night sky, mostly over urban areas, due to the electric lights of cars, streetlamps, offices, factories, outdoor advertising, and buildings, turning night into day for people who work and play long after sunset.

People living in cities with high levels of sky glow have a hard time seeing more than a handful of stars at night. Astronomers are particularly concerned with sky glow pollution as it reduces their ability to view celestial objects.

More than 80 percent of the world's population, and 99 percent of Americans and Europeans, live under sky glow. It sounds pretty, but sky glow caused by anthropogenic activities is one of the most pervasive forms of light pollution.

Artificial light can wreak havoc on natural body rhythms in both humans and animals. Nocturnal light interrupts sleep and confuses the circadian rhythm—the internal, twenty-four-hour clock that guides day and night activities and affects physiological processes in nearly all living organisms. One of these processes is the production of the hormone melatonin, which is released when it is dark and is inhibited when there is light present. An increased amount of light at night lowers melatonin production, which results in sleep deprivation, fatigue, headaches, stress, anxiety, and other health problems. Recent studies also show a connection between reduced melatonin levels and cancer. In fact, new scientific discoveries about the health effects of artificial light have convinced the American Medical Association (AMA) to support efforts to control light pollution and conduct research on the potential risks of exposure to light at night. Blue light, in particular, has been shown to reduce levels of melatonin in humans. Blue light is found in cell phones and other computer devices, as well as in light-emitting diodes (LEDs), the kinds of bulbs that have become popular at home and in industrial and city lighting due to their low cost and energy efficiency.

Studies show that light pollution is also impacting animal behaviors, such as migration patterns, wake-sleep habits, and habitat formation. Because of light pollution, sea turtles and birds guided by moonlight during migration get confused, lose their way, and often die. Large numbers of insects, a primary food source for birds and other animals, are drawn to artificial lights and are instantly killed upon contact with light sources. Birds are also affected by this, and many cities have adopted a "Lights Out" program to turn off building lights during bird migration.

A study of blackbirds (Turdus merula) in Germany found that traffic noise and artificial night lighting causes birds in the city to become active earlier than birds in natural areas—waking and singing as much as five hours sooner than their country cousins. Even animals living under the sea may be affected by underwater artificial lighting. One study looked at how marine animals responded to brightly lit panels submerged under water off the coast of Wales. Fewer filter feeding animals, such as the sea squirt and sea bristle, made their homes near the lighted panels. This could mean that the light from oil rigs, passing ships, and harbors is altering marine ecosystems.

Even in places meant to provide protected natural habitats for wildlife, light pollution is making an impact. The National Park Service (NPS) has made maintaining a dark night sky a priority. The NPS Night Skies Team has been monitoring night sky brightness in some one hundred parks, and nearly every park showed at least some light pollution.

There are three other kinds of light pollution: glare, clutter, and light trespass. Glare is excessive brightness that can cause visual discomfort (for example, when driving). Clutter is bright, confusing, and excessive groupings of light sources (for example, Times Square in New York City, New York). Light trespass is when light extends into an area where it is not wanted or needed (like a streetlight illuminating a nearby bedroom window). Most outdoor lighting is poorly positioned, sending wasted electricity up into the sky.

There are several organizations working to reduce light pollution. One of these is the U.S.-based International Dark Sky Association (IDA), formed in 1988 to preserve the natural night sky. IDA educates the public and certifies parks and other places that have worked to reduce their light emissions. In 2017, the IDA approved the first U.S. dark sky reserve. The massive Central Idaho Dark Sky Reserve, which clocks in at 3,667 square kilometers (1,416 square miles), joined eleven other dark sky reserves established around the world. As of December of 2018, IDA lists thirteen dark sky reserves on their site.

More people are taking action to reduce light pollution and bring back the natural night sky. Many states have adopted legislation to control outdoor lighting, and manufacturers have designed and produced high-efficiency light sources that save energy and reduce light pollution.

Individuals are urged to use outdoor lighting only when and where it is needed, to make sure outdoor lights are properly shielded and directing light down instead of up into the sky, and to close window blinds, shades, and curtains at night to keep light inside.

Questions 1–7

Do the following statements agree with the information given in Reading Passage 1?

In boxes 1–7 on your answer sheet, write

TRUE	*if the statement agrees with the information*
FALSE	*if the statement contradicts the information*
NOT GIVEN	*if there is no information on this*

1. The health of animals in the ocean is threatened by human-made material.
2. Light pollution exerts more negative influences on human health than on wildlife behavior.
3. The World Atlas of Night Sky Brightness was the first computer-generated map to show the use of artificial light.
4. Astronomers can view celestial objects more clearly due to sky glow.
5. There is a positive link between hormone melatonin production and the amount of light at night.
6. Blue light has led to reduction in human melatonin levels.
7. LEDs in computers result in blue light.

Questions 8–13

Complete the summary below.

*Choose **NO MORE THAN THREE WORDS** from the passage for each answer.*

Write your answers in boxes 8–13 on your answer sheet.

Light pollution exerts negative influences on how animal behave. Sea turtles and birds have difficulty distinguishing light pollution from **8** .... , and get lost during migration. A great number of insects are killed as soon as they touch **9** .... A study of blackbirds in Germany showed that urban birds wake and sing five hours earlier than those in natural areas, due to **10** .... as well as man-made lighting. Among three other types of light pollution, **11** .... is the one that make eyes uncomfortable, especially for people in cars. Organizations like IDA is dedicated to preserve the natural night sky and officially admits places like **12** .... , where light emissions have decreased. Outdoor lighting in some states have been controlled by law. In addition, **13** .... have been produced to reduce energy consumption and light pollution.

READING PASSAGE 2

*You should spend about 20 minutes on **Questions 14–26**, which are based on Reading Passage 2 below.*

How to raise the world's IQ

People today are much cleverer than they were in previous generations. A study of 72 countries found that average IQs rose by 2.2 points a decade between 1948 and 2020. This stunning change is known as the 'Flynn effect' after James Flynn, the scientist who first noticed it. Flynn was initially baffled by his discovery. It took millions of years for the brain to evolve. How could it improve so rapidly over just a few decades?

The answer is largely that people were becoming better nourished and mentally stimulated. Just as muscles need food and exercise to grow strong, so the brain needs the right nutrients and activity to develop. Kids today are much less likely to be malnourished than they were in past decades, and more likely to go to school. Yet there is no room for complacency.

Globally, 22% of under-fives—roughly 150m children—are malnourished to the point of stunting. That means their brains are likely to be stunted, too. Half the world's children suffer micronutrient deficiency, which can also impede brain development. Poor nutrition and a lack of stimulation can translate into a loss of as many as 15 IQ points. Damage incurred during the 'golden window' of the first 1,000 days after conception is likely to be permanent.

The world grows enough food, but several obstacles stop nutrients getting into young brains. One is war. Families sheltering from shrapnel cannot venture out to plant or harvest, and some governments intentionally starve restive regions into submission. Another is disease. Hungry children fall sick more often, and the energy they spend battling bugs cannot be devoted to growing grey matter.

Poverty is a big part of the problem. But global data from UNICEF, an aid agency, show that although half the children with very restricted diets (including no more than two food groups) are indeed from poor families, the other half are not. Other factors, such as poor eating habits, are also to blame.

Many parents, even in middle-income countries, think it is enough to stuff an infant with stodgy carbohydrates but neglect protein and micronutrients. Sexism plays a role, too. In patriarchal societies, husbands often eat first, wolf the tasty protein and leave their pregnant wives with iron deficiency. In some cultures, it is taboo for expectant mothers to eat certain highly nutritious foods, from eggs in parts of Ethiopia to shrimp in parts of Indonesia. Malnourished mothers are more likely to give birth to malnourished babies.

Demography adds urgency. Fertility is highest in countries where malnutrition is most widespread. Unless nutrition improves, the next generation will face greater cognitive challenges than the present one. That would be a dire outcome, especially because it is so easy to avoid. The World Bank estimates that it would cost a mere $12bn a year to fight malnutrition 'at scale'. That is slightly more than a third of what America wastes on farm subsidies.

Several tactics would work. The simplest is to fortify basic foods, such as flour, with micronutrients, such as iron, zinc and folic acid.

Another method is to give small sums of money to poor families with infants or pregnant mothers. Handing out cash is better than handing out food itself. It is more flexible—it can be spent on medicine as well as food. It costs less to distribute, since it can be sent digitally. And it is easier to monitor.

Some schemes make handouts conditional on other things that might help children, such as vaccinations or teaching parents about nutrition and hygiene. Changing people's habits is hard, but they have an incentive to learn, as most parents care that their children grow up healthy. Promoting better nutrition should be part of health-care systems, concentrating on those crucial first 1,000 days.

Meanwhile, more research is needed. Scientists in Bangladesh have found that most women in local slums have inflamed intestines, meaning they lack the right gut bacteria to absorb nutrients properly, and are testing cheap ways to promote benign bacteria. Researchers in Africa are working out how to treat anaemia (a lack of iron) without encouraging malaria (since the parasite thrives in iron-rich blood).

Some argue that human intelligence will matter less as people outsource their thinking to artificial intelligence. To assume this would be as foolish as betting 100 years ago that the invention of the car would make it unnecessary to walk. In the workplace, human intelligence and AI will probably complement each other. And brains are for the joy of thinking, as well as earning money. Steven Pinker of Harvard University calls intelligence 'a tailwind in life', helping people adapt rationally to new challenges or a changing environment. For a modest price, the next generation can have a stronger tailwind. It would not only be wrong to refuse them. It would be stupid.

Questions 14–17

Complete the sentences below.

Choose **NO MORE THAN TWO WORDS** from the passage for each answer.

Write your answers in boxes 14–17 on your answer sheet.

14 Food and physical exercise enable muscles to grow, similarly, in addition to appropriate activities, brain development also depends on proper ....

15 Children's brains tend to be stunted with inadequate ....

16 The energy starving children use to fight disease hardly can contribute to the growth of ....

17 According to UNICEF, there is a correlation between poverty and children's poor ....

Questions 18–22

Complete each sentence with the correct ending, **A–F**, below.

Write the correct letter, **A–F**, in boxes 18–22 on your answer sheet.

18 An infant fed mainly with stodgy carbohydrates
19 Husbands taking the tasty protein in patriarchal societies
20 The next generation in nations with widespread malnutrition
21 Women with inflamed intestines
22 Parents learning nutrition and hygiene

A may cause problems related to sexism.
B may encounter more cognitive difficulties than the current generation.
C may not provide the necessary nutrients for the infant's proper growth.
D may be related to the lack of some living organisms.
E may lead to a deficiency of a particular substance in pregnant women.
F may contribute to children's health.

Questions 23 and 24

Choose **TWO** letters, **A–E**.

Write the correct letters in boxes 23 and 24 on your answer sheet.

Which **TWO** are mentioned to help young brains develop?

A   distribute nutritious basic food

B   donate a small amount of cash to poor families with either young children or pregnant women

C   hand out medicine

D   monitor how the donated money is used

E   provide parents with necessary information relevant to children's health

Questions 25 and 26

*Choose **TWO** letters, A–E.*

Write the correct letters in boxes 25 and 26 on your answer sheet.

Which **TWO** of the following statements are correct according to the last paragraph?

A   human intelligence will become less important

B   it will be possible to make human intelligence and AI compatible when people work

C   there would be no need for people to walk because of the use of cars

D   AI could make think enjoyable

E   the next generation will make use of AI to adapt to challenges and changes

READING PASSAGE 3

*You should spend about 20 minutes on **Questions 27–40**, which are based on Reading Passage 3 below.*

Effects of Transportation on the Economy

A   The ability to transport goods and human beings safely and efficiently across long distances is fundamental to economic life in modern societies. A brief look at the early United States illustrates this principle dramatically. In the first half of the 19th century, Americans built a robust transportation network through new technologies and heroic engineering ventures. These investments in infrastructure, often described as 'internal improvements' in the political debate of the time, rapidly transformed the North American continent into a patchwork of overland roads, canals, and railways. These expanded transport links laid the foundation of a bustling nationwide economy of commercial agriculture and industry.

B   During the colonial and revolutionary periods, most of the nonindigenous population of North America lived near the Atlantic coast. Eighteenth-century America depended chiefly on water transportation to link small-scale farming and the artisan industry with transatlantic trade. Farmers living near the Hudson River or other river systems could float their crops downstream to the port cities. Upstream travel was slow and arduous. Post roads between the colonies had been built by the mid-1700s, but they were poorly built and not suitable for commercial transport. As a rule, the movement of agricultural produce and other goods was costly and took a great deal of time.

C   In 1794, a new road opened between Philadelphia, Pennsylvania, and Lancaster, Pennsylvania. It was the country's first toll road, financed and built privately by a corporation, which was chartered by the state. Soon, other groups of merchants were incorporating to pave more turnpikes, especially in the northeast. By the early 1820s, thousands of kilometers of graded paths crisscrossed the region. The toll roads usually failed to turn a profit for their investors, but they provided a major boost to regional commerce. The federal government paid for one major highway during this era, heading westward from Cumberland, Maryland, at the inland headwaters of the Potomac River. The Army Corps of Engineers began building the Cumberland Road, also called the National Road, in 1811. By 1818, it had crossed the Appalachian Mountains and reached Wheeling, West Virginia, permitting overland travel between the Potomac and Ohio rivers.

Meanwhile, river transport was aided immensely by the application of steam power. While American engineer Robert Fulton did not invent the steamboat, he was the first to make an unqualified success with the technology. In 1807, his paddle-wheeled vessel, the Clermont, achieved the astonishing speed of eight kilometers per hour (five miles per hour) on its first voyage up the Hudson River from New York City, New York, to Albany, New York. Steamboats made two-way river traffic a viable proposition—and they could haul a large amount of freight. Before long there were dozens of them, then hundreds, steaming along the Mississippi River and other major rivers.

D   Canals gave the maritime transportation system still greater reach. The largest and most important was New York's Erie Canal, approved by the state legislature in 1817 and completed eight years later. Extending from Buffalo to Albany at a width of 12.1 meters (40 feet) and a depth of 1.2 meters (4 feet), this mighty engineering feat created an artificial waterway connecting the Great Lakes to the Hudson River, which empties into the Atlantic. The Erie Canal drastically reduced both the travel time and the cost of shipping commodities such as grain and lumber from the Midwest to the eastern seaboard. It led to an immediate and dramatic increase in the shipment of such goods, and the state's investment in the monumental project paid off handsomely. Incoming toll revenues surpassed the entire cost of the canal's construction within 12 years. By the 1840s, New York City had become the nation's leading commercial port and well established as the country's financial and trade capital. The rest of the state of New York—especially cities along the canal route, such as Rochester and Syracuse—also prospered.

E   Other state governments hoped to replicate New York's success, leading to a furious round of publicly financed canal projects. By 1840, the United States had dug more than 4,828 kilometers (3,000 miles) of canals. Both Ohio and Indiana built systems connecting the Ohio River to Lake Erie at Cleveland and Toledo, respectively. The Illinois & Michigan Canal, completed in 1848, established a water link between the Mississippi River Valley and the Great Lakes. It spurred the city of Chicago, Illinois, to rise to prominence as the great Midwestern transport hub.

F   It was yet another innovation in transportation, the steam-powered locomotive, that ultimately had the furthest-reaching impact. Trains were a heavy-duty, fast, year-round transport solution, and in time they became the preferred option for commercial shipping. The earliest U.S. railroads covered only short distances, providing portage between two waterways. In 1827, a group of Baltimore, Maryland, businessmen formed a chartered corporation to build the first major railway between their city and the Ohio River. Many more private railway enterprises followed in the decades prior to the Civil War. Between 1840 and 1860, the nation saw a ten-fold increase in the amount of track laid, from 4,828 to 48,280 kilometers (3,000 to 30,000 miles). The majority of this development was in the northern states. Because competing companies built railways, the different lines used different rail gauges and track widths and were not interoperable until rails were standardized years later. The first transcontinental line was established in 1869 when the Central Pacific and Union Pacific lines met. Once their infrastructure was completed and initial problems resolved, the railways lowered the cost of transporting many kinds of goods. Railroads became a major industry, stimulating other heavy industries such as iron and steel production.

Questions 27–31

Reading Passage 3 has six sections, **A–F**.

Which section contains the following information?

*Write the correct letter, **A–F**, in boxes 27–31 on your answer sheet.*

NB   You may use any letter more than once.

27   mention of economic contribution to the local areas in spite of unprofitable outcomes to the sponsors themselves

28   reference to a term to describe the establishment of a form of infrastructure

29   mention of an organization was formed to build a transport system connecting city and a particular river.

30   a project not only increased the country's tax revenues but also made related cities thrived

31   how a person applied steam power to a form of transport

Questions 32–36

Look at the following statements(Questions 32–36) and the list of dates below.

Match each statement with the correct date, **A–F**.

Write the correct letter, **A–F**, in boxes 32–36 on your answer sheet.

32   a project was officially agreed
33   the first line crossing continent was set up
34   a road with different names began to be constructed
35   the first American toll road was put into use
36   the rate at which a means of transportation traveled on its first day made it a success

   A   1794
   B   1811
   C   1807
   D   1817
   E   1827
   F   1869

Questions 37–40

Do the following statements agree with the views of the writer in Reading Passage 3?

In boxes 37–40 on your answer sheet, write

> **TRUE**   if the statement agrees with the information
> **FALSE**   if the statement contradicts the information
> **NOT GIVEN**   if there is no information on this

37 In the 18th century, post roads were mainly used to transport commodities.

38 Erie Canal was the first artificial canal in New York.

39 Chicago became a Midwestern transport hub because of the connection between the Mississippi River Valley and the Great Lakes.

40 There were no standardized rails between 1840 and 1860 in the northern states.

Test 2

READING PASSAGE 1

*You should spend about 20 minutes on **Questions 1–13**, which are based on Reading Passage 1 below.*

Antonie van Leeuwenhoek(1632–1723)
The Dutch scientist invented the first practical microscope

Leeuwenhoek was born in Holland on October 24, 1632, and as a teenager he became an apprentice at a linen draper's shop. Although it doesn't seem a likely start to a life of science, from here Leeuwenhoek was set on a path to inventing his microscope. At the shop, magnifying glasses were used to count the threads and inspect the quality of cloth. He was inspired and taught himself new methods for grinding and polishing tiny lenses of great curvature, which gave magnifications up to 275x (275 times the subject's original size), the finest known at that time.

People had been using magnifying lenses since the 12th century and convex and concave lenses for vision correction since the 1200s and 1300s. In 1590, Dutch lens grinders Hans and Zacharias Janssen constructed a microscope with two lenses in a tube; though it may not have been the first microscope, it was a very early model. Also credited with the invention of the microscope about the same time was Hans Lippershey, the inventor of the telescope. Their work led to others' research and development on telescopes and the modern compound microscope, such as Galileo Galilei, Italian astronomer, physicist, and engineer whose invention was the first given the name 'microscope.'

The compound microscopes of Leeuwenhoek's time had issues with blurry figures and distortions and could magnify only up to 30 or 40 times.

Leeuwenhoek's work on his tiny lenses led to the building of his microscopes, considered the first practical ones. They bore little resemblance to today's microscopes, however; they were more like very high-powered magnifying glasses and used only one lens instead of two.

Other scientists didn't adopt Leeuwenhoek's versions of microscopes because of the difficulty in learning to use them. They were small (about 2 inches long) and were used by holding one's eye close to the tiny lens and looking at a sample suspended on a pin.

With these microscopes, though, he made the microbiological discoveries for which he is famous. Leeuwenhoek was the first to see and describe bacteria (1674), yeast plants, the teeming life in a drop of water (such as algae), and the circulation of blood corpuscles in capillaries. The word 'bacteria' didn't exist yet, so he called these microscopic living organisms 'animalcules.' During his long life, he used his lenses to make pioneer studies on an extraordinary variety of things—living and nonliving—and reported his findings in more than 100 letters to the Royal Society of England and the French Academy.

Leeuwenhoek's first report to the Royal Society in 1673 described bee mouthparts, a louse, and a fungus. He studied the structure of plant cells and crystals, and the structure of human cells such as blood, muscle, skin, teeth, and hair. He even scraped the plaque from between his teeth to observe the bacteria there, which, Leeuwenhoek discovered, died after drinking coffee.

He was the first to describe sperm and postulated that conception occurred when a sperm joined with an ovum, though his thought was that the ovum just served to feed the sperm. At the time, there were various theories of how babies formed, so Leeuwenhoek's studies of sperm and ovum of various species caused an uproar in the scientific community. It would be around 200 years before scientists would agree on the process.

Like his contemporary Robert Hooke, Leeuwenhoek made some of the most important discoveries of early microscopy. In one letter from 1716, he wrote,

'My work, which I've done for a long time, was not pursued in order to gain the praise I now enjoy, but chiefly from a craving after knowledge, which I notice resides in me more than in most other men. And therewithal, whenever I found out anything remarkable, I have thought it my duty to put down my discovery on paper, so that all ingenious people might be informed thereof.'

He did not editorialize on meanings of his observations and acknowledged he was not a scientist but merely an observer. Leeuwenhoek was not an artist either, but he worked with one on the drawings he submitted in his letters.

Van Leeuwenhoek also contributed to science in one other way. In the final year of his life, he described the disease that took his life. Van Leeuwenhoek suffered from uncontrollable contractions of the diaphragm, a condition now known as Van Leeuwenhoek disease. He died of the disease, also called diaphragmatic flutter, on August 30, 1723, in Delft. He is buried at the Oude Kerk (Old Church) in Delft.

Some of Leeuwenhoek's discoveries could be verified at the time by other scientists, but some discoveries could not because his lenses were so superior to others' microscopes and equipment. Some people had to come to him to see his work in person.

Just 11 of Leeuwenhoek's 500 microscopes exist today. His instruments were made of gold and silver, and most were sold by his family after he died in 1723. Other scientists did not use his microscopes, as they were difficult to learn to use. Some improvements to the device occurred in the 1730s, but big improvements that led to today's compound microscopes didn't happen until the middle of the 19th century.

Questions 1–7

Do the following statements agree with the information given in Reading Passage 1?

In boxes 1–7 on your answer sheet, write

> **TRUE** *if the statement agrees with the information*
> **FALSE** *if the statement contradicts the information*
> **NOT GIVEN** *if there is no information on this*

1 Hans and Zacharias Janssen made the first microscope in the world.

2 Galileo Galilei coined the word "microscope" to name his invention.

3 There were many similarities between Leeuwenhoek's early microscopes and those of today.

4   Leeuwenhoek's versions of microscopes were difficult for other scientists to learn to use.

5   Leeuwenhoek's studies of sperm and ovum were accepted by scientists immediately.

6   Robert Hooke were inspired by Leeuwenhoek's discoveries.

7   Leeuwenhoek regarded him an observer rather than a scientist.

Questions 8–13

Complete the notes below.

Choose **ONE WORD ONLY** from the passage for each answer.

Write your answers in boxes 8–13 on your answer sheet.

Antonie van Leeuwenhoek

Early life

- was born in Holland in 1632
- as an **8** .... in a shop selling linen drapery

Discoveries

- was the first to discover and give description of yeast plants, living organisms such as **9** .... in a waterdrop
- the creatures he discovered by microscopes were defined as **10** .... by him
- He removed the **11** .... from his teeth and discovered drinking coffee contributed to the death of the bacteria living there.
- studies on sperm and ovum were ahead of other scientists

Death and legacy

- suffered from painful contracting of the **12** .... and was dead in 1723 in Delft
- his instruments were made of precious metals and **13** .... of him sold the majority of them after his death

READING PASSAGE 2

You should spend about 20 minutes on **Questions 14–26**, which are based on Reading Passage 2 below.

Is it better to be an early bird or a night owl?

The promise and perils of waking before sunrise

A   Rare is the chief executive who extols the virtues of a lie-in. Tim Cook, boss of Apple, maker of the iPhone, wakes between 4am and 5am. So does Bob Iger, his counterpart at Disney, a media giant. According to one survey, two-thirds of the chief executives of large American companies are up by 6 o'clock; for average Americans the share is less than one in three. For those aspiring to corporate greatness, the message seems clear: you snooze, you lose.

Your guest Bartleby harbours no such ambitions. But he has, in the past, experimented with early starts, and can confirm that their benefits go beyond the smug sense of satisfaction that comes from arriving at your desk before your editor. Inboxes can be cleared and tricky problems mulled over before the onslaught of emails and meetings begins, leaving you feeling well prepared for the day ahead.

B   Those quiet hours of the morning need not be spent solely on work. In a popular genre of TikTok videos, influencers film themselves performing elaborate morning routines in which they submerge themselves in ice baths, recite affirmations and mindfully prepare nootropic coffees. In one widely pilloried video, Kris Krohn, a business coach, details how he wakes at 4 in the morning to 'align the pharmacy of the body and over-dopamine the mind'.

C   Although Mr. Krohn's routine may lack scientific rigour, plenty of research finds merit in early rising. In a study conducted in 2012 by Renée Biss and Lynn Hasher, then both at the University of Toronto, early birds reported feeling happier and healthier. Night owls, their nocturnal opposites, tend to have less sleep, which can weigh on their mood and health—as well as their productivity. Andrew Conlin of the University of Oulu, in Finland, and co-authors found that men who rose late made 4% less money than those who were up early (they did not test whether an extra 4% is enough to entice slumberers to throw off their duvets).

D   Early birds are certainly held in higher regard. Rolling into the office late continues to be frowned upon in most workplaces. A study published in 2022 by Jessica Dietch of Oregon State University and her co-authors found that night owls were perceived by respondents as being 'lazy', 'undisciplined' and 'immature'. To pile on the stereotypes, they are fatter, too, according to research by Lap Ah Tse of the Chinese University of Hong Kong and colleagues.

E Rising early is not, though, all upside. Those ready and waiting to receive work when the boss arrives may be given more of it. If the early bird gets the worm, the clever worm stays in bed. Urgent tasks often come up during the day, meaning that those who come in early may end up working just as late as their dawn-averse colleagues. And the more emails you send in the morning, the more responses you are bound to get back.

Waking before sunrise also risks turning you into a bore. Some larks cannot resist describing how much they got done while owls bashed the snooze button. Others go home early to tuck themselves in rather than socialise after hours. Night owls, by contrast, let loose. Research shows they drink more and take more drugs. Christoph Randler and colleagues at the Heidelberg University of Education found that men who stayed up later had 'higher dating success'. In the eyes of many, late nights are the preserve of youth, whereas early mornings are the domain of the geriatric.

F Efforts to alter your circadian rhythm are likely to end in sleepy frustration. A person's chronotype, to use the scientific lingo, is largely a product of their genes. Dimming your lights at night and buying a special alarm clock will not magically transform you into a morning person. Those early hours will be of little use if they are spent staring blankly at a screen through bleary eyes. This Bartleby abandoned his efforts at early starts after growing alarmed at the quantities of caffeine he required to stay awake. Early birds, for their part, lose out by never being the life of the party after the sun goes down. If nothing else, that gives them one fewer thing to feel smug about.

G Perhaps the best advice, then, is to stop worrying about your body clock. Most people are neither early birds nor night owls, but in between. They do not perform well first thing in the morning or late in the evening. Many, including your columnist, get sleepy in the afternoon, too. That is why most offices operate between 9 and 5—and why they ought to have nap rooms.

Questions 14–18

Reading Passage 2 has seven sections, A–G.

Which section contains the following information?

Write the correct letter, *A–G*, in boxes 14–18 on your answer sheet.

NB   You may use any letter more than once.

14   a mention of extra work may be assigned by supervisor

15   a reference to how a person felt other than being satisfied

16   an explanation why a person stopped getting up early

17   a reason why people come to work early may not finish work early

18   a mention of various activities people can do except for working in the morning

Questions 19–22

Complete the sentences below.

Choose **NO MORE THAN TWO WORDS** from the passage for each answer. Write your answers in boxes 19–22 on your answer sheet.

19   Less sleep may have negative impact on people's emotions, health and ……………… .

20   Many people believe that late nights are particular suitable for ……………… , while early mornings belong to the geriatric.

21   Changing circadian rhythm may lead to ……………… .

22   Chronotype is mainly influenced by one's ……………… .

Questions 23–26

Look at the following findings (**Questions 23–26**) and the list of researchers below.

Match each statement with the correct expert, *A–E*.

Write the correct letter, *A–E*, in boxes 23–26 on your answer sheet.

23   effect of the time to get out of bed on males' income

24   more likely to have romantic relationships

25   respondents from one group feel better mentally and physically while the opposite is true for the other group

26 stereotypical images held by respondents

    A Renée Biss and Lynn Hasher

    B Andrew Conlin

    C Jessica Dietch and her co-authors

    D Lap Ah Tse

    E Christoph Randler and colleagues

READING PASSAGE 3

*You should spend about 20 minutes on **Questions 27–40**, which are based on Reading Passage 3 below.*

How robots and AI change the meaningfulness of work

Machines might not take your job. But they could make it worse

July 19th was a day for help-desk heroes and support superstars. A routine software update by CrowdStrike, a cyber-security company, caused computer outages in offices, hospitals and airports worldwide. Most white-collar workers looked disconsolately at their screens and realised just how useless they are if they cannot log in. People in IT came to the rescue of helpless colleagues and stranded passengers. Their work that day was full of stress—but also full of meaning.

If machines can add purpose to some jobs when they fail, what about when they work properly? This is not an idle question. Discussions about artificial intelligence (AI) in particular easily get lost in hypothetical debates about wholesale job losses or, worse, the nature of consciousness. But technologies tend to spread in less dramatic ways, task by task rather than role by role. Before machines replace individuals, they change the nature of the work they do.

That is likely to affect job satisfaction. Many employees put a higher premium on non-monetary than monetary rewards. A recent Federal Reserve discussion paper by Katherine Lim and Mike Zabek surveyed American workers who had switched jobs to find out whether and why they thought their new positions were better; they found that interest in the work mattered more to people than pay and benefits.

Which is why another recent paper, from Milena Nikolova and Femke Cnossen of the University of Groningen and Boris Nikolaev of Colorado State University, makes for sobering reading. The authors looked at the prevalence of robots in industrial settings and how that affected workers. Robots reduced the perceived meaningfulness of jobs across the board, irrespective of age, gender, skills and the type of work. In theory, machines can free up time for more interesting tasks; in practice, they seem to have had the opposite effect.

In a separate paper, Ms Nikolova and Ms Cnossen, along with Anthony Lepinteur of the University of Luxembourg, explore why this might be. They find that industrial robots make jobs less physically taxing. But the number of tasks that remain open to humans dwindles, hurting both the variety of work and people's understanding of the production process. Work becomes more routine, not less.

Machines need not have a dulling effect. In their research Ms Nikolova and her co-authors found that people did not perceive a loss of autonomy if they were working with computers, where they have more control of the machine than the other way round. (Presuming, of course, you can turn it on.) And automation may well have a different impact on service industries like health care, where less time spent on drudge work might indeed mean more time with patients.

A paper from 2011 by Michael Barrett of the University of Cambridge and his co-authors found that the introduction of drug-dispensing robots into hospital pharmacies had disparate effects. Pharmacists felt the quality of their jobs had improved because they had more time for patient counselling. Like the IT administrators rolling back the CrowdStrike update, technicians enjoyed the enhanced status that came with knowing how to fix the robots. Pharmacy assistants had a more miserable time of it, however, as their role shrank to loading medicine into the machines.

Consumer reactions to automation can also vary. An experiment conducted by Eugina Leung, now of Tulane University, and her co-authors tested how customers reacted to different descriptions of a cooking set. People who prided themselves on being skilled chefs really didn't like products that promised to do everything at the touch of a button. A technology that cuts down on boring tasks is fine; one that threatens your sense of identity is not.

It is still too early to know how AI will affect the quality of work. Some will surely enjoy using a bot to brainstorm ideas and take care of menial tasks. Yet research by Pok Man Tang of the University of Georgia and his co-authors also suggests that workers who interact more with AI assistants feel lonelier and crave more social contact. The thing for managers to remember is that machines can make employees feel differently about their work. So it matters whether new technologies are introduced in collaboration with employees or imposed from above, and whether they enhance or sap their sense of competence. Bosses who ignore these issues are missing something meaningful.

Questions 27–30

Choose the correct letter, A, B, C or D

Write the correct letter in boxes 27–30 on your answer sheet.

27   The writer refers to the software update by CrowdStrike to illustrate the point that

   A   software updates often cause unexpected problems.

   B   cyber-security companies need to be more careful.

   C   technological advancements can have unforeseen consequences.

   D   global systems are vulnerable to software glitches.

28   The writer raises the question in the second paragraph in order to

   A   highlight the uncertainty of the impact of machines on jobs

   B   suggest that machines always perform better than humans do

   C   emphasize the positive effects of machines on work

   D   show that AI will replace humans in work

29   What can we know from the third paragraph?

   A   Monetary rewards are of greater significance for job satisfaction.

   B   Employees in USA change jobs frequently.

   C   Interest in the work may make employees feel more rewarding than pay does.

   D   Better positions bring about higher payment.

30   What does the paper of Milena Nikolova and Femke Cnossen's suggest?

   A   Robots have more impacts on certain professions.

   B   Robots enable workers to do more interesting tasks.

   C   The use of robots led to a decrease in how meaningful worker felt their jobs were.

   D   The effect of robots on job meaningfulness varies by worker characteristics.

Questions 31–36

Complete the summary using the list of phrases, A–H, below.

Write the correct letter, A–H, in boxes 31–36 on your answer sheet.

Ms Nikolova and Ms Cnossen, along with Anthony Lepinteur of the University of Luxembourg, find that although industrial robots can reduce physical **31** ...., they make work more **32** .... However, people did not feel unnecessary when they controlled the machine more. In addition, automated machines in some professions, such as **33** ...., may enable people to focus on more important tasks instead of taxing work. According to Michael Barrett and his team, the quality of pharmacists' work had enhanced, since they were more available to provide **34** .... for patients, while those whose work was limited to refill the machines felt even **35** .... Furthermore, an experiment carried out by Eugina Leung and her team suggests that although some technologies can be accepted, people tend to avoid those result in a sense of **36** ....

A	boring	**B**	relief	**C**	recognition	**D** professional advice
E	painful	**F**	burden	**G**	crisis	**H** medical service

Questions 37–40

Do the following statements agree with the claims of the writer in Reading Passage 3?

In boxes 37–40 on your answer sheet, write

    YES   *if the statement agrees with the claims of the writer*
    NO   *if the statement contradicts the claims of the writer*
    NOT GIVEN *if it is impossible to say what the writer thinks about this*

37 According to Ms Nikolova, Ms Cnossen, and Anthony Lepinteur, robots reduce both the number and the diversity of tasks humans can do.

38 People have less control of computers are more likely to have a sense of autonomy.

39 IT administrators enjoyed updating the software.

40 Pok Man Tang and his co-authors proves that interacting with AI assistants can improve workers' social ability.

Test 3

READING PASSAGE 1

*You should spend about 20 minutes on **Questions 1–13**, which are based on Reading Passage 1.*

Questions 1–7

*Reading Passage 1 has seven paragraphs, **A–G**.*

Choose the correct heading for each paragraph from the list of headings below.

*Write the correct number, **i–viii**, in boxes 1–7 on your answer sheet.*

i	Balancing water use and conservation in economic development
ii	Causes for illegal hunt
iii	Livelihoods of the natives and environmental threats
iv	International efforts to reduce demand for poached animals goods
v	Foreign poachers driven by illegal market demand
vi	A habitat for diverse species and home to several ethnic groups
vii	Devastating impacts on agriculture
viii	Fighting against poaching by cooperation

1 Paragraph A
2 Paragraph B
3 Paragraph C
4 Paragraph D
5 Paragraph E
6 Paragraph F
7 Paragraph G

Cracks in the Kalahari's Emerald: Threats to the Okavango Delta

Many species of plants and animals live in the Okavango Delta, but their well-being, and the well-being of the environment itself, is under threat from human activities

A The Okavango Delta is home to almost 2,000 plant and animal species that depend on the habitats of the delta for survival. Many threatened and endangered species, including the African wild dog (Lycaon pictus), the southern ground-hornbill (Bucorvus leadbeateri), the black rhinoceros (Diceros bicornis), and the white rhinoceros (Ceratotherium simum), call this inland delta their home. In addition to these animal populations, more than 100,000 people live in and around the Okavango Delta and depend on the resources it provides. The Okavango Delta Peoples of Botswana consist of five distinct ethnic groups: the Bugakwe, Dxeriku, Hambukushu, Wayeyi, and Xanekwe. Most people live on the outskirts of the delta, leaving huge uninhabited areas within it. Historically, some of these groups were grain farmers; others relied on hunting, gathering, and fishing to survive.

B Today, these indigenous groups continue to rely on subsistence farming, fishing, and other activities that have little impact on the environment or its ecosystems. There are, however, several other factors that threaten the integrity of the delta, including overdevelopment and poaching. The government of Botswana protects the land within Okavango Delta, but environmentalists worry that farming and industry just beyond its borders could have devastating impacts.

C One concern is water abstraction, or the removal of water for human use. Although abstraction from the upper part of the delta is not a major concern, increasing industrial demands pose a threat for the future. For example, Angola, which is north of Botswana and where the water in the delta originates, is planning a major initiative to increase commercial agricultural operations. This initiative would draw water from the Okavango Delta and possibly affect the surrounding environment. There are mechanisms in place, however, to protect the water supply to the delta. If Angola, Botswana, or Namibia wants to divert water from the Okavango River before it reaches the delta, their plans need to be approved by the Permanent Okavango River Basin Water Commission (OKACOM). OKACOM's mission is to promote economic prosperity, social justice, and environmentally conscious development of the Cubango-Okavango River Basin. To accomplish OKACOM's mission, all stakeholders need to work together to find a balance between supporting increased agriculture in the region and preserving the integrity of the delta.

D Poaching is a complex topic, and poachers hunt animals for reasons beyond simple economic gain. Thanks to conservation efforts, the population of African bush elephants (Loxodonta africana) in the delta has exploded. This can present problems for surrounding populations, as elephants that leave the protected land can destroy local crops and threaten the livelihoods of farmers, many of whom already live below the poverty line. Although rare, elephants have also been known to attack and even kill people. The residents near protected lands often view poaching as the only way to protect themselves and their crops. Others poach elephants, giraffes, and other animals to make bushmeat, which is then eaten or sold. As the population has increased and people have remained in poverty, demand for and prices of bushmeat have gone up, increasing the incentive for poaching.

E Not all poachers are inhabitants of the region. Local agencies report that many of the poachers who target rhinoceroses come to the delta from foreign countries, such as Zambia, and sell their wares on an underground, but well-organized, international market. These foreign poachers come to the area because of the high demand in some places of the world for rhinoceros horn, which some cultures believe to have medicinal properties. Additionally, although the sale of ivory is illegal in many places, in parts of Asia, there remains demand for elephant tusks to make jewelry and other items.

F   Combating poaching in the Okavango Delta will take joint efforts from a variety of sectors and both local and national governments. Some experts suggest that incentivizing the local community to become invested in the protection of wildlife would help decrease local poaching activity. This can mean sharing profits gained by preserves with the community or training and hiring more local members to work on preserves. Since many poachers have wilderness skills, they may be good candidates for legal jobs as wildlife managers.

G   Foreign governments and concerned citizens can also play a role in reducing demand for goods made from poached animals. Some experts suggest that increasing the availability of legal ivory and rhinoceros horns would weaken the underground market. Several countries in Asia are using marketing campaigns to decrease demand for ivory or other goods obtained from illegal poaching. There is evidence that these kinds of marketing campaigns can be effective in changing people's opinions.

Questions 8–13

Complete the notes below.

Choose **ONE WORD ONLY** from the passage for each answer.

Write your answers in boxes 8–13 on your answer sheet.

Factors threatening the integrity of Okavango Delta

Water abstraction

- Angola is planning to boost **8** .... farming activities
- drawing water from the delta; exerting effect on the **9** .... all around

Poaching

- residents poach elephants because **10** .... are ruined by those out of protected land
- population is increasing and people are living in poverty
- elephants, giraffes and other animals are made into **11** .... to eat or sell
- rhinoceros horns are in high demand because of their **12** .... value
- ivories are demanded in some places to make **13** .... and other artificial objects

READING PASSAGE 2

You should spend about 20 minutes on **Questions 14–26**, which are based on Reading Passage 2 below.

Putting Wind to Work

Wind energy is produced by the movement of air (wind) and converted into electricity.

A   Wind energy is produced by the movement of air (wind) and converted into power for human use. Wind has been used as a source of energy for more than a thousand years, but was largely replaced by fossil fuels for much of the 20th century. Today, wind is making a comeback as a source of electricity and power.

Wind energy is produced with wind turbines—tall, tubular towers with blades rotating at the top. When the wind turns the blades, the blades turn a generator and create electricity. Wind turbines can have a horizontal or vertical axis. The turbines do not actually produce wind energy, directly. The blades turn, convert the energy of wind into rotational energy, a form of mechanical energy, and this energy is in turn converted into electrical energy.

B   Horizontal-axis wind turbines (HAWTs) are the most familiar type of electricity-producing windmill. Most have three large blades that spin parallel to their towers, where the main rotor and generator are located. Most HAWT arrays are painted white, to promote visibility to low-flying aircraft. They stand about 60 to 90 meters (200 to 300 feet) tall, and the blades rotate at 10 to 20 rotations a minute. The enormous, stiff blades on a horizontal-axis wind turbine usually face the wind (upwind). A wind vane or wind sensor determines which way the wind is blowing, and turns the turbine to face the oncoming wind.

Vertical-axis wind turbines (VAWTs) have varied, unusually shaped blades that rotate in complete circles around their tower. The main rotor and generator are located near the ground, making maintenance easier and less expensive. VAWTs do not have to be upwind to generate electricity. Vertical-axis wind turbines can be much smaller than their horizontal counterparts. Standing only five meters (15 feet) tall, these VAWTs can be installed on the roofs of buildings.

C   Turbines cannot operate at every wind speed. If winds are too strong, they can be damaged. Therefore, the turbine has an automatic controller that turns on when winds are blowing at prime speed for generating electricity. This speed is usually 13 to 90 kilometers per hour (eight to 55 miles per hour). If the winds become stronger than that, the controller turns the turbine off.

In order to generate a large amount of electricity, wind turbines are often constructed in large groups called wind farms. Wind farms are made up of hundreds of turbines, spaced out over hundreds of acres. One of the largest wind farms in the world is Jaisalmer Wind Park, a series of connected facilities in the state of Rajasthan, India. In April 2012, Jaisalmer produced 1,064 megawatts of electricity, more than any other onshore wind farm in the world at the time.

D   Wind farms are often located in agricultural areas, where the land between the turbines can still be used for farming. Grazing animals are unaffected by the large, slow-moving turbines. In the U.S., the 'Corn Belt' overlaps with the 'Wind Belt,' an area across the Midwest that is ideal for harvesting crops and wind. Wind turbines tower over acres of corn, soy, and alfalfa in the states of Iowa, Nebraska, and Kansas. Some scientists suggest wind turbines may even improve the flow of carbon dioxide to surrounding crops.

Wind farms can also be located offshore. These turbines use the stronger, more predictable, and more frequent winds that develop as cool ocean breezes meet warmer continental winds. The world's most powerful offshore wind farms harvest the harsh winds off the coasts of Northern Europe. Walney Wind Farm, for example, is a farm of 102 turbines in the Irish Sea off the coast of Cumbria, England. Walney is the largest offshore wind farm in the world, generating 367 megawatts of power.

E   Technology is also being developed to create wind farms at extremely high altitudes. Jet streams are fast-moving winds that blow through the stratosphere at elevations of 9,754 meters (32,000 feet). Scientists and engineers are developing a wind turbine that would be tethered to the ground like a kite, but float thousands of meters in the air to capture jet streams' energy for electricity.

Single wind turbines can be purchased by individuals to generate electricity for their home or business. Progressive Field, home of the Cleveland Guardians baseball team in Cleveland, Ohio, U.S., had an enormous vertical-axis wind turbine. The corkscrew-shaped turbine was expected to generate about 40,000 kilowatt-hours per year, roughly the amount of energy needed to power four homes. However, the turbine was removed in 2013 after being damaged.

F   Wind turbines depend on wind, which is inconsistent and can be difficult to predict. Although wind is a renewable resource, its speed and direction change frequently, depending on other conditions of the atmosphere, such as temperature, humidity, and season.

Today, this unpredictability makes it a poor substitute for fossil fuels or more powerful renewable energy sources, such as solar energy. Due to most nations' increasing demands on the power grid, wind can be an excellent supplement to traditional power, but not the dominant component in most regions.

Questions 14–18

Reading Passage 2 has six sections, **A–F**.

Which section contains the following information?

*Write the correct letter, **A–F**, in boxes 14–18 on your answer sheet.*

14 an explanation of wind farms set up in specific areas due to natural features there
15 the reason why wind cannot take the place of some energy sources
16 a reference to a turbine with specific shape no longer in use
17 a reason why some wind turbines are painted in a particular colour
18 a mention of an ideal rate for electricity generation

Questions 19–22

Complete the summary below.

Choose **NO MORE THAN TWO WORDS** from the passage for each answer.

Write your answers in boxes 19–22 on your answer sheet.

Where can the wind farms be built

Wind farms are often found in zones where turbines rotating slowly have little influence on grazing animals, so the land between the turbines can be devoted to **19** .... Cron Belt and Wind Belt cover the same area in the USA. According to scientists, the movement of **20** .... toward plants in the vicinity may be improved by wind turbines there as well. Offshore turbines make use of **21** .... from ocean and less cool continental winds to generate stronger and more reliable winds. Scientists and engineers are working on a wind turbine attached to the ground, which resembles a **22** ...., to harvest the energy of jet streams and convert it into electricity.

Questions 23–26

Do the following statements agree with the information given in Reading Passage 2?

In boxes 23–26 on your answer sheet, write

    TRUE   *if the statement agrees with the information*
    FALSE   *if the statement contradicts the information*
    NOT GIVEN *if there is no information about this*

23   Wind energy began to be replaced by fossil fuels only since the 20th century.

24   Wind turbines convert the energy of wind into electrical energy directly.

25   Jaisalmer Wind Park once had the highest electricity production among all onshore wind farms in the world.

26   Walney Wind Farm generates more power than any other offshore wind farm.

READING PASSAGE 3

*You should spend about 20 minutes on **Questions 27–40**, which are based on Reading Passage 3 below.*

Why We Like People Who Ask Us for Favors

Here's a quick quiz. Person A does a favor for you. Person B asks you to do a favor for him. Who are you liable to like more? The answer: Person B. It seems counterintuitive. Wouldn't we favor those who do us favors? Not necessarily. Often, the opposite is true: We don't like people who are nice to us. We like people to whom we are nice. This quirk of human nature, known as the Ben Franklin Effect, explains a lot about how relationships work, and how we might improve them.

Benjamin Franklin stumbled across the phenomenon in 1736 when serving as clerk to the Pennsylvania Assembly. A powerful new member of the assembly didn't care for Franklin and threatened to make life miserable for him. What to do? Franklin could have kowtowed to this member and attempted to win him over with flattery. But he took a different approach. Having heard that the man owned a rare and valuable book, Franklin asked if he could borrow it for a few days. The man agreed, and Franklin returned it dutifully with a nice note. 'When we next met in the House he spoke to me, (which he had never done before) and with great civility,' Franklin recalled in his autobiography. The two became fast friends. Franklin's takeaway: 'He that has once done you a kindness will be ready to do you another, than he whom you yourself have obliged.'

Several studies have confirmed this. In 1969, psychologists Jon Jecker and David Landy enlisted 74 volunteers to take part in an academic contest, with cash prizes for the top performers. After the contest, they were (secretly) divided into three groups. The first group was approached by the lead researcher, purposely acting like a 'rather distasteful individual' who asked each contestant to do him a favor and return the money they won; he had been using his own funds and was running short. The second group was approached by an office assistant who also asked contestants to return the money, claiming it was a drain on the psychology department's anemic budget. The third group was simply allowed to keep their winnings. Participants were then asked to gauge the likability of the lead researcher. Those in the first group had a much more positive impression of him than did those in the third group. (The same did not hold true for those in the second group, suggesting that an indirect, outsourced request for a favor does not endear you to others.)

It mattered not how much money participants were asked to forsake. What mattered was the direct request for a favor. Jecker and Landy's conclusion: 'Under certain circumstances, when an individual performs a favor for another person, his liking for that person will increase.' Several subsequent studies reached the same conclusion, though with a few refinements. The Ben Franklin Effect is more pronounced when it involves a social request (asking for advice) rather than a transactional one (asking for money). Timing is important too: rather than waiting, it's best make a request soon after meeting someone for the first time.

But how can we explain the Ben Franklin Effect? Why do we like those who ask favors of us? Some psychologists point to cognitive dissonance as an explanation. It's difficult to hold two contradictory thoughts at the same time. It makes us uncomfortable. We resolve this tension by changing our mind. 'I don't like Joe, but I am doing a favor for Joe,' we might think. 'So maybe I do like him after all.'

While cognitive dissonance explains a lot, this concept alone doesn't explain the Ben Franklin Effect. One 2015 study found that it was, rather, the 'affiliative motive that the request conveys.' That is, we humans want to maintain good relations with other humans, and one way to achieve this is by doing favors for others. Known as the 'reciprocation bias,' it explains a lot about altruistic behavior. We like being useful and, by extension, we like those who give us the opportunity to do so. It is in our genes. As the archaeologist Richard Leakey wrote in his book *People of the Lake*, 'We are human because our ancestors learned to share their food and their skills in an honored network of obligation.' The Ben Franklin Effect supercharges that network of obligation.

The practical implications of the Ben Franklin Effect are profound and far-reaching. Those looking to make new friends would be wise to leverage the phenomenon. It works when two people know each other, and even among strangers, suggesting it 'could be a viable strategy not only for maintaining or strengthening a current relationship but also for initiating a new relationship,' said Yu Niya, a professor at Japan's Hosei University and author of a study on the Ben Franklin Effect.

In the business world, companies eager to attract loyal customers would be wise to ask something of them: helping design a new product for instance. That is exactly what Lay's Potato Chips did with their 2012 'Do Us a Flavor' campaign. Consumers were asked to suggest a new flavor. The company received nearly 4 million submissions. The winner: Cheesy Garlic Bread. Lay's, in return, saw a spike in sales after the campaign ran. Another word for the Ben Franklin Effect is engagement.

Perhaps the most fertile arena for deploying the Ben Franklin Effect is politics. Leaders from opposing parties could reach across the aisle not by dispensing favors but by requesting them. As behavior scientist Lauren Braithwaite writes in *The Decision Lab*, 'At its core, the Benjamin Franklin effect transforms adversaries into allies.' And it does so, remarkably, inexplicably, one favor at a time.

Questions 27–30

Choose the correct letter, A, B, C or D

Write the correct letter in boxes 27–30 on your answer sheet.

27 Why does the writer mention the Ben Franklin Effect in the first paragraph?

    A to show that people invariably like those who often help them

    B to explain that it is not necessary for people to be nice

    C to prove that human nature is always counterintuitive

    D to suggest that people tend to prefer those we are kind to

28 The writer refers to what happened to Benjamin Franklin in 1736 to suggest that

    A Flattery is the best way to deal with difficult people.

    B A person who has shown you kindness once is more likely to do so again.

    C Borrowing a book and returning it with a note is an effective way to make friends.

    D Kowtowing can help win over powerful individuals.

29 What does the writer find interesting about Jon Jecker and David Landy's study?

   A A direct request for favor made others have a better impression of a person.

   B Top performers in the first group returned the money they won.

   C Being distasteful was more effective to gain likability sometimes.

   D Asking favor indirectly could make others like you more.

30 Why does the writer refer to the 2015 study in the sixth paragraph?

   A to prove that cognitive dissonance is the sole cause of the Ben Franklin Effect

   B to show that the Ben Franklin Effect is related to altruism

   C to demonstrate that altruistic behavior is not related to reciprocation bias

   D to indicate that the Ben Franklin Effect does not work out in an honored network

Questions 31–34

*Look at the following people (**Questions 31–34**) and the list of statements below.*

Match each person with the correct statement, A–E.

Write the correct letter, A–E, in boxes 31–34 on your answer sheet.

31 Jon Jecker and David Landy

32 Richard Leakey

33 Yu Niya

34 Lauren Braithwaite

List of Statements

A Enemies become friends by requesting favors.

B Giving others the opportunity to show kindness could enhance interpersonal relationships.

C People will have a growing fondness to those who help them in some situations.

D It's best for people to perform a favor requested by others immediately.

E Being useful to others is an important element in a system where people are connected by responsibility and duty.

Questions 35–40

Do the following statements agree with the claims of the writer in Reading Passage 3?

In boxes 35–40 on your answer sheet, write

> **YES**   *if the statement agrees with the claims of the writer*
> **NO**   *if the statement contradicts the claims of the writer*
> **NOT GIVEN**   *if it is impossible to say what the writer thinks about this*

35   Benjamin Franklin's life was miserable when serving as clerk to the Pennsylvania Assembly.

36   The subsequent studies were not in line with Jecker and Landy's results.

37   According to cognitive dissonance people tend to change their mind when they hold contrasting thoughts in the meanwhile.

38   Richard Leakey referred to reciprocation bias in his book.

39   Ben Franklin Effect works only when people make new friends rather than maintain current relationship.

40   There was a boost in Lay's sales after the campaign.

IELTS
All-in-One Guide
(Basic Edition)

第三部分
雅思写作

1 雅思写作概述

写作是评估雅思考生英语书面表达能力的重要一环。它要求考生在有限的时间内，根据给定的话题或情境，运用恰当的词汇、语法和句式，清晰、连贯地表达自己的观点和想法。雅思写作不仅评估考生的语言运用能力、逻辑思维能力和批判性思维能力，更能全面考查考生的英语书面表达水平。为了更好地应对这一挑战，考生需熟悉考试结构，理解评分标准并掌握各类题型的特点，这将有助于考生更高效地准备，并在考试中取得优异成绩。

1.1 雅思写作考试结构解析

了解雅思写作考试的结构、时间限制和分值分配等将有助于考生明确每个部分需要花费的时间以及得分的关键因素。

雅思写作考试主要包含两个部分：Task 1（小作文）和 Task 2（大作文）。Task 1 通常是图表题，要求考生在有限的时间内准确理解图表信息并有效组织语言对其进行阐述。Task 2 是议论文或说明文，更侧重于观点表达和论证，需要考生就某一话题进行深入分析和论述。

在时间上，雅思写作考试的总时长为 60 分钟。考生需要合理分配时间，通常建议 Task 1 用时约 20 分钟，Task 2 用时约 40 分钟。这样的时间分配有助于考生充分思考和表达，确保两篇作文都能有足够的时间进行展开。

在分值上，雅思写作采用 9 分制评分。Task 1 和 Task 2 在总分中的比重不同。Task 1 占总分的 1/3，Task 2 占总分的 2/3。因此，考生在备考时应注重 Task 2 的训练，以提升整体写作得分。

1.2 雅思写作考试评分标准

雅思写作评分标准主要包括以下四个方面，这些标准分别应用于 Task 1（小作文）和 Task 2（大作文），但具体的要求和权重在小作文和大作文中有所不同。以下是详细的评分标准。

1.2.1 写作任务完成情况 / 回应情况

雅思写作的任务完成情况 / 回应情况评分标准包括内容完整性、准确性以及语言表达的恰当性。

考官主要关注考生是否全面、准确地完成了写作任务，是否充分回应了题目的要求。考生需要仔细阅读题目要求，确保自己完全理解题目的意图和指示。在写作过程中，考生需要时刻关注题目的要求，确保自己的文章全面、准确地回应了题目的要求。

Task 1 要求考生全面准确地描述、分析和总结图表信息，内容完整性体现在对图表关键数据和特征的无遗漏呈现，准确性在于图表解读正确，语言表达上要清晰准确地描述图表内容。

Task 2 要求考生清晰明确地阐述观点并进行有力论证，内容完整性体现在涵盖问题的各个重要方面，准确性方面要保证观点与题目契合且逻辑合理，语言表达要使观点鲜明且行文流畅自然。

1.2.2 连贯与衔接

雅思写作的连贯与衔接评分标准注重评估文章整体的逻辑性、段落间的关联性以及语句过渡的自然性。考官会关注文章信息和分论点是否安排连贯，论证过程是否清楚，是否有效运用衔接手段。考生需要注意在下笔前确定好文章思路和段落关系，正确使用衔接词，避免使用与自己想要表达的意思相反的逻辑关系词。

Task 1 要求图表描述具有清晰的逻辑顺序，段落之间过渡自然，各部分的衔接紧密合理，使读者能轻松跟随思路理解图表信息。

Task 2 要求文章结构层次分明，段落间存在明确的逻辑关系，论述循序渐进，过渡词运用恰当，文章的连贯性良好，思路流畅清晰。

1.2.3 词汇丰富程度

雅思写作的词汇丰富程度评分标准包含词汇的广度、准确性和多样性。考官会考查考生是否有能力使用丰富的词汇，应避免重复使用相同的单词来表达观点。考生需要灵活使用同义词汇，并尝试使用一些生动形象的单词，准确运用比喻、拟人等修辞手法。

Task 1 要求运用合适且准确的词汇来描述图表中的各种现象和数据，展现一定的词汇广度，不能局限于简单常用词汇，同时要确保用词的精确性，避免错误表达。

Task 2 要求使用广泛多样的词汇来清晰表达观点和进行论证，词汇的选择要贴切恰当，体现出丰富性，并且要准确无误，不能因词汇使用不当而影响文章的质量和理解。在论述不同层面和角度时，要灵活运用各种词汇来增强表达效果，展现出较强的词汇运用能力。

1.2.4 语法多样性及准确性

雅思写作的语法多样性及准确性评分标准涉及句子结构的丰富性、语法运用的正确性。考官会关注考生是否使用多种句子结构，如定语从句、名词性从句等句式，并检查是否有标点、单复数、时态、词性等错误。考生需要避免整篇作文都是简单的主谓宾或主系表结构的句子，要体现出语法的多样性，多使用复合结构，另外还需注意正确使用标点符号。

Task 1 要求描述图表时语法准确无误，避免出现诸如主谓不一致、时态混乱等错误，同时还要尝试运用多种不同的复杂句式来提升表达的丰富性，比如使用各类从句、分词结构等，使描述更具逻辑性，更加生动。

Task 2 要求考生在阐述观点和论证过程中确保语法的精准，不能有明显的语法错误影响读者的理解。同时，要积极使用不同类型的句子来展现语法多样性，如复合句、强调句、倒装句等，以增强文章的表现力和感染力，让文章在语法层面既准确又富有变化。

雅思写作考试评分标准的四个维度权重相同，但具体要求和权重在小作文和大作文中有所不同。考生在备考时需要分别对 Task 1 和 Task 2 进行有针对性的训练，以提升自己在各个方面的写作能力。同时，考生还需要注意时间管理，合理分配时间，以确保两篇作文都能得到充分的展开。

1.3 雅思写作考试题型综述

了解雅思写作题型能帮助考生明确考试的方向和重点，让备考更具针对性，同时还有助于考生构建起系统的写作思维框架，根据题型特点更好地组织语言和内容，展现出逻辑的连贯性和观点的合理性，进而提升写作水平，增加获得理想分数的可能性。

1.3.1 Task 1（小作文）

Task 1 主要考查考生能否在图表中选择最重要和最相关的信息，并对这些信息进行清晰的描述。题目通常会给出一个或多个互相关联的图表，这些图表可分为三类：数据图表、流程图、地图，考生需对其中的事实或数据进行描述对比或对其运作方法进行解释等。

1.3.1.1 数据图表

数据图表是 Task 1 中最为常见且重要的一种类型。数据图表主要包括柱状图、线形图、饼状图、表格、混合图表等，这些图表通常用于展示不同数据之间的关系、趋势或比例。

（1）柱状图：柱状图是一种直观展示不同类别数据的图，通过矩形的长度或高度来展示不同类别或时间点的数值差异。下图是一张典型的柱状图，展示了从 1995 年到 2002 年间英国不同类型的电话呼叫数量情况及变化趋势。

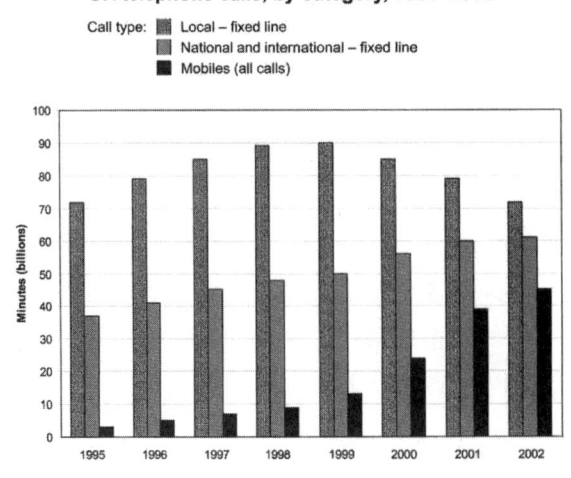

（Cambridge ESOL，2013：53）

（2）线形图：线形图用于展示数据随时间或其他连续变量的变化趋势，通过连接数据点的线条揭示数据间的关联和周期性规律。下图是一张典型的线形图，展示了自 1980 年到 2030 年美国的能源消耗情况及变化趋势。

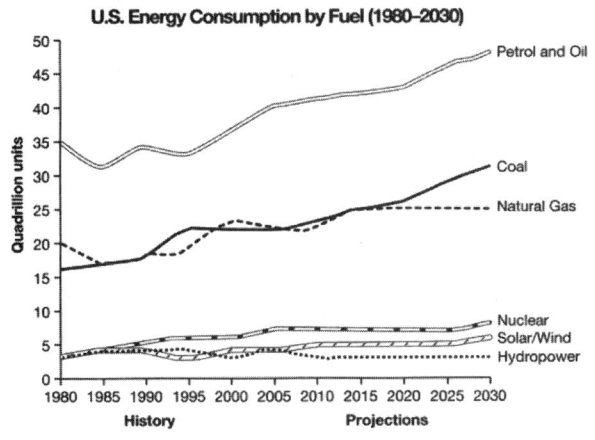

(Cambridge ESOL, 2013: 101)

(3)饼状图:饼状图以扇形的面积表示不同类别在总体中所占的比例,直观显示分类数据的分布情况。下图是饼状图的示例,对比了也门和意大利两个国家2000年不同年龄人口的占比以及对2050年的预测。

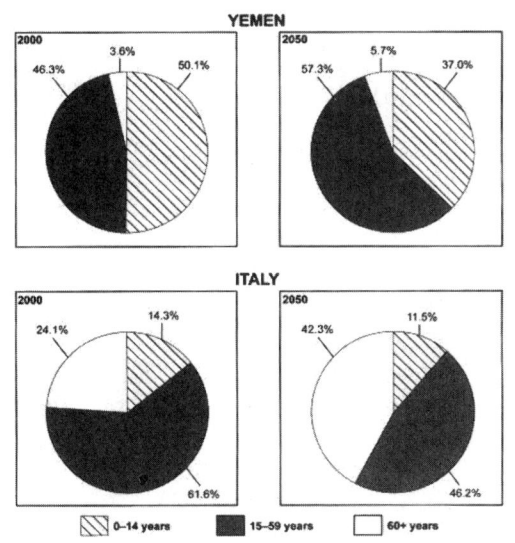

(Cambridge ESOL, 2013: 76)

(4)表格:表格是一种用于组织和展示数据的结构化方式,它以行和列的形式来呈现数据。以下表格描述了1999年和2004年五个欧洲国家"公平贸易"咖啡和香蕉的销售情况。

Sales of Fairtrade-labelled coffee and bananas (1999 & 2004)

Coffee	1999 (millions of euros)	2004 (millions of euros)
UK	1.5	20
Switzerland	3	6
Denmark	1.8	2
Belgium	1	1.7
Sweden	0.8	1

Bananas	1999 (millions of euros)	2004 (millions of euros)
Switzerland	15	47
UK	1	5.5
Belgium	0.6	4
Sweden	1.8	1
Denmark	2	0.9

（Cambridge ESOL，2015：54）

（5）混合图表：混合图表题型在一个题目中同时出现两种或两种以上的数据图表，要求考生对图表内容进行描述和分析。混合图表题型在雅思写作 Task 1 中的出现频率虽然不如其他单一图表题型高，但考生仍需对此题型有所准备。

以下混合图表由一张柱状图和一个表格构成，柱状图显示了某国 2015 年和 2016 年不同类别的商品出口价值，而表格显示了 2015—2016 年各出口类别的百分比变化。

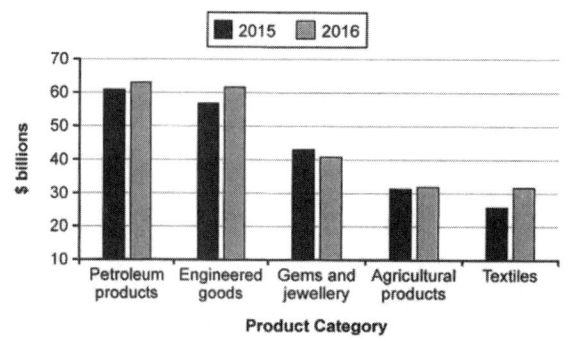

（Cambridge ESOL，2019：50）

1.3.1.2 流程图

雅思写作中的流程图是一种特殊的图表形式，流程图主要考查考生对流程信息的理解、描述和解释能力。题目通常会给出一个流程图，展示某个过程或事件的步骤和环节，如产品制造、科学实验、决策过程等。考生需要仔细阅读流程图，理解其中的信息，并清晰地描述这个过程。如下图所示，该流程图展示了回收塑料瓶的过程。

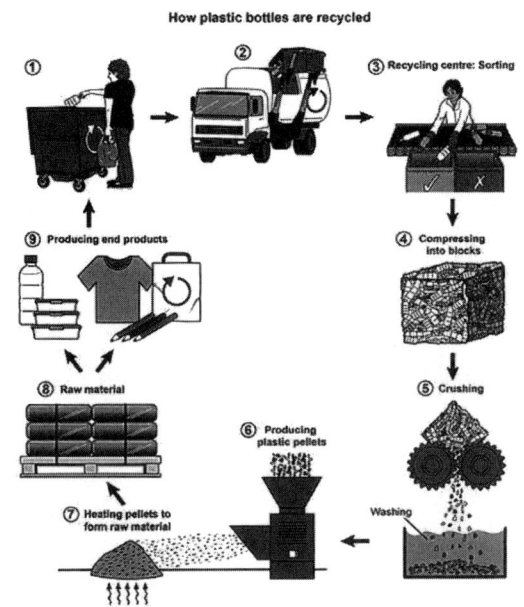

（Cambridge ESOL，2021：95）

1.3.1.3 地图

地图题虽然不如其他图表题型常见，但仍然是可能遇到的一种题型。地图题主要考查考生对地图信息的理解、描述和对比能力。通常，题目会给出一张或多张地图，显示某一地区在不同时间点的变化，如城市规划、建筑物位置、道路网络等。考生需要分析地图中的信息，对这些变化进行描述或对比。下图包含两个地图，展示了同一个岛屿在旅游设施建设前后的变化。

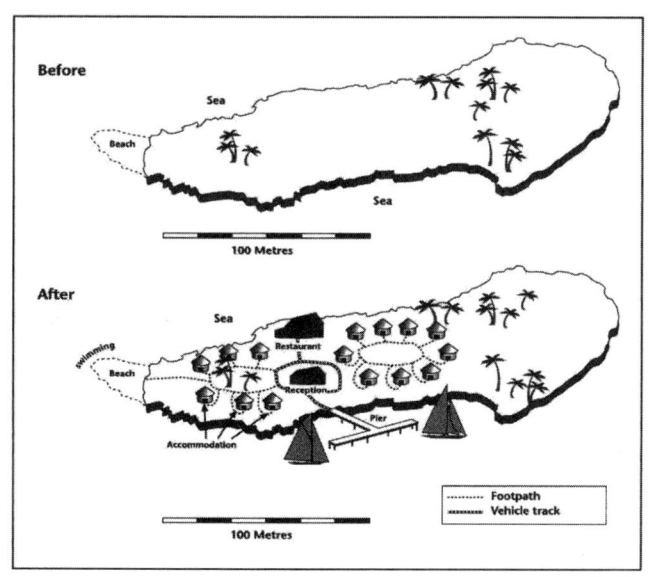

（Cambridge ESOL，2013：30）

1.3.2 Task 2（大作文）

雅思写作 Task 2 要求考生根据给定话题或问题进行分析、论证和表达。它涵盖了观点表达、问题讨论、现象描述等，旨在评估考生的逻辑思维、语言表达和批判性思维能力。考生需要在规定时间内，清晰、连贯地阐述自己的观点，分析问题的各个方面，或根据题目要求提出合理的解决方案或建议。

1.3.2.1 观点类题型

（1）明确立场型（Do you agree or disagree?）：这类题型直接要求考生就某一观点或陈述表达个人的同意或不同意立场，并给出相应的理由来支持自己的观点。例如，题目可能询问：Do you agree that technology has had a more positive than negative impact on society?

（2）权衡利弊型（Do the advantages outweigh the disadvantages?）：此题型要求考生评估某个事物或现象的优点和缺点，并判断其利是否大于弊。考生需要列出正反两面的论据，并进行比较和权衡。例如：Do the advantages of globalization outweigh its disadvantages?

（3）性质判断型（Do you think this is a positive or negative development?）：这类题型让考生判断某一发展或变化是积极的还是消极的，并阐述判断的依据。考生需要明确表明立场，并通过具体事例或分析来支持自己的观点。例如：Do you think the rise of e-commerce is a positive or negative development for traditional retail businesses?

1.3.2.2 列举类题型

（1）双重观点讨论型（Discuss both views and give your opinion）：此题型要求考生先概述并讨论两个或多个不同的观点或立场，然后给出自己的看法。考生需要展现对不同观点的理解和尊重，并清晰地表明自己的立场。例如：Discuss both the view that universities should offer vocational courses and the view that they should focus solely on academic subjects, and give your own opinion.

（2）报告式双问题型（Reports with two questions）：这类题型需针对题目提出的两个问题进行探讨。重点在于客观分析，如阐释现象的原因、影响及措施等，不侧重个人观点表达。虽然它不完全属于传统的列举类，但因为涉及对多个方面的讨论，故在此一并提及。例如：What are the main causes of environmental pollution? How can we effectively tackle this issue?

1.3.2.3 混合类题型

混合类题型结合了观点类和列举类题型的特点，要求考生同时处理多个相关的问题或观点。这类题型可能既要求考生表达个人观点，又要求列举相关论据或分析不同观点。例如，题目可能先描述一个社会现象，然后询问：What are the reasons behind this trend? Do you believe this is a positive or negative development? 考生需要同时分析原因和提出解决方案，展现出全面的思考和分析能力。

2 雅思写作基本要素与技巧

雅思写作考试要求考生在有限的时间内,用恰当的词汇和准确的语法表达自己的观点。因此,掌握一些基本要素和技巧对于提高雅思写作成绩至关重要。下面将详细介绍雅思写作的基本要素和技巧,包括语法、词汇、句子结构、逻辑连贯性、段落结构等。学习这些内容有助于考生提高自己的写作水平,在考试中取得更好的成绩。

2.1 基本要素

在雅思写作中,正确的语法、丰富的词汇、合理的句子结构、连贯的逻辑以及良好的段落结构是构成一篇优秀作文的基本要素。对这些要素的深入理解和熟练运用,有助于考生写出高质量的文章,准确地表达自己的观点,展现出扎实的英语语言能力。

2.1.1 语法准确性

语法准确性影响文章整体质量,关系到考生的语言表达能力和逻辑思维能力。了解常见的语法错误,尽量避免犯这些错误,对于提高雅思写作成绩具有重要意义。接下来将详细讲解时态、语态等表达中常见的语法问题,并通过实例分析来帮助考生避免常见的语法错误,提高语法准确性。

1) 常用时态

时态是英语语法的基石,它直接影响句子的含义和上下文的逻辑关系。英文中共有十六大时态,不同的时态可以传达不同时间概念,涵盖过去、现在和将来。雅思写作中的常用时态有七种,应根据具体情况对时态进行灵活调整,同时要保持时态的一致性。在写作过程中,可以根据题目要求和文章内容,合理运用不同的时态来表达准确的意思。下面介绍七种常用时态及其在雅思写作中的用法。

(1) 一般现在时(Simple Present Tense):一般现在时是英语中最基本的时态之一,它可以表示现在经常发生的动作或存在的状态,现在的状态、特征、能力、性格等,以及客观事实、普遍真理等。这个时态通常使用动词的现在时 do/does。以下是一般现在时的用法和例句。

①表示现在经常发生的动作或存在的状态。

例如:We constantly <u>interact</u> with various technological devices, and this has become a common occurrence in our daily routines.

②表示现在的状态、特征、能力、性格等。

例如：AI possesses the ability to analyze vast amounts of information quickly and adapts to new data in real-time.

③表示客观事实、普遍真理等。

例如：It is an undeniable truth that the earth revolves around the sun.

（2）现在进行时（Present Progressive Tense）：用于表示现在正在发生的动作。这个时态通常使用"be（am/is/are）+ doing"的形式。

例如：Technology is revolutionizing the way we live.

（3）现在完成时（Present Perfect Tense）：着眼于过去发生的动作与现在的联系，用于表示过去发生的动作对现在造成的影响或产生的结果，或者表示过去的动作或状态一直持续到现在。这个时态通常使用"have/has + done"的形式。

例如：Recently, scientists have made groundbreaking discoveries in the field of artificial intelligence, paving the way for exciting advancements in robotics and automation.

（4）一般过去时（Simple Past Tense）：表示过去某个具体时间发生的动作或状态。这个时态中动词通常使用过去式。

例如：When Steve Jobs founded Apple in 1977, he never imagined how much his company would revolutionize the technology industry.

（5）过去进行时（Past Progressive Tense）：表示过去某个具体时间正在进行的动作。这个时态通常使用"was/were + 动词的现在分词"的形式。

例如：While researchers were conducting experiments in the lab, they observed unexpected results that led to a new scientific discovery.

（6）过去完成时（Past Perfect Tense）：表示过去某个动作之前已经完成的动作。这个时态通常使用"had + 过去分词"的形式。

例如：Before the software update was released, the development team had tested it extensively to ensure compatibility and stability.

（7）一般将来时（Simple Future Tense）：表示将来某个具体时间会发生的动作或状态，常与表示将来的时间状语连用，如 tomorrow（明天），next week（下周），in the future（在未来）等。这个时态通常使用"be（am/is/are）going to"和"will/shall + 动词原形"的形式。

例如：New technologies will bring more convenience and changes to our lives in the years to come.

NB　在雅思写作中，如何避免时态错误？

A　仔细审题：明确题目要求的时间背景，根据具体情况选择时态。

B　理清思路：在写作前先规划好文章的结构和内容，确定每个部分应使用的时态。

C　检查修正：完成写作后，仔细检查时态的使用是否一致和正确。

D　多做练习：通过大量的写作练习，提高对时态的敏感度和运用能力。

E　学习规则：熟练掌握各种时态的用法和特点，避免混淆。

在雅思写作中，选择合适的时态至关重要。不同的时态能准确地展现事件发生的时间及逻辑关系，确保文章表达准确。时态一致可使文章更连贯，避免出现混淆与歧义。恰当的时态还能有力传达作者的观点与态度，增强文章的说服力。此外，合适的时态能让文章更贴近现实，真实反映事件的情况与发展，使读者更易感受到文章的可信度与现实感。

时态练习题

1. 请在以下段落中对现在时态进行标记。

In today's rapidly evolving technological landscape, technology plays an increasingly important role in our lives. It has revolutionized the way we communicate, work, learn, and play. Scientists and engineers have made remarkable breakthroughs, pushing the boundaries of what was once thought possible. For example, researchers have developed AI systems that can learn and adapt in real-time, revolutionizing industries such as healthcare and finance. Meanwhile, tech companies are currently exploring the potential of quantum computing, a field that promises unparalleled computational power and could transform the way we solve complex problems in the future.

2. 请在以下段落中对过去时态进行标记。

Researchers in the field of technology were always passionate about their work. They were dedicatedly exploring new frontiers while experiments were ongoing. Numerous significant discoveries and innovations had already been accomplished before.

3. 请在以下段落中对将来时态进行标记。

In the future, technology will bring about tremendous changes. We are going to see more advanced artificial intelligence systems that will revolutionize various industries. Robots will play a significant role in our daily lives, and we shall experience a new era of convenience and efficiency. The development of technology will continue to advance at an astonishing pace, bringing us even more exciting possibilities.

2）语态的运用

在英语中，语态是动词的一种形式，用来表达主语和谓语之间的关系。英语动词包含两种语态，即主动语态和被动语态。主动语态表示主语是动作的执行者，而被动语态则表示主语是动作的承受者。

（1）主动语态（Active Voice）：强调动作的执行者，句子结构为"主语 + 谓语动词 + 宾语"。

例如：Students study hard. （这里 students 是动作 study 的执行者。）

　　　Students should actively participate in class discussions. （这里 students 是动作 participate 的执行者。）

（2）被动语态（Passive Voice）：强调动作的承受者，句子结构为"宾语 +be 动词 + 过去分词（+by+ 执行者）（括号内容可省略）"，其用法如下。

①不知道或无须提及动作执行者：保持句子的简洁性。

例如：The letter was posted yesterday. （可能不知道是谁寄的信）

　　　Mistakes were made. （可能不知道是谁犯的错误）

②强调动作承受者：突出动作影响的对象。

例如：A lot of mistakes were made in the exam.（这里更关注和强调错误）

The cake was eaten yesterday.（这里更突出"蛋糕"被吃的事实）

（3）表达客观事实：普遍的观点或说法。

例如：It is said that the new policy will be implemented soon.（表达一种普遍的观点或说法：据说新政策很快会被执行）

The law is obeyed by most people.（这是一个普遍存在的事实：大多数人遵守法律）

（4）使句子更正式：在正式场合或书面语中常用。

例如：The proposal will be considered by the committee.

The policy is being reviewed carefully.

NB 使用主动语态和被动语态的建议

A 根据表达需要选择：明确想要强调的是动作的执行者还是承受者，从而选择合适的语态。

B 保持一致性：在同一篇文章中，不要频繁切换语态，以免造成混乱。

C 灵活运用：不要过度使用某一种语态，适当变换语态能增加句子的多样性。

D 注意逻辑连贯：确保语态的转换符合文章的逻辑和语义。

E 多练习：通过写作练习，逐渐熟悉并掌握主动语态和被动语态的运用技巧。

在雅思写作中，灵活地运用不同的语态，能够让文章的语言表达更加丰富多彩，富有层次感，提升整体写作水平。

语态练习题

请用两种不同的语态翻译以下句子。

1. 互联网极大地改变了人们获取信息的方式。

   主动语态：_____

   被动语态：_____

2. 环境污染对我们的健康造成威胁。

   主动语态：_____

   被动语态：_____

3. 应该鼓励人们采取可持续的生活方式，以减少对环境的负面影响。

   主动语态：_____

   被动语态：_____

4. 人们强烈要求采取行动来解决城市交通拥堵问题。

   主动语态：_____

   被动语态：_____

5. 科学家们一直在努力探索新能源，以应对日益严峻的能源危机。

   主动语态：_____

   被动语态：_____

6. 有效的教育政策可以提高国民素质，促进国家的发展和进步。

主动语态：_____

被动语态：_____

7. 许多人认为，家庭教育对于孩子的成长起着至关重要的作用。

主动语态：_____

被动语态：_____

8. 学校应该提供更多的课外活动，以帮助学生培养兴趣爱好和社交能力。

主动语态：_____

被动语态：_____

3）其他常见雅思写作语法错误

（1）句子残缺：句子在结构上不完整，缺少了必要的成分，导致句子意思表达不明确或无法理解。

①缺主语：句子中缺少主语。

例如：On the global stage, have a profound impact on our lives.（缺主语）

②缺谓语：句子中缺少谓语。

例如：In the era of rapid technological advancements, numerous innovative ideas and solutions.（缺谓语）

③缺并列连词：在两个或多个应该用并列连词连接起来的句子成分之间，没有使用相应的并列连词，常见并列连词有 and，or，but，so 等。

例如：We need to take action to protect the environment, promote sustainable development.（缺并列连词 and）

People should raise awareness of environmental protection. Encourage recycling.（缺并列连词 and）

（2）从句单独成句：从句需要与主句结合在一起，共同表达一个完整的意思。如果从句单独作为一个句子，就会导致句子结构不完整，语义不明确。

例如：The economy has been growing slowly in recent years. Because the global market conditions have been rather challenging.（Because 引导的从句单独成句）

While we are facing the challenges brought about by climate change. It is essential to take immediate actions to protect our environment.（While 引导的从句单独成句）

（3）双重谓语：在一个句子中出现了两个或两个以上的谓语动词，这种错误会导致句子结构混乱，逻辑不清晰。

例如：<u>Lack</u> sleep can <u>affect</u> your mood and cognitive function.

There <u>are</u> many celebrities <u>live</u> in the residential area.

（4）主语重复：在一个句子中，不必要地多次使用同一个主语，会使句子显得啰唆、不简洁，也可能导致逻辑不清晰。

例如：Writing poetry, it allows expressing emotions in a profound and creative way.（it 和 writing poetry 重复）

Exploring the art museum, the exhibits on display, they showcase a diverse range of artistic styles and techniques.（the exhibits 和 they 重复）

(5) 主谓不一致：句子中主语和谓语在人称和数上不对应，主语的单复数形式与谓语动词的形式需要保持一致。

①集体名词作主语时的错误：集体名词应视为一个整体，谓语动词用单数。

例如：The team of scientists have discovered a new phenomenon.（主语是由科学家组成的团队，强调整体，谓语动词应该用单数）

The committee of experts, which consist of renowned scholars from various fields, have different opinions on the research methodology.（主语是由专家组成的委员会，强调整体，谓语动词应该用单数）

②不定代词作主语时的错误：如 someone, anyone 等不定代词作主语，谓语动词通常用单数。

例如：Anyone who want to learn English well must work hard.（不定代词 anyone "任何人"作主语，谓语动词应用单数）

Everyone have their own opinions.（不定代词 everyone "每个人"作主语，谓语动词应用单数）

③并列主语时的错误：当并列主语由 and 连接时，通常谓语动词用复数。

例如：Renewable energy and sustainable agriculture plays a crucial role in environmental conservation.（主语是 renewable energy 和 sustainable agriculture 两者，主语为复数则谓语动词用复数）

④从句作主语时的错误：主语为从句时，谓语动词的数通常根据从句所表达的意义来确定。

例如：What scientists believe that technology can solve environmental problems are not always true.（这里主语从句表达的是一个整体概念，即"科学家们认为技术可以解决环境问题的说法"，谓语动词应该用单数形式）

How much pollution are caused by new technologies are a concern.（这里主语从句表达的是一个整体的量，即"新科技带来的环境污染"，谓语动词应用单数形式）

(6) 冠词使用不当：在句子中冠词（a、an、the）的运用不符合语法规则或语境要求，通常包括漏用冠词、滥用冠词、错用冠词。

①漏用冠词。

例如：Idea of equality is deeply rooted in our culture.（idea of quality 属于抽象概念，idea 前面要加 the）

The student who is best in the top class has the right to go to any university in this city.（who is best，best 为最高级，前面要加 the）

Access to education is fundamental right for every citizen.（fundamental right 前面要加 a，表泛指）

②滥用冠词。

例如：In the modern society, people are facing various challenges.（society 是泛指，modern

前不用加 the）

The many researchers believe that climate change is a pressing issue. （many researchers 是泛指，many 前不用加 the）

③错用冠词。

例如：Many students choose to study at an university which is known for its research facilities. （university 的第一个音节为 /ju/，/ju/ 是辅音，所以 an 应改成 a）

The students who is a best in the top class has the right to go to any university in this city. （best 是最高级，前面加 the 而不是 a）

（7）代词使用错误：在句子中使用代词时，出现了不恰当、不准确或不符合语法规则的情况。

①指代不明：代词所指代的对象不明确，导致读者难以理解句子的意思。

例如：The government should take measures to protect the environment, which is crucial for our future. However, some people argue that these policies will have negative impacts on the economy, and they ignore the long-term benefits. ［政府应该采取措施保护环境，这对我们的未来至关重要。然而，一些人认为这些政策会对经济产生负面影响，并且他们忽视了长期的好处。这里的 they 指代不明，既可理解为 some people（一些人），也可理解为 policies（这些政策）］

②前后不一致：代词与它所指代的名词在数、性或人称上不相符。

例如：Each student has their own strengths and weaknesses. （每个学生都有他们自己的长处和短处。这里的 their 应该与 Each student 保持一致，改为 his 或 her）

The team members are working hard to achieve their goals, and they believe that success is within its reach. （团队成员正在努力实现他们的目标，并且他们相信成功就在他们的掌握之中。这里的 its 应该与 The team members 保持一致，改为 their）

③多余代词：不需要使用代词时却使用了，造成语义混乱。

例如：Composing music, it delivers ideas in a profound and creative way. （删除 it）

The actors on stage, they displayed exceptional talent in their performances. （删除 they）

改错练习题

1. In the city center, many buildings and streets.

2. During the summer vacation, a lot of activities and fun.

3. The government should take measures to improve the economy. Because it is crucial for the country's development.

4. We need to protect the environment. While it is our responsibility to ensure a sustainable future.

5. The situation change quickly affect our plans.

6. The number of tourists continue to increase.

7. Reading books, it is a great way to expand your knowledge.

8. Going to the gym, the exercise, it helps to keep fit.

9. We should reduce waste, protect the environment.

10. People need to be more aware of climate change, take action.

11. The family of five have moved to a new city.

12. The class of students are excited about the field trip.

13. Someone in the audience want to ask a question.

14. Everyone in the room have their own agenda.

15. The teacher and the student is discussing the assignment.

16. The singer and the dancer has their own talents.

17. What we need to do are to take action immediately.

18. How many people are involved in this project are unknown.

19. Reading is important skill for personal growth.

20. We should respect the human rights.

21. Importance of education cannot be overstated.

22. History is the fascinating subject.

23. She is an university student.

24. The students who are best in the top class have the right to choose which universities to go.

25. The class has many students, and each of them have their own unique ideas.

26. The company is facing some challenges that are causing operational difficulties, but it is not clear which departments will be most affected by them.

27. We need to buy some supplies, but it's not clear which store has it in stock.

28. The development of technology has brought many benefits, but some people argue, that it has also caused some negative impacts on society.

29. Some people believe that money can buy happiness, but I think, there are more important things in life than money.

30. Traveling can bring us a lot of pleasure and inspiration, it allows us to experience different cultures and landscapes; yet, many people don't have enough time or money to travel.

2.1.2 词汇的积累与运用

在雅思写作中，词汇是不可或缺的核心元素。它不仅是文章表达的基础，还直接关系着文章的准确性、清晰度、丰富性、深度以及说服力。考生通过积累和运用多样化的词汇，可以更加精准地传达自己的观点，增强文章的说服力，并提升文章整体的流畅性和连贯性。

1）积累不同主题的词汇

雅思写作涉及的主题较为广泛，包括教育、科技、环境、社会现象、经济发展、文化差异等。因此，考生需要积累不同主题的词汇，以应对考试中可能出现的各种主题。积累不同主题词在以下几个方面具有重要作用。

（1）提高表达的准确性和专业性：每个主题都有其特定的专业词汇和表达方式，不同的主题需要使用特定的专业词汇来准确表达概念。积累这些词汇能够使考生在写作时更加准确地表达自己的观点，避免用词不当导致的误解。

例如："气候变化"（climate change）误翻为 weather change（天气变化，令读者误解），"温室气体"（greenhouse gas）可能被误翻成 warm house gas，"二氧化碳排放"（carbon dioxide emission）误翻成 carbon discharging。

（2）丰富文章内容：使用与主题相关的专业词汇和表达方式可以使文章更加丰富、生动、有趣，并展现出考生对主题的深入理解和具备的广泛知识。这有助于提高文章的整体质量，吸引阅卷老师的注意力。

例如，以环境保护为主题，假设主题词汇积累不够，考生若想提到环境保护和污染的问题，可能会写出句子：Pollution is bad for us. We should take actions to protect our environment. 这个句子虽然意思正确，但表达较为笼统，缺乏具体的环境保护术语。

积累主题词汇后可改进为：Air pollution and deforestation are serious threats that impact our health and ecosystems. Measures like reducing waste, using renewable energy, and planting more trees can help mitigate these effects and create a more sustainable future. 在这个句子中，考生使用了如 air pollution, deforestation, health, ecosystems, reduce waste, renewable energy, plant trees, mitigate effects, sustainable future 等具体的环境保护主题词汇。这些词汇不仅使内容更加具体，还展示了学生对环境保护问题的认识。句子提出了减少污染、使用可再生能源、植树造林等具体措施，使观点更具说服力。

（3）增强话题的相关性：词汇是语言的基本单位，也是理解文本的基础。当考生面对一个涉及特定主题的写作任务时，如果对该主题的词汇不熟悉，就很难深入理解题目的真正意图或无法充分展开论述。例如，如果题目要求讨论"可持续发展"的相关问题，但考生对"可持续性""生态平衡"等词语缺乏了解，就可能导致对题目要求的误解，从而偏离主题。积累不同主题的词汇可以帮助考生更好地理解题目要求，准确把握写作主题。

（4）提高写作速度：熟悉不同主题的词汇可以减少思考和选择词汇的时间，提高写作速度。在考试中，时间非常紧张，快速准确地表达自己的观点至关重要。如果考生对某个主题的词汇不熟悉，就可能会在写作过程中出现卡顿或表达不清的情况，从而影响文章的质量和阅卷老师的评分。

词汇翻译练习题

请翻译以下环境话题词汇。

中文	英文	中文	英文
气候变化	_____	全球变暖	_____
环境污染	_____	空气污染	_____
噪声污染	_____	环境退化	_____
荒漠化	_____	森林砍伐	_____
水资源短缺	_____	生态平衡	_____
自然资源	_____	生物多样性	_____
环保意识	_____	塑料污染	_____
回收和再利用	_____	减少碳排放	_____

保护野生动物及其栖息地＿＿＿＿＿＿	节约能源和资源＿＿＿＿＿＿＿＿＿＿
可持续发展＿＿＿＿＿＿＿＿＿＿＿＿	建立自然保护区＿＿＿＿＿＿＿＿＿＿

2）词汇的搭配和用法

雅思写作中，词汇的搭配和用法是评价考生语言水平的重要指标之一。恰当的词汇搭配和准确的词汇用法不仅能让考生的文章更加流畅、自然，还能增加文章的说服力和专业性。

（1）词汇的搭配。

①同义词与反义词的使用：同义词的替换可以避免文章单调，而反义词的对比则能突出观点。通过合理使用同义词，可以避免重复使用相同的词汇，使文章更加丰富多彩。同时，反义词的对比使用可以突出观点，增强说服力。考生应学会在文章中适时运用同义词和反义词，使表达更加精准、生动。

例如：prosperous，同义词 wealthy，反义词 poor。

②动词与名词的搭配：动词和名词的恰当搭配能让句子焕发活力。正确的动词和名词搭配可以使句子更加准确、生动，考生需关注动词与名词之间的逻辑关系，确保搭配的合理性。

例如：initiate 与 project（启动项目），boost 与 economy（促进经济）。

③形容词与名词的搭配：形容词用来修饰名词，使名词更加具体、生动。恰当的形容词与名词搭配可以增强文章的表现力。

例如：美丽的风景（beautiful scenery），关键的决定（crucial decision）。

（2）词性的正确使用。

①准确运用不同词性的词汇：在雅思写作中，正确使用不同词性的词汇至关重要。名词、动词、形容词、副词等在句子中扮演着不同的角色，正确使用词性可以避免语法错误，使句子结构更加清晰。名词在句子中作主语或宾语，动词作谓语，形容词修饰名词等。

例如：He is an excellent athlete. （He 是主语，is 是谓语，excellent 是形容词，修饰名词 athlete）

②短语和固定搭配的使用：短语和固定搭配是英语中常见的语言现象。掌握一些常用的短语和固定搭配可以让考生的语言更加地道、自然。

例如：as a result（结果），in addition（此外），in other words（换句话说）。

③同义词的辨析与使用：同义词之间往往存在细微的差别，了解这些差别并在写作中恰当使用同义词可以使考生的表达更加准确，词汇更加丰富。

例如：big room → spacious room，large population → dense population。

词汇搭配练习题

以下句子中均出现词性错误或搭配错误的情况，请一一指出并改正。

1. None can negative the importance of money.
2. Pollution effects the citizens' living standards negatively.
3. The forests are destroyed, but few people concern about it.

4. On the one hand, technology brings convenient; on the other hand, it also causes some problems.

5. The government plays a crucial role in promote economic development.

6. Scientists make great contributions in the progress of society.

7. Succeed is often associated with hard work and determination.

8. The government should give prior to the development of education.

9. The government should make effective measures to reduce crime.

10. The lacking of exercise contributes to the increase in obesity rates.

2.1.3 句子结构

在雅思写作中，句子结构的学习是提升写作能力的关键。通过学习和掌握英文中不同类型的句子结构，考生可以更加灵活地运用语言，提高写作水平和表达能力。在雅思写作中，合理使用这些句子结构可以使文章更加清晰、连贯和有说服力。良好的句子结构可以使文章更易于理解，避免信息混淆，同时展现出考生较高的语言运用能力和思维深度。

1）简单句（Simple Sentence）

简单句是最基本的句子类型，它由主语和谓语构成，表达一个完整的思想。简单句是英语句子的基础，具有直接明了、易于理解的特点。在雅思写作中，正确运用简单句能够确保信息的准确传达，同时使文章结构清晰。简单句的基本构成可以分为以下五种类型。

（1）"主语 + 谓语"：句子仅由主语和谓语构成，表达"某人或某物如何动作"或"某人或某物自身怎样运动"。

例如：She smiled. （她笑了。）

（2）"主语 + 谓语 + 宾语"：句子由主语、谓语和宾语构成，表达"某人或某物做什么事情"。

例如：I love music. （我爱音乐。）

（3）"主语 + 谓语 + 间接宾语 + 直接宾语"：句子由主语、谓语、间接宾语（通常为人）和直接宾语（通常为物）构成。

例如：He gave me a book. （他给了我一本书。）

（4）"主语 + 谓语 + 宾语 + 宾语补足语"：句子中宾语后还有补充说明宾语状态或动作的补足语。

例如：They found the house empty. （他们发现房子是空的。）

（5）"主语 + 系动词 + 表语"：句子中谓语是系动词，后接表语说明主语的状态或特征。

例如：She is beautiful. （她很漂亮。）

在雅思写作中，简单句是不可或缺的基础句子类型。通过合理运用简单句，可以确保文章结构清晰、内容准确、易于阅读。同时，也要注意避免空洞、重复和过长的句子，使文章更加生动有趣、具有说服力。

2）复合句（Compound Sentence）

复合句由两个或多个独立子句（Independent Clauses）组成，这些句子通过并列连词（如and,

or, but 等）连接，每个句子都是完整的简单句。复合句可以表达多个相对独立的思想，同时保持句子之间的逻辑关系。

常见的并列连接词有：

and	but	or	so	yet
for	while	as well as	not only... but also...	
neither ... nor...	either ... or ...	although	however	

例如：Many parents believe that traditional classroom teaching is more effective, and they argue that it allows teachers to monitor students' progress more closely.（并列关系）

Although primary education is compulsory in most countries, the quality of education can vary significantly.（转折关系）

3）复杂句（Complex Sentence）

复杂句是由一个主句（Principal Clause）和一个或多个从句（Subordinate Clause）组成的句子。其中从句作为主句的一部分，通过特定的连词、关系词或引导词与主句连接，不能独立存在。

雅思写作有严格的时间限制以及字数要求，使用复杂句能够在有限的篇幅内传达更多的信息。考生能通过有效使用不同类型的从句表达更丰富的信息和更复杂的逻辑关系，还可以显著提升作文的复杂度和表达清晰度。以下是雅思写作中常用从句类型及其运用。

（1）名词性从句：在句子中起名词作用的从句，可以作主语、宾语、表语等。

例句1：What the latest technology advancements mean for our future remains unclear.（最新的科技进展对我们未来的意义仍不清楚。）

由 what 引导的从句 What the latest technology advancements mean for our future 在整个句子中作主语，回答了"什么仍不清楚"的问题。

例句2：I don't know whether artificial intelligence will ultimately replace human jobs.（我不知道人工智能最终是否会取代人类的工作。）

由 whether 引导的从句 whether artificial intelligence will ultimately replace human jobs 在句子中作宾语，是 I don't know 的内容。

例句3：The question is what impact the new technology will have on our daily lives.（问题是新技术将如何影响我们的日常生活。）

由 what 引导的从句 what impact the new technology will have on our daily lives 在句子中作表语，回答了 The question 是什么。

（2）定语从句：用于修饰主句中的某个名词或代词，提供关于该名词或代词的额外信息。

例句1：The smartphone that has a built-in camera with high megapixels is very popular.（具有内置高像素摄像头的智能手机非常受欢迎。）

这个定语从句使用了关系代词 that 来引导，它修饰了主句中的 smartphone。通过定语从句，我们了解到这个智能手机具有一个内置的高像素摄像头。这个额外的信息使得读者或听者能够更具体地理解这个智能手机的特点，即它是具有高级摄像功能的智能手机。

例句 2：The smartphone, which has become an essential tool in our daily lives, has numerous functions.（智能手机已经成为我们日常生活中必不可少的工具，具有许多功能。）

这个定语从句使用了关系代词 which 来引导，它同样修饰了主句中的 smartphone。通过定语从句，我们了解到智能手机已经成为我们日常生活中必不可少的工具。这个额外的信息强调了智能手机在我们生活中的重要性，并帮助读者或听者了解智能手机在日常生活中扮演的重要角色。同时，主句还进一步补充了智能手机具有许多功能的信息。

（3）状语从句：状语从句用于描述主句事件发生的时间、条件、原因等背景信息，使句子内容更加丰富。

例句 1：When new technology is introduced, it often takes time for people to adapt to it.（当新技术被引入时，人们通常需要一段时间来适应它。）

这个状语从句使用 when 引导，表示"当……时"的时间关系。它描述了新技术被引入这一时间点，而主句则说明了在这个时间点之后通常会发生的情况，即人们需要一段时间来适应新技术。

例句 2：We should invest in renewable energy because it helps reduce carbon emissions and protect the environment.（我们应该投资可再生能源，因为它有助于减少碳排放并保护环境。）

这个状语从句使用了 because 来引导，表示"因为……"的原因关系。它解释了为什么我们应该投资可再生能源，即因为它有助于减少碳排放并保护环境。这个状语从句为主句提供了充分的理由和背景信息。

4）其他常见句型

在雅思写作中，除了简单句、复合句和复杂句之外，还有其他一些常见的句型，这些句型能够增强文章的表现力，使文章更加生动有趣。

（1）倒装句。

倒装句是一种改变句子正常语序的句式，通常用于强调某个信息或保持句子平衡，以下是其具体用法。

①完全倒装句：将整个谓语提到主语之前。

例如：In the middle of the lake stands a beautiful pavilion.（湖中央矗立着一座漂亮的亭子。）

In the middle of the lake 是表示地点的介词短语，置于句首，需要将谓语 stands 完全置于主语之前，形成完全倒装，起到强调地点"湖中央"的作用。

②部分倒装句：只将情态动词或 be 动词等提到主语之前。

例如：Not only are textbooks expensive, but also they are often outdated.（教科书不仅昂贵，而且往往过时。）

在这个句子中，not only 位于句首，导致 are 这一助动词提前到主语 textbooks 之前，形成了部分倒装句。

（2）强调句。

强调句用于突出句子中的某个部分，通常使用 "it is/was + 被强调的部分 + that/who ..." 的结构。

例如：It is the rapid development of technology that has transformed our lives in the past few decades.（正是科技的快速发展在过去的几十年里改变了我们的生活。）

这个句子使用了 it is ... that ... 的结构来强调 the rapid development of technology 这一关键信息，

突出了科技发展对生活的重要影响。

（3）It引导的形式主语句。

It引导的形式主语句的基本形式为"It + be + 形容词 / 名词 +（for/of sb.）+ to do sth."。it只是形式上的主语，其使用是为了使句子结构更平衡，避免头重脚轻，真正的主语是后面的to do sth.。

例如：It is crucial for individuals to maintain a balanced diet.（对个人来说，保持均衡的饮食是至关重要的。）

这个句子使用了"It + be + 形容词 + for sb. + to do sth."的结构，其中It是形式主语，真正的主语是to maintain a balanced diet。形式主语句使得句子结构更加平衡，同时强调了"维持均衡饮食"对于个人的重要性。

句子结构练习题

翻译以下简单句，并将简单句合并成复合句或复杂句。

1. 简单句1：气候变化是一个严峻的问题。

翻译：＿＿＿＿＿＿＿＿＿＿＿＿＿＿＿＿＿＿＿＿＿＿＿＿＿＿＿＿＿＿＿

简单句2：气候变化问题急需全球关注和一致努力。

翻译：＿＿＿＿＿＿＿＿＿＿＿＿＿＿＿＿＿＿＿＿＿＿＿＿＿＿＿＿＿＿＿

合并：＿＿＿＿＿＿＿＿＿＿＿＿＿＿＿＿＿＿＿＿＿＿＿＿＿＿＿＿＿＿＿

＿＿＿＿＿＿＿＿＿＿＿＿＿＿＿＿＿＿＿＿＿＿＿＿＿＿＿＿＿＿＿＿＿＿

2. 简单句1：教育对个人成长至关重要。

翻译：＿＿＿＿＿＿＿＿＿＿＿＿＿＿＿＿＿＿＿＿＿＿＿＿＿＿＿＿＿＿＿

简单句2：教育帮助人们开发潜能和实现梦想。

翻译：＿＿＿＿＿＿＿＿＿＿＿＿＿＿＿＿＿＿＿＿＿＿＿＿＿＿＿＿＿＿＿

合并：＿＿＿＿＿＿＿＿＿＿＿＿＿＿＿＿＿＿＿＿＿＿＿＿＿＿＿＿＿＿＿

＿＿＿＿＿＿＿＿＿＿＿＿＿＿＿＿＿＿＿＿＿＿＿＿＿＿＿＿＿＿＿＿＿＿

3. 简单句1：环保是每个人的责任。

翻译：＿＿＿＿＿＿＿＿＿＿＿＿＿＿＿＿＿＿＿＿＿＿＿＿＿＿＿＿＿＿＿

简单句2：我们应该减少废物排放和能源消耗。

翻译：＿＿＿＿＿＿＿＿＿＿＿＿＿＿＿＿＿＿＿＿＿＿＿＿＿＿＿＿＿＿＿

合并：＿＿＿＿＿＿＿＿＿＿＿＿＿＿＿＿＿＿＿＿＿＿＿＿＿＿＿＿＿＿＿

＿＿＿＿＿＿＿＿＿＿＿＿＿＿＿＿＿＿＿＿＿＿＿＿＿＿＿＿＿＿＿＿＿＿

4. 简单句1：全球化促进了国际贸易。

翻译：＿＿＿＿＿＿＿＿＿＿＿＿＿＿＿＿＿＿＿＿＿＿＿＿＿＿＿＿＿＿＿

简单句2：全球化使各国能够共享资源和知识。

翻译：＿＿＿＿＿＿＿＿＿＿＿＿＿＿＿＿＿＿＿＿＿＿＿＿＿＿＿＿＿＿＿

合并：＿＿＿＿＿＿＿＿＿＿＿＿＿＿＿＿＿＿＿＿＿＿＿＿＿＿＿＿＿＿＿

5. 简单句1：全球变暖问题不容忽视。
翻译：_____
简单句2：全球变暖对生态系统产生了严重的影响。
翻译：_____
合并：_____
_____

6. 简单句1：学生需要掌握多门语言。
翻译：_____
简单句2：掌握多门语言可以帮助他们在国际舞台上取得成功。
翻译：_____
合并：_____
_____

7. 简单句1：健康越来越受到人们的关注。
翻译：_____
简单句2：饮食和运动习惯对人们的健康有很大影响。
翻译：_____
合并：_____
_____

2.1.4 逻辑连贯性

雅思写作中，逻辑连贯性至关重要。通过合理安排逻辑顺序、巧妙使用过渡词和连接词以及妥善处理句与句之间的逻辑关系等方法，可以显著提升文章的条理性和连贯性。

1）合理安排逻辑顺序

合理安排逻辑顺序能够使文章各部分紧密相连，形成一个有机整体。先因后果、先总后分等逻辑顺序能够确保读者在阅读过程中能够清晰地跟随作者的思路，理解文章的各个部分是如何相互关联、相互支持的。

在雅思写作中，考生需要阐述自己的观点并说服读者。合理的逻辑顺序安排能够使考生的观点更加有力、更具说服力。例如，通过先因后果的顺序，考生能够展示出自己的观点是基于合理的推理和论证得出的；通过先总后分的顺序，考生能够先概括出核心观点，再逐步展开论述，使观点更加深入、全面。

除了先因后果和先总后分，还可以根据文章的具体内容和需要采用其他逻辑顺序，如时间顺序、空间顺序等。无论采用何种顺序，都应确保文章条理清晰、易于理解。

2）段落之间的衔接

雅思写作中，过渡词（transitional words and phrases）和连接词（linking words）在段落间的使用有助于增强文章的连贯性和可读性，还能够明确逻辑关系、加强论证力度并展现考生的语言水平。例如：

In discussing the impact of technology on modern society, it is crucial to consider both its advantages and disadvantages. **Firstly**, technology has significantly improved the efficiency of our daily lives. Tasks that once required hours of manual labor can now be completed in mere minutes with the help of advanced machinery and software. **Secondly,** technology has changed the way people communicate with each other.

However, there is a flipside to this coin. While technology has brought about immense convenience, it has also caused a decline in human interaction. People are increasingly relying on digital communication, which often lacks the warmth and depth of face-to-face conversations. **Furthermore,** excessive screen time has been linked to various health issues, such as eye strain and poor posture.

To sum up, while technology offers numerous benefits, it is essential to strike a balance and avoid its potential downsides.

在上面的段落中，第一段的 Firstly 和 Secondly 用于表示段落中的顺序和层次，使得读者能够清晰地理解作者首先讨论的是技术的两个优势。第二段开头的 However 表示话题的转折，从讨论技术的优势转向探讨其劣势，帮助读者意识到接下来将讨论相反的观点。最后一段的 To sum up 用于总结全文，表明作者即将结束讨论并给出结论。

3）句与句之间的逻辑

明确句与句之间的逻辑关系在雅思写作中能够增强文章的条理性。构建明确的因果关系、处理转折关系以及构建并列关系等都是提升雅思写作质量的关键。

（1）因果关系的表达。

在雅思写作中，清晰地表达因果关系是非常重要的。当想说明某个现象的原因和结果时，可以使用 because 和 therefore。

例如：As the government has increased its investment in environmental protection, the air quality has been significantly improved.（因为政府加大了对环保的投入，所以空气质量得到了显著的改善。）

在这个例子中，As（因为）用于表示原因，使句子的逻辑关系更加明确，空气质量得到改善是因为政府加大了对环保的投入。

（2）转折关系的处理。

在处理转折关系时，使用 although 或 however 等词语可以表达不同的观点或事实之间的对比和差异。

例如：Although e-commerce brings convenience to consumers, it also brings a series of security risks.（虽然电子商务为消费者带来了便利，但是同时也带来了一系列的安全隐患。）

在这个例子中，Although（虽然）用于表示让步关系，而后引入与前面观点相反的另一个观点，例句中电子商务为消费者带来便利和安全隐患是截然不同的两个角度的观点。

（3）并列关系的构建。

在构建并列关系时，使用 and 等词语可以连接多个并列项，表达并列关系。

例如：A successful leader has great communication skills, excellent leadership and adequate professional knowledge.（一个成功的领导者具备出色的沟通技巧、卓越的领导才能和足够的专业知识。）

在这个例子中，and 用于连接三个并列项：沟通技巧、领导才能和专业知识。

（4）常用逻辑连接词。

正确使用过渡词和连接词衔接文章段落和句子有助于考生获得高分。以下是常用的过渡词和连接词或短语：

• 表示顺序和层次 首先：first, firstly, to begin with, first of all, in the first place 其次：second, secondly, then, next, also, after that 此外（递进）：what's more, moreover, furthermore, besides, in addition, additionally 最后：finally, at last, last but not least
• 表示转折 对比：in contrast, on the contrary, conversely, on the other hand, … while/whist…, nevertheless 让步：although, though, even though, despite, in spite of, nonetheless, nevertheless, yet, however, after all, even if
• 表示原因和结果 因为：because, due to, owing to, for this reason, since 因此／结果：therefore, thereby, consequently, hence, as a result, so, thus, as such, accordingly
• 表示例证和说明 例如：for example, for instance, such as, a good case in point 也就是说：that is (to say), namely, in other words, specifically speaking, to be more specific, to put it simple 在这种情况下：in this case, particularly, in particular, by way of illustration
• 表示总结和结论 总之：in conclusion, to conclude, in summary, in short, on the whole, overall, generally speaking, to sum up, in a word, all in all, to put it briefly

- 表示观点和态度

在我看来：in my opinion, in my point of view, from my perspective, from my standpoint, as far as I'm concerned, personally

我认为：I believe/hold/contend/maintain

坦白说/实际上：frankly/honestly/strictly speaking, in fact, in reality, as a matter of fact

- 表示条件和假设

如果/假设：if, in case, provided that, supposing, assuming, on the assumption that, on condition that

考虑到：given that, considering, in view of, owing to the fact that

逻辑连贯性练习题

添加逻辑连接词重组下列句子，使意思通顺完整。

1. 句子 1: Education is essential for personal development.
   句子 2: It provides individuals with the knowledge and skills they need to succeed.
   重组后：_____
   _____

2. 句子 1: The Internet has revolutionized the way we access information.
   句子 2: It has also led to the spread of misinformation.
   重组后：_____
   _____

3. 句子 1: Many cities are facing serious traffic congestion.
   句子 2: Public transport should be improved.
   重组后：_____
   _____

4. 句子 1: The demand for renewable energy is increasing.
   句子 2: Fossil fuels are becoming scarce and polluting.
   句子 3: Solar energy and wind energy are viable alternatives.
   重组后：_____
   _____

5. 句子 1: Poverty is a major challenge in many developing countries.
   句子 2: Education can be a powerful tool in the fight against poverty.
   句子 3: Education helps individuals gain skills and knowledge that lead to better job opportunities.
   重组后：_____
   _____

2.2 Task 1 写作技巧

雅思写作考试中，Task 1 篇幅较短，但对考生语言运用和数据分析能力要求较高。本小节聚焦 Task 1 写作技巧，深入探讨图表作文，包括图表结构解读、审题方法、段落构建及不同图表题应对策略。系统学习和大量练习有助于考生在 Task 1 中提升表现，取得优异成绩。

2.2.1 图表作文简介

雅思写作图表类作文 Task 1 是测试考生理解和分析图表能力的一种方式，旨在考查考生将图表信息转化为文字信息的能力。Task 1 要求考生在 20 分钟内至少写 150 个词，根据图表中的数据进行描述、分析、比较和对比，并以客观的方式用完整的句子呈现信息，不包含个人观点、假设、推理或结论。在撰写过程中，考生应运用丰富多样的词汇和句式，以生动、准确的语言描绘图表内容，使信息传达既清晰又富有表现力。雅思常见图表题型详见本部分 1.3.1。

图表作文的写作通常遵循清晰、逻辑有序的模式，考生应系统地分析和阐述图表中的数据，作文通常可以分为三个部分，包含四到五个段落。以下是典型的雅思图表作文结构：

引言段 Introduction	**主题概括**：简要介绍图表研究的主题、研究对象、时间范围及数据形式。
概述段 Overview	**整体描述**：对图表进行整体性的描述，概括图表中的主要趋势、特点或显著数据。 **总结要点**：用一两句话总结图表中最关键的信息，为读者提供一个清晰的预览。
主体段（描述段）Body	（通常 2-3 段） **分段分析**：根据图表的具体内容，将描述段细分为多个部分，每个部分专注于图表中的一个方面或数据组。 **具体数据**：详细阐述每个描述段中的具体数据，包括数值、百分比、比例等，并进行必要的解释和说明。 **对比分析**：在描述数据的同时，进行必要的对比分析，如不同时间段、不同类别或不同国家和地区之间的比较。

2.2.2 数据图表作文写作技巧

图表作文不仅考验考生对数据的敏感度与解析能力，更要求考生能够将这些复杂的数据信息转化为条理清晰、逻辑严密的文字。审题、段落构建、语言运用等核心技巧能帮助考生掌握高效实用的方法，以应对各种图表作文题型。

2.2.2.1 审题技巧

在雅思写作 Task 1 的图表作文题中，审题是第一步也是至关重要的一步。准确的审题能够帮助考生明确写作方向，避免偏离主题。考生需要仔细阅读题目要求，明确以下几点。

（1）明确任务要求：首先，仔细阅读题目和图表说明，确保理解需要描述的内容。考生要确定所给图表的具体类型，是柱状图、线形图、饼状图、表格，还是其他特殊类型的图表。不同类型的图表在数据呈现和关注重点方面可能存在差异。例如，柱状图通常侧重不同柱子间的高度对比，以凸显数据的差异；线形图则需关注线条的起伏走向及关键转折点，从而洞悉变化趋势。

（2）识别和理解图表信息：注意图表中的标题、标注、时间轴等信息，图表的标题往往体现了图表的核心主题，而标注等则可能包含重要的背景信息或数据单位。譬如，若图表呈现的是不同城市的气温，标题可能为"某年度不同城市气温对比"，标注则可能注明测量气温的具体仪器及精度。

（3）关注关键信息并确定描述重点：图表通常存在一些极为显著的数据或鲜明的趋势，它们是考生需要重点描述的内容。同时，考生也需要关注图表中的异常值或特殊情况，这些都可能成为写作的亮点。举例来说，在关于某公司销售业绩的图表中，某个季度销售额的陡然飙升或急剧下跌，或者某款产品的销售表现与整体趋势大相径庭，都应成为重点关注的对象。

（4）排除干扰信息：图表中可能存在一些次要或无关紧要的信息，考生要学会辨别并排除这些干扰，集中精力处理与题目要求紧密相关的数据和内容。

（5）思考逻辑框架：在审题过程中，初步构思文章的结构和段落安排。根据题目要求和关键信息，确定开头如何引入、概述段的阐述要点以及描述段如何展开描述和分析。

例如：

You should spend about 20 minutes on this task.

> *The graph below shows the consumption of fish and some different kinds of meat in a European country between 1979 and 2004.*
>
> *Summarise the information by selecting and reporting the main features, and make comparisons where relevant.*

Write at least 150 words.

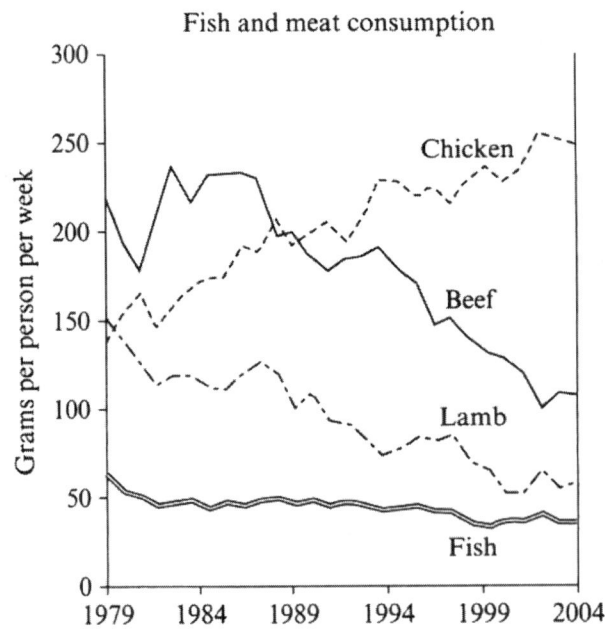

（Cambridge ESOL，2009：53）

审题分析

图形类型：线形图，数据随时间而变化。

时　　间：1979 年至 2004 年，每隔五年有一个标记点。

主题对象：Fish and meat consumption，four types (Fish, Lamb, Beef, and Chicken)

趋势概述：Chicken 的消费量呈显著上升趋势，而 Beef 和 Lamb 消费量变化趋势相似，均呈下降趋势，Fish 的消费量保持相对稳定（25 年间在四个品类中始终消费量最低）。

细节描述：逐一描述每种肉的变化趋势，从起点到终点（包括交点和最值等）使用具体的年份和数据来支撑观点。通过对比不同肉之间的消费量，突出它们之间的差异和相似之处。1979 年 Beef 的消费量远高于其他三种肉，同年 Lamb 和 Chicken 消费量接近（150g 左右）。第一个五年，只有 Chicken 的消费量增长。1989 年每人每周 Beef 和 Chicken 的消费量接近（190g 左右），Chicken 的消费量从 1979 年的排名第三上升到 2004 年的第一。

2.2.2.2 段落写作技巧

1）开头段

首先，开头段应简短而有力，避免冗长和复杂的句子；其次，要明确主题，用一两句话说明图表的主题或主要内容，让考官一目了然。可以通过改写题目实现。例如：

题目 1：The graph shows the demand for energy and the energy available from fossil fuels in Freedonia from 1985 to 2005.

改写：The line chart illustrates the changes of energy demand and energy available from fossil fuels in Freedonia over the period between 1985 and 2005.

题目 2：The bar chart shows the different modes of transport used to travel to and from work in one city, in 1970, 1990, 2010.

改写：The column graph compares the percentage of total travelers using different modes of transport to and from work in one city in 1970, 1990, 2010.

例图作文的开头段可以这样写：

The line graph compares the amount of fish, lamb, beef and chicken consumed per person per week in a European country from 1979 to 2004.

☆ 开头段常用句型及单词替换：

	图表类型	显示（动词）	（某类型）数据
The	chart	illustrate	the number/quantities of...
	graph	present	the amount of...
	table	reflect	the figure for
	pie/line/bar (chart/graph)	describe	the proportion/percentage/rate/ratio of
	flow chart/diagram	compare	information/data on
	maps/graphs/pictures	give information about	

2）概述段

（1）总体趋势概括：用简洁的语言描述图表中数据的总体变化趋势是上升、下降、波动还是保持稳定。

（2）关键数据提及：指出图表中的重要数据，如最高值、最低值、转折点等。

（3）主要特点总结：总结图表的主要特点，如数据的分布规律、不同数据之间的关系等。

例图作文的概述段可以这样写：

It is clear that people's weekly consumption of chicken experienced the sharpest increase in the given time, while both beef and lamb decreased significantly. Overall, fish consumed the least by consumers per week throughout the whole period of 25 years.

3）描述段

描述段是图表作文的核心部分，用于详细阐述图表中的具体数据、趋势或对比关系。

（1）分段描述：根据图表的不同部分或时间段，将描述内容分成 2～3 个段落。每个段落应专注于图表的一个方面或特征，注重总结和对比。

（2）数据支持：在描述段中，应使用具体的数据，数据应尽量准确。

（3）逻辑连贯：描述段内部应保持逻辑连贯，使用连接词（如 moreover, however, in contrast 等）来表明不同信息之间的关系。

（4）语言丰富：避免使用单调的语言描述数据。尝试使用不同的词汇和句式来表达相同的意思，以增加语言的多样性和文章的可读性。

例图作文中的描述段可分为两段，Beef 和 Lamb 的变化趋势类似，故而归为一组（在一个段落中进行描述），那么 Chicken 和 Fish 自然归为一组。可以这样描述：

描述段 1（Beef & Lamb）

Prior to 1989, beef held the top position as the most favored meat, with an average weekly per capita consumption of approximately 200 grams. However, from 1989 onwards, a steady decline ensued, culminating in the bottom of 100 grams in 2003. Similarly, lamb consumption, though initially lower than beef, mirrored a similar downward trend over time.

描述段 2（Chicken & Fish）

The consumption of chicken stood in sharp contrast to the trends observed for other meats. It kept increasing, surpassing beef in popularity in 1989 and subsequently establishing itself as the most consumed meat. In stark contrast, fish consumption remained consistently modest, fluctuating narrowly around 50 grams per week for the entire 25-year period, positioning it as the least popular choice among the four meats examined.

2.2.2.3 图表作文习作分析

1）柱状图作文

You should spend about 20 minutes on this task.

> *The chart shows the number of mobile phones and landlines used per 100 people in selected countries.*
>
> *Write a report for a university lecturer describing the information given.*

You should write at least 150 words.

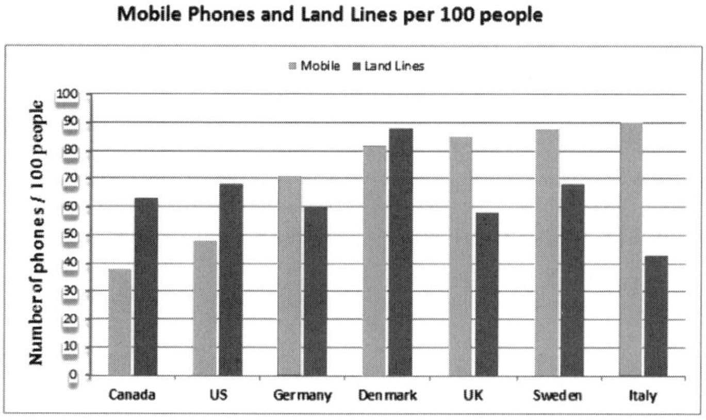

Mobile Phones and Land Lines per 100 people

(From: ielts-mentor.com)

学生习作：

The chart presents the number of mobile phones and landlines per 100 people in selected countries. Canada has approximately 38 mobile phones per 100 people. In the US, it's around 48, and in Germany, about 70. Italy has only around 90 mobile phones per 100 people, much higher than in Canada.

Regarding landlines, the situation is different. Denmark has nearly 90 landlines per 100 people, while in the UK, it's around 60. Interestingly, in some countries, the number of landlines may be decreasing while the number of mobile phones is increasing.

In general, the chart shows differences in the two things among the selected countries, indicating that the popular of them can vary greatly from one country to another. For example, in Canada and the US, mobile phones appear to be more popular than landlines, but in some other countries, the situation might be different.

评分：Band 4.5

评价：文章基本能够描述图表中的主要信息，虽然涵盖了一些数据信息，但不全，且部分图中具有重要意义的数据并未提及。各组数据之间未进行归纳和对比，使用的词汇较为简单，能够表达基本意思，但缺乏多样性和准确性。句型相对单一，多为简单句，缺少复杂句的运用，存在一些语法错误。文章有一定的组织结构，但段落之间的过渡不够流畅，文章的逻辑性和连贯性较弱。

参考范文：

The bar chart compares the quantity of mobile phones and landlines per 100 users in selected countries.

It is notable that most of the countries included have more mobile phone subscribers than landlines. Italy is the country who witnessed the highest number of mobile phones users and lowest landline users.

Canada, Denmark, and the US had more landlines users than mobile phones. Mobile phone use is the lowest in Canada, with only around 40 users per 100 people, whereas the highest number of landline users are found in Denmark which is almost 90 per 100 people. In the USA, the number of mobiles is around 50 per 100 people, which is much lower than the number of landlines (almost 70).

In contrast, in the other four countries, the number of landlines is smaller than the number of mobile phones. Italy has twice as many mobile phones as landlines, with 90 mobiles per hundred people in contrast to 42 for landlines. The number of mobile phones used per 100 people in Sweden is similar to, but slightly lower than, Italy. Mobile phone and landline ownership in Germany and the UK was 70, 60, 85, 58 respectively.

2）饼状图作文

You should spend about 20 minutes on this task.

The two graphs show the main sources of energy in the USA in the 1980s and the 1990s.
Write a report for a university lecturer describing the information shown below.

Write at least 150 words.

Sources of Energy, USA, in the 1980s and 1990s.

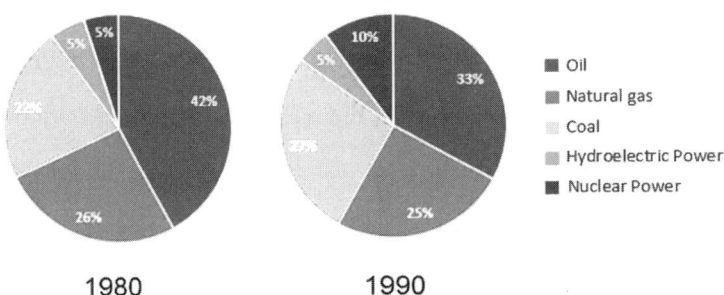

(From: ielts-mentor.com)

学生习作：

The pie charts shows many types of energy sources used in the USA in the 1980s and 1990s.

In the 1980s, oil was 42% of the energy, and natural gas was 26%. Coal was 22%, and hydroelectric power and nuclear power were 5% and 5% each.

In the 1990s, the numbers changed a little. Oil was 33%, natural gas was 25%. Coal was at 27%, and hydroelectric power and nuclear power were 19% and 13%.

In general, these charts give some informations about the energy in the USA in these two decades. The use of hydroelectric power remianed unchanged in 1980 and 1990. Natural Gas was only slighted changed.

评分：Band 4.0
评价：文章长度不够，内容基本符合任务要求，但对于图内部分重要信息的描述过于简略，几乎没有展开。整体行文推进较为简单，衔接手段使用有限；文章词汇使用较为简单且范围有限，能够表达基本意思，但缺乏变化和丰富性。例如，多次重复使用 was 来表示占比。句子结构基本正确，主要使用简单句，缺乏复杂句式的运用。存在语法错误，语法多样性不足。

参考范文：

The two pie charts compare the use of different sources of energy in the USA in the 1980s and 1990s.

It is obvious that oil remained the predominant energy source in the USA throughout both 1980 and 1990, while coal, natural gas, and hydroelectric power maintained relatively stable proportions. In contrast, nuclear power witnessed a remarkable surge, doubling its percentage over the course of the ten years.

Oil consistently supplied the largest proportion of energy, albeit with a slight decrease from 42% in 1980 to 33% in 1990. Coal emerged as the second-largest energy source in 1990, with its proportion rising from 22% in the previous decade to 27%. Natural gas, which was the second-largest source in 1980 at 26%, experienced a very minor decrease in its share, providing 25% of America's energy a decade later.

The percentage contributed by hydroelectric power remained unchanged at 5% of the total energy utilized. Nuclear power exhibited the most significant change: in 1990, it accounted for 10%, twice the percentage it had in 1980.

3）表格作文

You should spend about 20 minutes on this task.

> *The table below gives data on the hour of leisure time per year for people in Someland.*
> *Write a report for a university lecturer describing the information in the table below.*

You should write at least 150 words.

Hours of leisure time per year in Someland							
	Teens	**20s**	**30s**	**40s**	**50s**	**60s**	**70s+**
Watching TV/Videos	1200	700	400	500	600	700	1100
Socialising with 4 or less people	150	150	300	250	250	200	200
Socialising with 4 or more people	350	350	50	50	25	25	25
Individual exercise	150	100	200	200	50	75	150
Group exercise/sport	450	350	200	150	50	0	0
Cinema	100	75	50	25	25	50	75

(From: ieltsdata.org)

学生习作：

The graph illustrates how long people in Someland spend on a variety of methods of relaxing in leisure time per year.

It is clear that the types of watching TV and videos are the most popular in Someland, while going to the cinema in leisure time is not a choice to citizens in Someland. Moreover, the people in 60s and 70s no one choose group exercise and sport to unwind themselves.

It notable that teens spend 1200 hours in watching TV and videos and the elderly who over 70 years old spend 1100 hours in this way. What's more, the relax time on TV in 700 hours was spend same in 20s and 60s. The others three age stages 30s, 40s and 50s spend 400, 500 and 600 hours individually. The next ways is socialising with 4 or less people, the hours is similar at 150 in teens and 20s and it is also same at 250 in 40s and 50s. Both the 60s and 70s spend 200 hours in the per year.

评分：Band 4.5
评语：基本符合任务要求，能够描述图表中关于不同年龄段人们在各种休闲方式上花费的时间，但表述不够准确和完整。连贯性较差，句子之间的连接不够流畅。使用了一些简单的连接词，但整体行文推进不够清晰。词汇范围有限，表达较为简单，缺乏变化。语法错误较多。

参考范文：
The table presents how many hours people in different age groups spent on various leisure activities in a year in Someland.

Generally speaking, watching TV and videos is the activity that people of all ages like the most in their free time, but the time spent on other activities changes depending on people's age.

Socialising with 4 or more people was liked by teenagers, but as people get older, they preferred to socialise with fewer people, with the number of hours decreasing from 350 to 25. Teenagers and young adults liked group exercise, but people over 60 avoided it. People aged 30 to 40 seemed to spend about 200 hours a year on individual exercises.

For entertainment activities, on one hand, going to the cinema took up 100 leisure hours for teenagers, and the time kept decreasing as people get older, except for people over 70 who spent more time on this activity than people aged 30 to 70. On the other hand, young and old people spent more time watching TV and videos than people in other age groups, with teenagers spending 1200 hours and older people aged above 70 1100 hours.

4）混合图表作文
You should spend about 20 minutes on this task.

> *The chart below shows the amount of money per week spent on fast foods in Britain. The graph shows the trends in consumption of fast foods.*
> *Write a report for a university lecturer describing the information shown below.*

You should write at least 150 words.

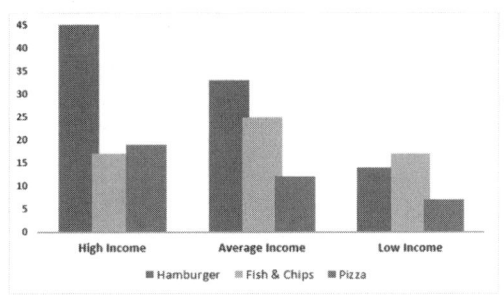

Expenditure (Pence per person per week) on fast foods, by income groups, UK 1990

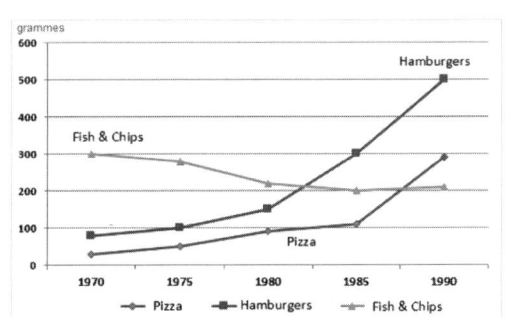

Consumption of fast food per person in gram (1970-1990)

(From: ieltsdata.org)

在雅思混合图表作文的写作中，需要注意以下几点。

（1）整体规划：在开始写作之前，先对两个图表进行整体观察和理解，明确它们之间的关系和重点信息；规划好文章的结构，确定如何合理地安排两个图表的描述顺序，有时一个图写一个主体段。

（2）分别描述：为每个图表分配适当的篇幅，确保对每个图表的关键特征和数据进行准确和清晰的描述。

（3）关联对比：寻找两个图表之间的联系和对比点。这可能是时间上的关联、数据的相互影响或者主题上的呼应。

学生习作：

The two graphs illustrate a variety of fast food including hamburger, fish & chips and pizza and show the consumption of these foods.

Generally speaking, the bar chart shows that the high income group has the lowest interest in fish & chips, while the low income group has more interest in fish & chips. And the expenditure on hamburgers decreases as the income group level goes down. Moreover, the line chart demonstrates that the hamburger and pizza always show an upward trend. Yet, fish & chips shows a downward trend.

The high income group spent 45 dollars per person per week on hamburgers, however the low income group just spent 15 dollars a week. But the low income group spent more money on fish & chips, 20 dollars a week. It's notable that the average income group spent on this different types of food (hamburger, fish &

chips and pizza) 33, 25 and 13 dollars respectively.

For the other graph, starting at 5 grammes in 1970, the consumption of pizza increased to 300 grammes in 1990. The hamburger was in the same trend; it was at 99 grammes in 1970 and climbed to the peak at 500 grammes in 1990. On the contrary, fish & chips had a downward trend from 300 in 1970 to 200 in 1990. And in the period in 1980, it was close to the consumption of hamburger. What's more, it was surpassed by pizza in the beginning of 1990.

评分：Band 5.5
评语：文章基本涵盖了题目要求的信息，对两张图表进行了描述，包括不同收入群体的快餐支出及消费趋势等，但在数据总结和对比上做得不够好。文章使用了一些衔接词，逻辑较为连贯，信息和观点组织合理。词汇使用基本恰当，能基本表达图表信息，但语言丰富性有待提升。语法错误较少，句子结构基本正确，能传达基本信息，但某些表达不够准确自然。

参考范文：
The bar chart illustrates the weekly expenditure of people in the UK on fast food in 1990 while the line graph presents how much fast food they ate from 1970 to 1990.

It is notable that expenditures on fast food varied depending on people's income class, with the rich consuming considerably more fast foods than the low-income class in 1990. Overall, hamburgers gained popularity during the 20-year period while fish & chips started to be consumed by less British people.

As the bar graph suggests, the high-income group spent around 44 pence per person per week on hamburgers, while only about 16 pence on fish & chips and 20 pence on pizza. The average income group also favored hamburgers, spending approximately 33 pence on it, followed by 25 pence on fish & chips and 11 pence on pizza. The low-income group, on the other hand, spent the least on fast foods, with around 16 pence on fish & chips, 14 pence on hamburgers, and 6 pence on pizza.

Regarding the line graph, fish & chips was the most consumed item in 1970, with a consumption of around 300 grammes per person, which is much higher than hamburgers (90 gramms) and pizza (30 gramms). However, over the years, the consumption of hamburgers steadily increased, and by 1990, it became the most popular fast food, with a consumption of 500 grammes per person. Meanwhile, the consumption of fish & chips gradually declined. For pizza, it shared a similar pattern to hamburger, rising from 20 to almost 300 grammes.

2.2.3 其他图表作文题写作技巧

在雅思 Task 1 写作考试中，除了要求根据数据图表写作文之外，有时还要求根据流程图和地图等非数据图写作文。

流程图侧重于展示某个过程或流程的具体步骤和顺序，考生需要清晰地阐述每个环节的操作、环节的转换以及它们之间的逻辑关系。流程图作文考查考生的逻辑思维和组织能力，检验他们是否能够准确地描述复杂的过程。

地图作文题要求考生准确描述地图中所展示的地理信息、地点布局以及相关变化，这不仅考验考生的语言表达能力，还考查考生的空间感知和分析能力。通过完成地图作文题，考生能够展示自己对地理空间的理解和描述能力。

本节将深入剖析这两种题型的审题和写作要点，通过详细的讲解和丰富的示例，帮助考生提升写作技巧，准确、清晰地传达图中的信息。

2.2.3.1 流程图作文

1）审题与分析

（1）理解题目要求和流程图所展示的内容。

认真阅读题目要求，明确流程图展示的对象和相关背景信息。接着，仔细观察流程图的整体布局和各个元素。注意流程图中的起始点和终点，以及箭头的指向，确定流程的顺序。同时，留意流程图中出现的各种图标、符号和文字说明，它们对于理解流程的具体内容至关重要。

（2）确定流程图的主题和主要步骤。

首先，通过对流程图的观察，明确其主题。例如，一张流程图展示的是从原材料到成品的生产过程，那么主题就是该产品的生产流程。然后，梳理出流程图中的主要步骤。这些步骤通常是按照一定的逻辑顺序排列的，可以通过箭头的走向来判断。将每个步骤的关键动作或事件提取出来，例如生产过程可能包括原材料的采集、加工、组装等主要步骤。

（3）分析步骤之间的关系和逻辑。

深入分析每个步骤之间的关系，判断它们是依次进行的线性关系，还是存在并行、循环或分支的情况。例如，在某些流程中，有多个步骤同时进行，或者在某个步骤之后会根据不同的条件采取不同步骤，即出现步骤分支。

（4）关注细节和关键环节。

注意流程图中是否存在关键的节点或环节，它们往往对整个流程的顺利进行起着重要作用。例如，某些步骤可能需要特定的条件或有时间限制，又或者会产生特定的结果或产物。

以以下流程图为例：

You should spend about 20 minutes on this task.

> ***The diagram below shows the process by which bricks are manufactured for the building industry.***
>
> ***Summarise the information by selecting and reporting the main features, and make comparisons where relevant.***

You should write at least 150 words.

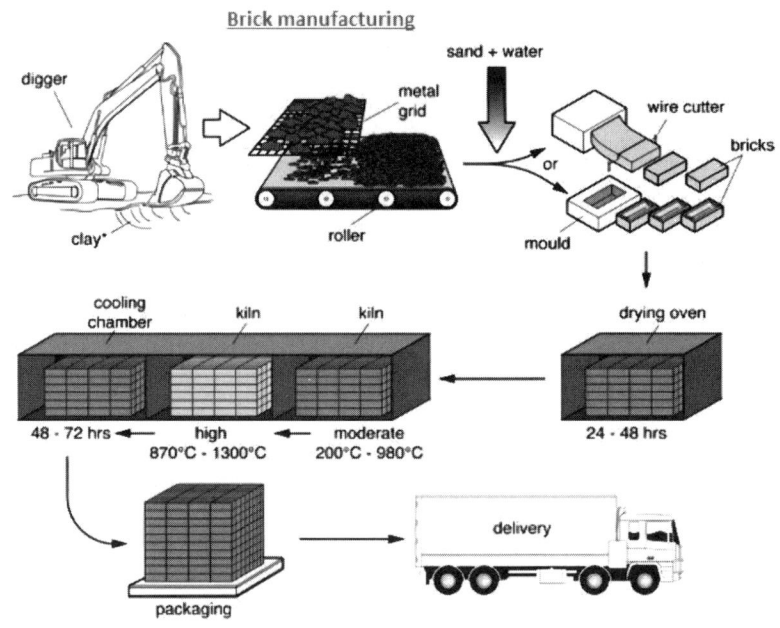

(From: IELTSMaterial.com)

解析：

（1）理解题目要求和流程图所展示的内容。

通过阅读题目，明确该流程图展示的是砖块的制造过程。仔细观察流程图的整体布局，起始点为黏土（clay）、沙子（sand）、水（water）的混合，终点为砖块的包装（packaging）和交付（delivery）。箭头的指向清晰地展示了流程的顺序。考生应留意流程图中出现的各种图标、符号和文字说明，如金属网格（metal grid）、切线机（wire cutter）、碾轧机（roller）、模具（mould）、冷却室（cooling chamber）等。

（2）确定流程图的主题和主要步骤。

主题为砖块的制造，主要步骤包括原材料的混合（沙子、水和金属）、材料的处理（通过网格、切线机等）、成型（黏土经过碾轧机进行模具中加工）、冷却（在冷却室中）、烧制（在窑中，温度为870℃～1300℃，持续48～72小时）、干燥（在干燥烤箱中，温度为200℃～980℃，持续24～48小时）、包装和交付。

（3）分析步骤之间的关系和逻辑。

通过分析每个步骤之间的关系，发现它们是依次进行的线性关系，没有明显的并行、循环或分支情况。原材料经过一系列的加工和处理，逐步转化为成品砖块。

（4）关注细节和关键环节。

注意到流程图中存在关键的节点或环节，如烧制和干燥阶段，它们对整个流程的顺利进行和保障砖块的质量起着重要作用。同时，每个阶段都有特定的时间和温度要求，如烧制阶段在870℃～1300℃之间持续48～72小时，干燥阶段在200℃～980℃之间持续24～48小时，这些细节丰富了对流程图的描述，使文章更加准确和完整。

2）写作要点与方法

（1）按照流程的顺序依次描述。

流程图的描述要按照流程的先后顺序进行，从流程图的起始点开始，有条不紊地介绍每个步骤的具体内容和操作。在描述过程中，要注意对关键步骤或复杂环节进行详细阐述，以突出其重要性和复杂性。而对于一些简单或次要的步骤，则可以简要带过，以避免文章过于冗长。

（2）连接步骤的过渡语言。

过渡语言在连接流程图的各个步骤中起着关键作用。使用 First（首先）、Then（接着）、Next（然后）、Finally（最后）等表示顺序的词汇，可以清晰地展示步骤之间的先后关系，使考官能够轻松跟上文章的节奏。

常用过渡语如下：

表示顺序	to begin with, initially, at the outset, first/firstly, second/secondly, third/thirdly, next, then, after that, afterwards, subsequently, later, in the following stage, finally, eventually, lastly, at the end
表示同时	at the same time, simultaneously, meanwhile
表示补充	in addition, additionally, besides, also, too, furthermore, moreover, what's more
表示因果	therefore, thus, as a result, consequently, hence, accordingly, as a consequence, for this reason
表示在……之前/之后	prior to, before, beforehand after, subsequent to, following

（3）适当添加解释和说明。

为了帮助读者更好地理解流程图的原理和意义，适当添加解释和说明是非常必要的。在描述流程图的过程中，可以对某个步骤的目的进行解释，让读者明白为什么要采取这样的操作。例如："在这个步骤中，我们进行加热处理，目的是使原材料达到一定的温度，从而满足后续加工的要求。"

以上流程图参考范文：

The diagram illustrates different stages of brick manufacturing for the building industries.

It is notable that brick production involves 7 steps, starting from digging clay and ending at the delivery stage.

The first step in brick manufacturing, as shown in the diagram, is the digging of clay from the ground using a large digger. The clay is then filtered and processed through a metal grid onto a roller machine before being mixed with sand and water. In the third stage, the mixture is either placed in a mould or cut using a wire cutter to form the raw shape of the bricks. Subsequently, the raw bricks are dried in a drying oven for 24～48 hours, before being baked in a kiln, initially at a moderate temperature of 200～980℃, followed by an extremely high temperature of 870～1300℃. They are then further cooled for 48～72 hours in the cooling chamber. Later the finished products are packed and loaded onto trucks, and the final stage is to deliver bricks to various locations.

2.2.3.2 地图作文

1）审题与分析

（1）理解题目要求和地图所展示的内容。

考生需认真阅读题目中的文字说明并聚焦地图的细节，留意地图中的标注，关注自然地貌（如山脉、河流等，它们可能影响城镇的发展方向和布局），道路的形态、宽窄和连接情况，建筑物的位置、类型和规模。

（2）确定地图的主题和变化焦点。

明确地图的主题是读懂地图的关键。如：地图可能展示的是一个城市的扩张与现代化进程，也可能展示了某个乡村地区为发展旅游业而进行的重新规划。在确定主题后，就要找出变化焦点。如：变化焦点可能是一座新建成的大型体育场馆，其规模和现代化设计在整个区域中格外突出；或者是原本分散的商业区逐渐集中，形成了商业中心。

以以下地图为例：

You should spend about 20 minutes on this task.

> *The two maps below show road access to a city hospital in 2007 and in 2010.*
> *Summarise the information by selecting and reporting the main features, and make comparisons where relevant.*

You should write at least 150 words.

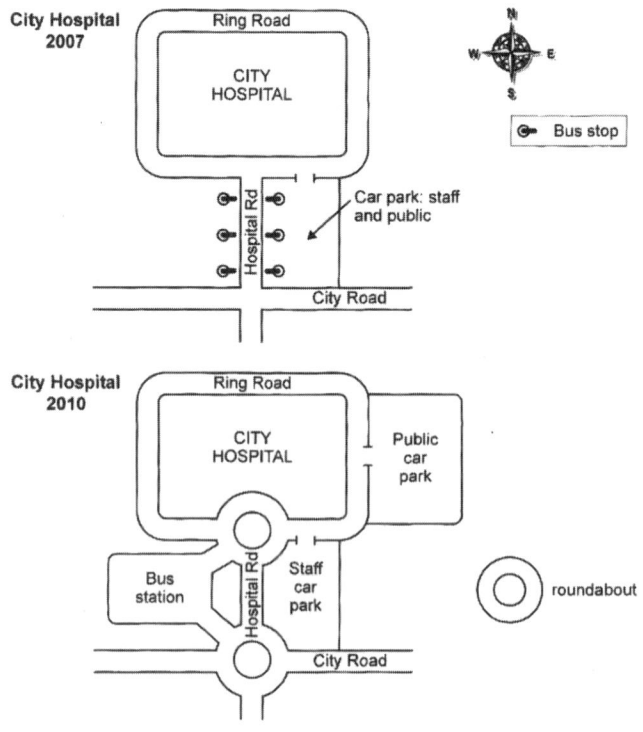

（Cambridge ESOL，2018：29）

解析：

（1）理解题目要求和地图所展示的内容。

- 图片展示了某城市医院 2007 年和 2010 年周围道路和设施的变化，重点在于布局的转变。
- 观察地图细节：主要道路为 City Road，Hospital Road 和 Ring Road，Hospital Road 连接 City Road 和 Ring Road，Ring Road 环绕 City Hospital 而建。2007 年，Hospital Road 周边设有一个公交停靠站（Bus stop）以及东边一个供员工和公众使用的停车场（Car park: staff and public）。到 2010 年，在道路交汇处 Hospital Road 的两端设置了环形交叉路口（roundabout），公交停靠站变为长途汽车站（bus station），City Hospital 的东边新增了一个公共停车场（Public car park），之前的停车场改为员工专用。

（2）确定地图的主题和变化焦点。

- 地图的主题是 City Hospital 道路和基础设施的完善和优化。
- 变化焦点：①停车场的增加与改变：新增公共停车场，设置员工专用停车场；②交通设施的改进：环形交叉路口的设置有助于优化交通，减少拥堵；③交通站点的集中：公交停靠站变为长途汽车站，有利于车辆的集散。

2）写作要点与方法

（1）准确描述地图信息：按照一定的逻辑顺序进行描述，如从整体到局部、从主要到次要等。使用准确的方位词和其他词汇来描述建筑物、道路、设施等的位置、形状和大小。注意细节，包括地图中的标注、颜色等信息，以确保描述的准确性。

（2）突出变化：对比不同时间段的地图，明确变化的内容和程度。在描述变化时，使用恰当的动词和短语。

（3）时态正确：描述地图中的现状使用一般现在时，描述过去的情况使用一般过去时，描述未来的规划使用一般将来时或其他表示未来的时态。保持时态的一致性，避免时态混乱。

（4）结构清晰：开头段引出主题，概述段总结主要变化，主体段详细描述地图信息和变化。

（5）逻辑连贯：使用连接词和短语来连接段落和句子，使文章过渡自然，逻辑连贯。

参考范文：

The given maps illustrate the layout changes of the area named City Hospital from 2007 to 2010.

It is clear that there are some noticeable alterations in the infrastructure and facilities during this period. The main roads (City Road, Hospital Road and Ring Road) remain unchanged, but new additions and modifications to the surrounding areas can be found.

In 2007, there was only one car park, with a single access in the south-east of the Ring Road. By 2010, this had become a car park for staff only and a public park was added next to the City Hospital, to the right of the eastern section of the Ring Road.

To the southern part of the map, there was a roundabout newly constructed in 2010 at the junction with Hospital Road. At the other end of the road, another roundabout was built at the crossroads with City Road, which likely aims to improve traffic circulation and safety. The upgrade of the bus stop to a bus station implied an improvement in the public transportation system.

2.2.4 Task 1 写作技巧练习

Task 1 写作技巧练习

1. 仔细阅读题目要求，理解表格中展示的内容，指出表格中的关键信息和数据并思考写作框架。

The table below shows the number of medals won by the top six countries in the 2020 Tokyo Olympic Games.

2020 Tokyo Olympic Games Medal Table

Rank	Country	Gold	Silver	Bronze	Total
1	United States	39	41	33	113
2	China	38	32	18	88
3	Japan	27	14	17	58
4	Great Britain	22	21	22	65
5	Russian Olympic Committee	20	28	23	71
6	Australia	17	7	22	46

(From: Olympics.com)

基本情况：_____

_____

关键信息和数据点：_____

_____

写作框架：_____

_____

2. 写出开头段（一句话改写题目）

_____

_____

3. 写出概述段

_____

_____

4. 写出描述段

_____

_____

2.3 Task 2 写作技巧

雅思写作 Task 2 旨在评估考生的批判性思维能力、逻辑论证能力以及书面表达能力。该任务通常要求考生针对一个给定的论题或问题，在 40 分钟内撰写一篇不少于 250 字的议论文。Task 2 的题目范围广泛，可能涉及教育、科技、社会、环境、文化、政府政策等多个领域，要求考生深入分析问题，提出个人见解，并给出充分的理由和例证来支持自己的观点。

2.3.1 Task 2 题型分类及作文结构

雅思 Task 2 写作题型较为多样，详见本部分 1.3.2。

雅思 Task 2 写作通常包括三个部分：开头段（introductory paragraph）、主体段（body paragraph）和结论段（concluding paragraph）。其基本结构如下：

开头段	• 背景介绍：通过对题目的背景进行简要描述，引入话题、主题所处的大环境。 • 题目改写：用不同的词汇和句式重新阐述题目中的观点或问题，展示对题目的理解。 （根据题目要求进行个人观点陈述：明确表明自己的立场。）
主体段	通常包括 2～4 段 主体段 1 • 主题句：提出本段的核心观点，与文章的总体观点相关。 • 解释和论证：通过举例子、提供数据、引用权威观点等方式对主题句进行详细的解释和论证。 主体段 2 • 主题句：提出另一个支持总体观点的分论点。 • 解释和论证：同样进行详细的阐述和论证。 （如有需要，可以增加更多主体段，论证方法同上）
结论段	• 总结观点：再次强调文章的核心观点，对主体段的主要内容进行概括总结。 • 适当展望：可以对未来的情况进行简要的展望，或者提出一些建议。

2.3.2 Task 2 写作技巧

雅思 Task 2 的写作并非简单的文字堆砌，而是一项需要精心构思和巧妙表达的任务。掌握一系列有效的写作技巧有助于在这部分取得高分。以下将详细剖析各个关键写作技巧环节。

2.3.2.1 审题技巧

（1）仔细阅读题目，理解题目的要求和重点。

仔细阅读题目并理解题目的要求和重点不仅能帮助考生确保论述方向与题目紧密相连，避免偏离主题或误解题意，还能使考生在写作过程中更加集中地围绕核心议题展开论证，提升论述的针对性和深度，从而增加文章的说服力，提升质量。

以下题为例：In modern society, people increasingly rely on technology for social interaction. Some people believe that technology has a positive effect on interpersonal relationships, while others believe that it leads to estrangement. Discuss both views and give your own opinion.

通过仔细阅读题目，明确题目要求我们讨论关于科技对人际关系影响的两种对立观点（一种认为科技有积极影响，另一种认为科技导致疏远），并给出自己的看法。重点在于对 positive effect（积极影响）和 leads to estrangement（导致疏远）这两个核心观点的深入探讨，不能只简单提及，而要充分阐述各自的理由和依据。

（2）确定题目中的关键词和主题词。

关键词是题目中具有关键指示作用、对写作内容有决定性影响的词汇，而主题词则是能够概括整个题目的核心词汇。准确识别关键词和主题词，有助于在写作过程中紧扣题目，不偏题、不跑题。

以上题为例。

- 主题词：科技（technology）、影响（effect）。
- 关键词：现代社会（modern society）、社交互动（social interaction）、人际关系（interpersonal relationships）、积极影响（positive effect）、疏远（estrangement）。

（3）分析题目类型及涉及的观点和角度，确定写作方向和重点。

不同类型题目需要采用不同写作策略和结构，明确类型有助于迅速选择合适的方法，使文章结构清晰、逻辑连贯。通过分析能更好地理解题目，避免遗漏重要信息或在次要细节上耗时，提高写作效率和质量。此外，确定写作方向和重点能在有限字数内有效传达关键信息，避免内容混乱、主次不分，还能在语言表达上更精准和有针对性，运用恰当词汇和句型，突出重点，增强文章可读性和专业性。

以上题为例。

- 题目类型：这是一个列举型问题，要进行双边讨论并给出个人观点，其重点是双边讨论。
- 涉及的观点和角度。

    观点一：科技对人际关系有积极的影响。

    观点二：科技导致了人际关系的疏远。

- 确定写作方向和重点：科技在社交互动和人际关系中的角色，分析阐述两种对立的观点并给出个人观点。

2.3.2.2 构思技巧

雅思写作前的文章构思能帮助考生明确文章的主旨、论点与论据，合理安排文章结构，确保内容逻辑清晰、条理分明。构思过程包括确定立场、规划段落分布、筛选并组织相关论据，从而有效避免写作过程中的跑题或思路混乱，提升文章的整体质量和说服力。头脑风暴和构建思维导图是构思文章确定立场的重要方法。

1）头脑风暴：激发创意与全面思考

头脑风暴是一种快速而有效的方法，用于在构思阶段激发思维活力，收集尽可能多的观点和论据。考生在平时练习中可以设定时间限制，比如 5～10 分钟，专注于题目主题，不评判任何想法的优劣，只负责将其记录下来。在头脑风暴过程中，鼓励自己从不同角度思考，包括正面、反面、实际影响、未来趋势等，这样可以帮助自己全面理解问题，并为后续的写作提供丰富的素材。头脑风暴的过程中一定要紧扣题目关键词、限定词和主题。

以上节雅思题目为例，通过头脑风暴展开思考和准备的具体操作如下。

（1）明确题目的核心要求：探讨科技在现代社会中作为社交互动手段的影响，特别是它对人际关系产生的两种截然不同的影响——正面影响和导致疏远，并给出个人见解。

（2）自由联想、发散思维：在头脑风暴过程中，鼓励自己从各个角度进行思考，不一定形成完整的观点，可以是一些词或者短语等。如：

Positive	Negative
convenience/instant messaging/online shopping/rich information/remote work/news information/learning resources/improve work/study efficiency/expand social network/promote innovation/technological innovation/new product development/cross-border integration	over-reliance is bad/decreased face-to-face communication/privacy concerns-personal information leakage/social anxiety/cyberbullying/threaten physical health/decreased vision/decreased physical activity/limited communication/misleading information/identity theft/inauthentic display

（3）初步扩展（将词汇／短语转化为初步观点）。

①正面影响的初步观点。

· The development of technology has greatly improved the convenience and efficiency of people's living and working. (e.g. instant messaging, video conferencing, online shopping and remote working)

· Technology-based social media and online platforms break down national boundaries and make it easy for people to make friends from all over the world.

②负面影响的初步观点。

· Over-reliance on technology for social interaction leads to a decreased face-to-face communication, a limitation in authentic emotional exchange, and a negative impact on the depth and quality of human relationships.

· Prolonged use of technological devices has adverse effects on vision, sleep and physical health, such as vision loss, sleep disorders and reduced physical activity.

· Using the Internet to communicate may bring great threats to personal privacy, such as the exposure of personal information on the Internet, data abuse and identity theft.

2）构建思维导图：梳理逻辑与结构

思维导图是一种图形化的思维工具，通过中心主题向外辐射出各级子主题，直观地展示文章的结构和逻辑关系。在雅思写作 Task 2 中，构建思维导图可以帮助考生明确文章的主旨、分论点及其支撑论据，确保论述条理清晰、逻辑严密。

构建思维导图时，首先确定文章的中心论点（如"对人际关系来说，科技是把双刃剑"），然后围绕中心论点列出主要分论点（如"积极影响"和"消极影响"），再为每个分论点添加具体的论据和例子。

例如：

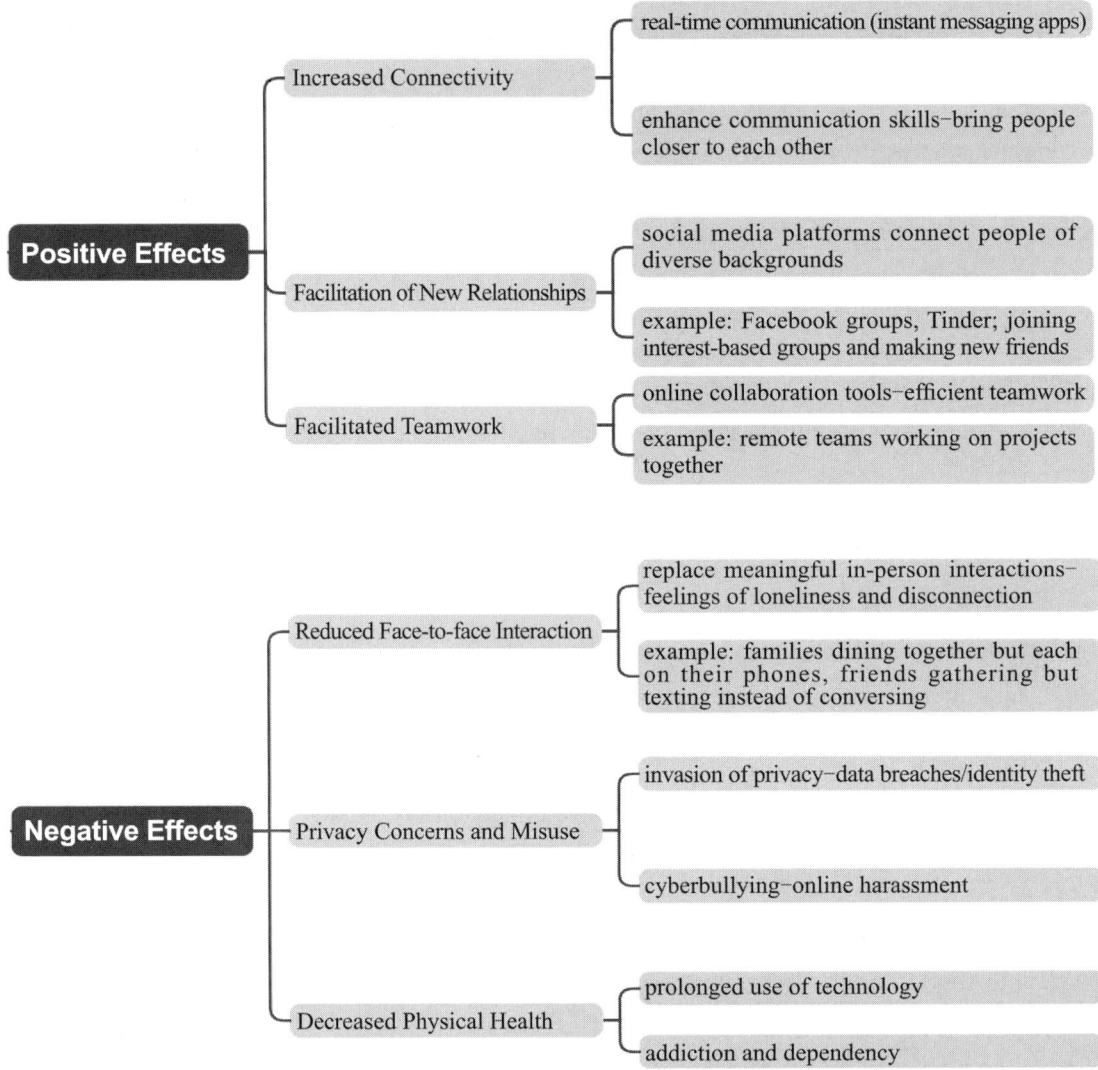

基于上述思维导图，考生可以进一步形成自己的论点。

Positive Effects：

·Online technology, such as instant messaging apps, enables real-time communication, enhancing communication skills and bringing people closer together.

·Social media platforms increase connectivity, allowing people to easily connect with those from diverse backgrounds.

·Online collaboration tools, a product of technology, promote efficient teamwork, enabling remote teams to work on projects together seamlessly.

Negative Effects：

·The over-reliance on technology for social interaction leads to reduced face-to-face interaction, causing feelings of loneliness and estrangement.

· Technology also raises privacy concerns, with the risk of data breaches and identity theft, and facilitates cyberbullying.

· Prolonged use of technology can have negative impacts on physical health and lead to addiction and dependency.

2.3.2.3 论述技巧：包括举例、对比和其他论证方法

在雅思写作 Task 2 中，论述技巧的运用是考生展现逻辑思维、分析能力和语言组织能力的关键。有效的论述不仅能够清晰传达观点，还能深深吸引并说服考官，从而助力考生获得高分。以下将详细探讨三种核心论述技巧：举例、对比以及多种论证方法的运用。

1）举例：具体生动，强化论点

（1）具体：在举例时，务必确保所选例子具体而翔实，避免泛泛而谈。一个生动的例子能够让抽象的论点变得具体可感，使读者能够迅速理解并产生共鸣。例如，在讨论"科技对人际关系的影响"时，与其泛泛地说"科技让人们变得疏远"，不如具体描述在家庭聚会中大家各自低头玩手机而忽视彼此交流的场景，这样的例子更具说服力。

（2）恰当：所选例子应与论点紧密相关，能够直接支持或反驳观点。避免使用与主题脱节或模糊不清的例子，以免削弱论证效果。

（3）结合紧密：在叙述例子时，要清晰地展示它是如何支撑论点的。通过适当的过渡句或分析，使例子与论点无缝连接，让整个论述过程流畅自然。

2）对比：凸显差异，增强说服力

（1）明确对比对象：在进行对比时，首先要明确想要对比的两个方面或观点。这些对比对象应当是同一类别中相对立或存在差异的两方，以便读者清晰地看到其中的不同。

（2）突出差异：通过详细阐述对比对象之间的区别，突出其某一方面的优势或劣势。使用对比性的词汇和句式，如 by contrast, however, although 等，强化对比效果。

（3）增强论证力度：对比不仅仅是为了展示差异，更重要的是通过对比来突出立场和观点。在对比的过程中，引导考官看到考生所支持观点的合理性和必要性，从而增强整个论证的说服力。

3）运用其他论证方法：归纳法与演绎法并重

（1）归纳法：从个别到一般，通过列举多个具体事例，归纳出普遍性的结论。这种方法适用于那些需要使用大量实例来支撑论点的情况。在运用归纳法时，要注意所选事例的广泛性和代表性，以确保归纳出的结论具有普遍意义。

（2）演绎法：从一般到个别，以普遍性的原理或假设为出发点，推导出特定情况下的结论。这种方法逻辑严密，适用于那些已经有明确前提或理论框架的情况。在运用演绎法时，要确保前提的正确性和推理过程的严谨性，以避免出现逻辑错误。

以以下雅思写作题目为例：Some people believe that international tourism brings more benefits than problems to the local community and environment. To what extent do you agree or disagree?

（1）举例子。

在探讨这个题目时，为了支持或反驳"国际旅游对当地社区和环境带来更多益处"的观点，可以举出具体的例子来强化你的论证力度。

①支持观点的例子：可以提到某个著名旅游城市，如巴厘岛，通过发展旅游业，当地居民获得了更多的就业机会，改善了生活质量。同时，旅游业的发展也带动了当地文化的保护和传播，使得传统手工艺品和民俗表演得以保留并展示给全世界。

②反对观点的例子：为了反驳这个观点，可以提及威尼斯这样的城市，过度旅游开发导致当地生活成本上升，居民被迫搬离市中心，文化遗产受到破坏，环境压力增大，水体污染、噪音污染等问题日益严重。

（2）对比。

通过对比国际旅游带来的好处与问题，更加鲜明地表达立场。好处与问题的对比：首先列举国际旅游为当地带来的经济收益、文化交流等好处，然后转而讨论它带来的负面影响，如环境破坏、文化同质化、居民生活质量下降等。通过这种对比，可以突出强调更关注的方面，从而增强论证力度。

（3）运用其他论证方法。

①归纳法：在总结多个类似案例的基础上，归纳出国际旅游对当地社区和环境的普遍影响。例如，列举多个因旅游而受益或受损的社区案例，然后归纳出旅游业发展的双刃剑特性。

②演绎法：从一个普遍性的原理或假设出发，推导出特定情境下的结论。例如，可以从"旅游业发展需要平衡经济收益与环境保护"这一普遍原则出发，推导出某个具体旅游城市应该如何制定可持续发展策略的结论。

2.3.2.4 段落写作技巧：段落的结构、主题句的写法等

在雅思写作 Task 2 中，段落作为构建文章的基本单元，其质量直接关系到内容层次的清晰度和整篇文章的说服力。因此，掌握段落写作技巧有助于考生在有限的时间内展现出最佳的写作水平。

（1）明确段落主题，以主题句引领全段。

每个段落都应有其主题或核心观点，而这一主题应通过段落的第一句话即主题句明确表达出来，主题句是段落的灵魂。一个有效的主题句应当简洁、直接，并能准确概括段落的中心思想。考生应避免在主题句中引入过多细节或偏离主题的信息，以保持段落的聚焦性和清晰度。

（2）内容紧密围绕主题，逻辑清晰地展开。

一旦主题句确立了段落的方向，接下来的内容就应当紧密围绕主题进行阐述。考生需要运用逻辑推理、事实例证、对比分析等方法逐步展开论述，深化对主题的理解。在阐述过程中，要注意段落内部结构的合理性，确保各句子之间形成有机的联系，共同支撑主题句的观点。同时，要保持论述的连贯性，避免出现跳跃式思维或无关紧要的插叙，以免扰乱读者的阅读思路。

（3）句子间相互关联，逻辑链条紧密。

段落中的每个句子都不是孤立存在的，它们之间应当通过一定的逻辑关系相互连接，形成一条清晰的逻辑链条。为了实现这一目标，考生可以运用连接词、指示代词等语言手段来加强句子间的联系。

（4）结尾句总结或过渡，完美收官。

一个成功的段落不仅要有引人入胜的开头和充实的内容，还需要有画龙点睛的结尾。总结性结尾句可以简要回顾段落中的主要观点或论据，强调主题句的重要性；过渡性结尾句则可以引出下一个段落的主题或论点，实现段落间的自然衔接。无论采用哪种方式，结尾句都应紧扣段落主题，保持语言的简洁和准确性，以给读者留下深刻的印象。

以以下雅思写作 Task 2 题目为例：Some people think success of life is based on hard work and determination but others think there are more important factors like money and appearance. Discuss both sides and give your own opinion.

- 段落一：开头段

The debate surrounding the defining factors of success in life has long been a contentious issue, with some advocating the paramountcy of hard work and determination, while others argue that factors such as money and appearance hold greater sway.

这一句明确提出了文章要讨论的主题，即成功生活的决定因素，并简要概述了正反两方的观点。

- 段落二：正方观点段

主题句：Proponents of hard work and determination as the cornerstone of success contend that these qualities enable individuals to overcome obstacles and achieve their goals.

随后，可以使用具体例子或论据等来支持这一主题句，如：For instance, the numerous athletes who have risen to the top of their fields through relentless training and perseverance, despite facing numerous setbacks along the way.

- 段落三：反方观点段

主题句：On the contrary, those who argue for the significance of money and appearance in determining success maintain that these factors often open doors that would otherwise remain closed.

同样，通过具体实例来加强论述，如：In the entertainment industry, for example, actors and performers with striking appearances and financial backing often find it easier to secure leading roles and projects, thereby accelerating their path to success.

在每个段落中，通过使用连接词、指示代词等语言手段，确保句子之间的逻辑联系紧密。例如，在正方观点段中，可以使用 furthermore, additionally 等词语来进一步阐述努力工作和决心的重要性；在反方观点段中，则可以用 similarly, conversely 等词语来对比说明金钱和外貌对成功的影响。

结尾句要对段落内容进行总结和过渡。

- 段落二结尾句：Thus, it is evident that hard work and determination play a pivotal role in shaping an individual's success story.
- 段落三结尾句：As such, it is also undeniable that in certain contexts, money and appearance can serve as catalysts for success, particularly in fields where these factors are highly valued.

2.3.2.5 结尾技巧：如何总结文章并给人留下深刻印象

在雅思写作 Task 2 作文的尾声，一个强有力的结尾不仅能够为整篇文章画上圆满的句号，还能在考官心中留下深刻的印象，成为提升分数的关键。

（1）总结文章的主要内容和观点。

结尾的首要任务是回顾并总结全文的核心信息和主要观点。考生可以简要概括每个段落的主题，强调文章的中心思想，确保读者对文章的整体框架和主要论点有清晰的认识。

（2）提出一些建议或展望未来。

在总结完文章后，考生可以进一步提出个人见解、建议或对未来发展趋势的展望，以展现自己的批判性思维和前瞻性。这些建议或展望应与文章主题紧密相连,既体现了考生对问题的深入思考,也增加了文章的深度和广度。

(3) 避免在结尾处引入新的观点或内容。

结尾是文章的收尾部分,应保持其简洁性和与上文的一致性。因此,考生应避免在结尾处突然引入新的观点或内容,以免破坏文章的整体结构和连贯性。如果确实有新的想法或发现,建议在正文中适当位置进行阐述,而非留待结尾处理。保持结尾的紧凑和聚焦,是确保文章质量的重要一环。

以上节题目为例,总结段(段落四)可以像下面这样写。

主题句(总结性陈述):In conclusion, while hard work and determination undoubtedly form the bedrock of success, it is equally important to recognize that factors such as money and appearance can also play a significant role, depending on the specific context and industry.

随后,可以给出自己的观点,如:Ultimately, I believe that a balanced approach that acknowledges the importance of both internal qualities and external factors is key to achieving sustainable success in life.

2.3.3 不同题型作文的写作要点

雅思写作 Task 2 涉及多种题型,每种题型都有其独特的要求和挑战。

2.3.3.1 观点类题型

(1) 明确立场型(Do you agree or disagree?)。

题目示例:Some people believe that private tutoring is essential for students' academic success, while others think it may have negative effects. To what extend do you agree or disagree?

- 开头段:清晰地表明自己的立场,简要介绍讨论的话题背景。

例如:In the contemporary educational landscape, the debate on whether private tutoring is beneficial for students' academic performance is highly contested. Personally, I strongly disagree with the notion that private tutoring is always a positive factor.

- 主体段1:阐述支持自己立场的第一个主要理由,可以进行拓展或提供具体例子和详细解释。

例如:One key reason for my disagreement lies in the potential for over-reliance. Students who constantly depend on private tutors may fail to develop independent learning skills. For instance, they might get used to having tutors explain every concept in detail and solve problems for them, instead of trying to figure things out on their own. When faced with new challenges in higher education, they may struggle to solve problems independently. This situation suggests that excessive reliance on tutors can undermine students' autonomous learning abilities, which is detrimental to their long-term development.

- 主体段2:提出支持自己立场的第二个重要理由,同样可以列举相关的例子、事实或个人经验。

例如:Another significant drawback is the financial burden it imposes on families. The cost of private tutoring can be substantial, putting a strain on household budgets. A survey conducted in our local community revealed that many families had to cut back on other essential expenses to afford tutoring for their children. This not only affects the quality of life of the family but also creates an unequal playing field for students from different socioeconomic backgrounds. Those who can afford private tutoring may have an advantage over those who cannot, which goes against the principle of equal educational opportunities.

- 结尾段：重申观点，总结论点，可适当展望未来。

例如：In conclusion, I insist that private tutoring is not invariably beneficial. The problems of students' over-reliance and the financial stress on families should not be neglected. Clearly, a more balanced approach to education is needed, reducing the excessive reliance on private tutoring.

（2）权衡利弊型（Do the advantages outweigh the disadvantages?）。

题目示例：With the increasing demand for energy such as oil and gas, people start to look for their sources in remote and untouched places. Do the advantages outweigh the disadvantages?

- 开头段：简要介绍题目中讨论的事物或现象，表明自己将对其优点和缺点进行权衡，并给出自己的观点，即自己认为到底是"利大于弊"还是"弊大于利"。

例如：As the demand for energy like oil and gas keeps escalating, the search for these resources has extended to remote and untouched places. Although exploitation of resources can satisfy people's current needs, I firmly believe that the disadvantages outweigh the benefits.

- 主体段：分别阐述优点和缺点。在阐述优点时，要具体说明其带来的好处；在阐述缺点时，要指出可能存在的问题或可能造成的负面影响。同时，要对优点和缺点进行比较，说明自己认为利是否大于弊的理由，如：如果认为利大于弊，可以强调弊可以被优化或带来的影响较小等。

a. One of the advantages of exploring energy sources in these remote and untouched areas is that it can increase the supply of energy to meet the current high demand. This can support economic growth and various industries, ensuring the smooth operation of modern life. For example, it can provide sufficient fuel for transportation and power generation. Additionally, the development of energy sources in these areas can potentially create job opportunities for local communities, boosting their economic well-being and living standards.

b. However, the disadvantages are overwhelming. Firstly, the environmental impact is huge. The extraction process can cause irreversible damage to the local ecosystem, including soil erosion, water pollution, and the destruction of natural habitats. This can lead to the extinction of rare species and disrupt the ecological balance. Secondly, it poses a threat to the rights and livelihoods of indigenous communities living in these areas. Their ancestral lands might be exploited, and their traditional cultures and ways of life could be disrupted.

c. When comparing the two, I do believe that the advantages are short-term and limited, while the disadvantages have long-lasting and widespread effects. The damage to the environment and communities is difficult to repair and has significant implications for future generations.

- 结尾段：重申自己的观点，总结主体段论述的优点和缺点，可提出一些建议或改进措施，以减少缺点的影响或增强优点的发挥。

In conclusion, the exploration of energy sources in remote and untouched places brings more disadvantages. The environmental degradation and social injustices are unacceptable. To mitigate these negative effects, we should take measures such as prioritizing the development of renewable energy sources such as solar and wind power.

（3）性质判断型（Do you think this is a positive or negative development?）。

题目示例：In recent years, there has been a significant increase in the number of people working from home. Do you think this is a positive or negative development?

- 开头段：引出讨论的发展或变化，针对该发展或变化是积极的还是消极的表明自己的看法。

例如：The recent surge in the number of people working from home, fueled by advancements in technology, has become a noteworthy trend. I firmly believe that this development is overwhelmingly positive, offering numerous benefits that go beyond individual convenience and impact society at large.

- 主体段：提供具体的事例或分析来支持自己的判断。可以从经济、社会、环境等多个角度进行分析。

例如：To illustrate the positivity of this trend, several key aspects can be considered. From an economic perspective, remote work has broadened job opportunities, allowing individuals to secure positions that might not be geographically feasible otherwise. This flexibility has not only increased productivity for many businesses but also facilitated a more diverse and inclusive workforce. For instance, companies can now tap into global talent pools, enhancing innovation and competitiveness.

Socially, working from home has promoted a healthier work-life balance. Reduced commuting time translates to more time for family, hobbies, or personal development. Moreover, it has accommodated individuals with specific needs, such as those with disabilities or caregiving responsibilities, enabling them to participate more fully in the workforce.

Environmentally, the shift towards remote work has contributed to reducing carbon emissions associated with daily commuting. With fewer cars on the road, there is a tangible improvement in air quality and a step towards mitigating climate change.

- 结尾段：总结自己的观点，并强调该发展或变化的重要性或影响。

例如：In conclusion, I do believe that the rise of working from home is a decidedly positive development, fostering economic growth, social inclusivity, and environmental sustainability. Its impact extends beyond mere convenience, reshaping the way we work and live for the better.

2.3.3.2 列举类题型

（1）双重观点讨论型（Discuss both views and give your opinion）。

题目示例：Some people believe that the best way to improve public health is by increasing spending on education about healthy lifestyles. Others, however, argue that the key to better public health lies in providing better access to healthcare services. Discuss both views and give your opinion.

- 开头段：简要介绍题目中涉及的两个观点，表明自己将对它们进行讨论并给出个人看法。

例如：The debate surrounding the most effective means of enhancing public health has garnered significant attention, with two primary viewpoints emerging: increasing spending on education about healthy lifestyles and improving access to healthcare services. While both approaches have their merits, I believe that a comprehensive strategy combining both education and healthcare access is the most effective way forward.

- 主体段1：详细阐述第一种观点的合理性和支持论据。

例如：Advocates for increased spending on education about healthy lifestyles argue that well-educated citizens are more likely to make wiser decisions about their health. By educating individuals on the importance of balanced diets, regular exercise, and avoiding harmful substances like tobacco and alcohol, society can empower people to make informed decisions that positively impact their health. This approach fosters a sense of personal responsibility and encourages long-term behavioral changes.

- 主体段2：深入分析第二种观点的要点和依据。

例如：On the other hand, those who prioritize improving access to healthcare services contend that preventive measures alone are not sufficient. They emphasize that even with the best intentions, individuals may still fall ill or face health crises. Therefore, ensuring accessible and quality healthcare becomes crucial. Timely medical interventions, regular check-ups, and affordable treatments can significantly reduce the burden of diseases and improve overall life expectancy.

- 主体段3：给出自己的观点，结合前两种观点的优点进行综合论述，并提供进一步的理由和例子。

例如：In my opinion, both viewpoints hold merit, and a comprehensive approach combining education and healthcare access is ideal. Education provides the foundation for individuals to make healthy choices, while accessible healthcare acts as a safety net when prevention fails. This blend ensures that citizens are equipped with knowledge and have the support system in place when needed.

- 结尾段：总结全文，再次强调自己的观点。

例如：In conclusion, while both increasing spending on education about healthy lifestyles and improving access to healthcare services contribute to better public health, I contend that a holistic approach that integrates both strategies is most effective.

（2）报告式双问题型（Reports with two questions）。

题目示例：The issue of traffic congestion in urban areas has become a pressing concern. What are the main causes of traffic congestion in cities? How can these problems be alleviated?

- 开头段：简要介绍报告的主题和背景，引出两个相关问题。

例如：As populations continue to grow and urbanization accelerates, the problem of traffic congestion has exacerbated, so the concerns of traffic congestion in urban areas have become a pressing issue for many cities worldwide. In this essay, I'm going to examine the main reasons behind it and suggest effective measures to alleviate this issue.

- 主体段1：分析回答第一个问题，如造成交通拥堵的主要原因。

例如：One of the primary reasons for traffic congestion in urban areas is the increasing number of vehicles on the road. As cities become more populous, the demand for personal transportation rises, resulting in a higher number of cars, buses, and trucks on the roads. Additionally, inadequate public transportation systems often force individuals to rely on private vehicles, further contributing to congestion.

主体段2：分析回答第二个问题，如提出有效缓解交通拥堵的措施，结合实际案例和可行方案进行阐述。

例如：To alleviate traffic congestion, several effective measures can be implemented. Firstly, improving public transportation systems is crucial. By providing efficient, reliable, and accessible public transport, cities can reduce the reliance on private vehicles. Secondly, implementing congestion pricing or tolls in high-traffic areas can discourage private vehicle use during peak hours. Lastly, investing in smart traffic management systems, such as real-time traffic monitoring and intelligent transportation systems, can help optimize traffic flow and reduce congestion.

- 结尾段：总结两个问题的回答，可适当展望未来。

例如：In conclusion, traffic congestion in urban areas is a complex issue with multiple contributing factors, including the increasing number of vehicles and inadequate public transportation system. However, by implementing effective measures such as improving public transportation, introducing congestion pricing, and investing in smart traffic management systems, cities can alleviate this problem.

2.3.3.3 混合类题型

题目示例：In recent years, it has become increasingly common for people in many countries to adopt modern, international styles of clothing, such as suits, dresses, and jeans, instead of traditional attire. What are the reasons behind this trend? Do you believe this is a positive or negative development?

- 开头段：仔细阅读题目，理解题目中所涉及的现象、问题以及要求回答的问题。

例如：In recent years, a notable shift in clothing preferences has emerged globally, with many individuals embracing modern, international styles of clothing such as suits, dresses, and jeans, often replacing traditional attire. This trend reflects a complex interplay of factors and I think generally it is a positive development.

- 主体段：根据题目要求，分别回答各个问题。要注意各个问题之间的逻辑关系，使文章连贯流畅。

例如：a. The reasons behind this shift in clothing preferences are multifaceted. Firstly, globalization has played a significant role in breaking down cultural barriers and promoting the exchange of ideas and styles. As people become more exposed to diverse cultures and fashion trends, they are naturally inclined to adopt clothing that reflects their personal tastes and aspirations for modernity. Secondly, modern clothing is often associated with convenience, comfort, and practicality. Suits, dresses, and jeans are versatile and adaptable to various settings, making them suitable for the fast-paced lifestyles of many individuals today.

b. One of the reasons why I believe this trend is generally a positive development is that it fosters a sense of global unity and inclusivity. By embracing modern, international styles of clothing, individuals from different cultures can connect and identify with each other on a more universal level. This promotes understanding and respect for diversity. Another cause is that the availability of diverse clothing options allows individuals to express their unique personalities and identities. Clothing has always been a form of self-expression, and this trend enables people to do so in a more globalized context.

- 结尾段：总结文章的主要内容，再次强调自己的观点和解决方案。可以对未来的发展进行展望，或者提出一些建议。

例如：In conclusion, the notable shift in clothing preferences towards modern, international styles is a complex phenomenon driven by globalization, practicality, and fashion influences. I believe this trend is generally a positive development as it fosters global unity and promotes individual expression.

2.3.4 范文分析

通过深入剖析不同分数段的范文，考生能够清晰地了解优秀作品的特质以及不足之处，从而汲取经验，避免常见的错误。

（1）题目一：Some people say the best way to improve road safety is to increase the minimum legal age for driving a car or a motorbike. To what extent do you agree or disagree?

学生习作：

Road safety is very important, it affect many people. We need to improve traffic safety. Nowadays, some people think that the best way to improve road safety is to increase the minimum legal age for driving a car or a motorbike. I strongly disagree about the idea.

First, drive cars shows mature of many young people. Many young people need to driving to work place and other place. If we improving the traffic safety by increase the minimum legal age for driving a car. It's limits their actions. They must relying on others for travel. It is not convenient. What's more. Many young people rely on driving for work or education as mentioned, so increase the minimum legal age for driving is also cause some economic problems for them. They must pay more on the transport. Because they don't know how to drive. They need to take taxis.

Increasing the driving age is not the best solve of improve the road safity. We can improve driving education or use some more strict laws to solve the problem. Last but not least. Age is not related to responsibility. Some young people have a strong responsibility, but some old men even have less responsibility when driving. This kind of less responsible may lead to car accidents sometimes.

评分：Band 4.5

评价：文章最低限度回答了题目中的问题，然而，论证不够清晰和充分，观点阐述较为简单。文章在连贯和衔接方面，句内和句间的衔接有时不流畅，指代和替换的使用不够准确，段落划分不够明确，逻辑推进不够清晰。词汇使用较为有限，存在一些错误和不恰当的表达，仅能够使用一些简单的词汇来表达观点，用词缺乏丰富性和准确性。语法错误较多，影响理解，简单句和复杂句的使用都存在问题，句子结构不够准确和灵活。

参考范文：

Road safety is a critical issue that affects millions of people worldwide. Some argue that increasing the minimum legal age for driving cars and motorbikes is the most effective way to improve road safety. However, I disagree with this approach for several reasons.

Firstly, the ability to drive represents independence and maturity for many young people. Raising the minimum driving age would significantly limit their mobility and autonomy. For many who rely on driving to commute to work, school, or other activities, forcing them to depend on others for transportation could be highly inconvenient and potentially hinder their personal development and career prospects, potentially causing economic hardship.

Secondly, age alone is not an accurate predictor of driving ability or responsibility. While it's true that inexperience can contribute to accidents, many young drivers are cautious and law-abiding. Conversely, older drivers can also be reckless or irresponsible. Rather than implementing a blanket age restriction, a more nuanced approach focusing on individual competence and behavior would be more effective.

Instead of raising the driving age, there are alternative strategies that could significantly improve road safety. Enhanced driver education programs, for instance, could better prepare new drivers of all ages for the challenges they'll face on the road. These could include more rigorous training in defensive driving techniques and hazard perception. Additionally, implementing stricter penalties for dangerous driving behaviors, regardless of the driver's age, could serve as a more effective deterrent.

In conclusion, while road safety is undoubtedly important, increasing the minimum legal driving age is not the most effective solution. Instead, a multifaceted approach focusing on education, enforcement, and individual responsibility would likely yield better results in creating safer roads for all users, regardless of age.

（2）题目二：Some people think that in this modern world people are getting dependent of each other. Others think the modern world gets people more independent of each other. Discuss both views and give your own opinions.

学生习作：

Nowadays, there are two perspectives with in modern world whether people becoming more dependent of or more independent on each other, that bring highly discussing around citizens.

On the one hand, a series of living problems lead to people become more and more dependent of each other.

The first problem about modern world's pace of life is too fast, people can easily become too tired and lead to emptiness. Acompany of each other is much valuable. We often depend on experts and professionals for specialized knowledge or turn to online communities for advice.

on the other hand, people are getting more independent on each other point to several factors. Firstly is most important that technology improve in amazing speed, so people found it's more convenience to social and talk online that they gradually rely on information than each other. Then, 'no trust' frequent appears in the society. Cmpare to depend on each other, people prefer to choose themselves. Last but not least, in modern world, people tend to have more free time and vacant space to be alone that useful to relax and enhance themselves.

In conclusion, i agree with the them. Half and half. We have to adopt communicate with friends, colleagues, even the strangers every day. And we have to admit they give us much emotions both positive and negative, let us live more vivid. Over-dependence can cause harm, so we also should be rely on ourselves. The modern world provided us with the tools and opportunities to more dependent or more independent, depending on how we utilize these offerings.

评分：Band 5.5

评价：该文章基本完成了写作任务，讨论了两种观点并给出了自己的看法，但对话题的讨论和延伸缺乏深度，且部分内容重复。文章总体上是连贯的，但部分句子表达不流畅。词汇使用基本满足需求，但较简单，出现较多单词拼写错误。语法错误出现得较为频繁，如句子结构不完整、时态和词性使用不当，给读者阅读带来一些困难。尝试使用复杂句，但未能正确使用。

参考范文：

In today's rapidly evolving world, there is an ongoing debate about whether people are becoming more interdependent or independent of one another. This essay will look at both sides of the argument and explain why I think that people in today's society are facing a combination of both dependence and independence.

On one hand, there are compelling arguments suggesting that people in contemporary society are increasingly interdependent. The fast-paced nature of modern life often necessitates relying on others' expertise and support. For instance, we frequently turn to professionals such as doctors, financial advisors, and technology specialists to navigate various aspects of our lives. Additionally, the rise of social media and online communities has created new forms of connection, allowing people to seek advice, emotional support and a sense of belonging from a wider network.

Conversely, there is evidence to suggest that modern life is fostering greater independence. Technological advancements have made it possible for individuals to access information, services, and entertainment without direct human interaction. Online learning platforms, for example, enable self-directed education, while e-commerce and digital banking reduce the need for face-to-face transactions. Furthermore, more people place greater emphasis on individual autonomy and self-reliance. The gig economy and remote work opportunities allow individuals to shape their careers with greater flexibility and independence.

In my view, the modern world has strangely brought about both more independence and interdependence at the same time. Technology and social changes have made us more self-reliant, yet also formed new ways of connection and mutual dependence.

To sum up, this dual situation shows how complex modern society is. Independence and interdependence aren't opposites; they complement each other in modern life. The challenge for everyone is to learn when to be independent and when to depend on others, finding a balance that helps both personal growth and social harmony.

（3）题目三：In many countries, people are now able to eat out-of-season vegetables at any time due to the development of modern agricultural technology. Do the advantages outweigh the disadvantages?

学生习作：

Nowadays, with the development of modern technology, people can eat out-of-season vegetables. Some people think this is good, but others think it has problems. In this essay, I will discuss the advantages and disadvantages of eating out-of-season vegetables.

Now, people can eat many kinds of vegetables all year. For example, in winter, people can eat tomatoes and cucumbers, which are usually summer vegetables. This makes food more interesting and gives people more choices. Also, it is good for health because people can get different things from different vegetables. Another advantage is that farmers can make more money. When they grow out-of-season vegetables, they can sell them at higher prices because they are not common. This helps farmers to improve their lives and support their families.

However, there are also disadvantages. Out-of-season vegetables may not taste as good as in-season ones. This is because they are often grown in artificial conditions, like greenhouses, and may not have the same natural taste. Also, some people think these vegetables are not as healthy because they may have more chemicals to help them grow. Moreover, it may destroy the environment. Growing out-of-season vegetables often requires a lot of energy, like electricity for greenhouses and transportation to move the vegetables to different places. This can increase pollution and harm the environment.

In conclusion, eating out-of-season vegetables has both advantages and disadvantages. It gives people more food choices and helps farmers earn money, but it may affect the taste and healthiness of the vegetables and harm the environment. In my opinion, the disadvantages are more important because health and the environment are very important for everyone.

评分：5.0

评价：这篇文章围绕现代技术发展下人们能吃到反季节蔬菜这一现象，对其优缺点进行了讨论，结构较为清晰，能完成基本的写作任务。然而，语言表达和语法准确性方面存在明显不足，词汇使用较为基础且重复较多，缺乏多样性和准确性。语法错误较多，有句子结构简单、标点符号使用不当、时态不一致等问题。此外，论点的展开较为简单，缺乏深入的分析和具体的例子支持，导致论证不够充分，段落之间的衔接也不够自然，逻辑连接词使用较少，影响了整体的连贯性。

参考范文：

In many countries, the advancement of modern agricultural technology has made it possible for people to access out-of-season vegetables throughout the year. This development has its own set of advantages and disadvantages. Personally, I think this do more good than harm.

The entire business chain associated with out-of-season vegetables stands to benefit from modern agricultural technology. Farmers, for instance, can enjoy increased income by diversifying their crops and meeting the demand for off-season produce. Similarly, salesperson can expand their market reach and profit margins by supplying a variety of vegetables year-round. Consumers, on the other hand, enjoy a wide range of fresh produce regardless of the season, promoting a healthier lifestyle and dietary diversity. In essence, the widespread benefits extend to farmers, traders, and consumers, making the accessibility of out-of-season vegetables a positive development.

Admittedly, there are some temporary disadvantages associated with the availability of out-of-season vegetables. Farmers may face challenges in acquiring the necessary technology, which could increase production costs. However, these challenges can be addressed through government support programs, subsidies, and training initiatives to help farmers adapt to new agricultural practices. On the consumer side, concerns about the use of hormones and pesticides in out-of-season vegetables may arise. Nevertheless, consumers can make informed choices by learning about food safety practices and opting for organic alternatives. It's important to note that the higher prices of out-of-season vegetables may only affect a small portion of the population, and as the industry evolves, prices are likely to decrease over time.

In conclusion, while there are some initial hurdles and concerns regarding the availability of out-of-season vegetables through modern agricultural technology, the benefits of year-round access to fresh produce far outweigh the drawbacks. By ensuring that all relevant stakeholders are supported and informed, we can harness the advantages of year-round access to fresh produce while mitigating any potential negative impacts.

2.3.5 Task 2 写作技巧练习

练习1：审题技巧练习

请分析以下题目中的关键词、主题词、题目类型以及涉及的观点和角度，并确定写作方向和重点。

（1）题目一：Some people think that the main purpose of education is to prepare individuals for the job market, while others believe that education should focus on personal development. Discuss both views and give your opinion.

主题词：_____

关键词：_____

题目类型：_____

涉及的观点和角度：_____
_____

写作方向和重点：_____
_____
_____

（2）题目二：Some people think that the government should spend more money on providing affordable housing rather than improving the transportation system. Do you agree or disagree?

主题词：_____

关键词：_____

题目类型：_____

涉及的观点和角度：_____
_____

写作方向和重点：_____
_____
_____

练习2：构思技巧练习

（1）题目一：Recently, a notable surge has been observed in the employment of artificial intelligence in the workplace. Some people believe that it brings convenience, while others argue that it could lead to job losses. Discuss both views and give your own opinion. 针对以上题目进行头脑风暴，记录所有与题目相关的想法，进行整理，形成自己初步观点。

_____
_____

（2）题目二：Cultural diversity is an important aspect of a society. Some people think that it is essential to preserve and promote local cultures, while others believe that global cultural integration is inevitable and beneficial. Discuss both views and give your own opinion. 针对以上题目构建思维导图，明确中心论点、分论点及论据。

练习3：论述技巧练习

（1）举例子。

阅读以下题目：Some argue that social media has a positive impact on individual lives, while others claim it brings negative consequences。请选择一个立场（正面或负面），使用至少两个具体例子来支持你的观点。

（2）比较和对比。

阅读以下题目：Telecommuting is increasingly adopted in modern society. Some believe it enhances work efficiency, while others suggest it reduces team collaboration. 请分别阐述两种观点的优势或劣势，使用对比性词汇和句式来强化对比效果。

练习4：段落写作技巧练习

1. 请为以下段落写出主题句。

（1）Topic: Social media

_____. In recent years, there has been a significant increase in the use of social media. People of all ages are spending more time on platforms like Facebook, Instagram, and Twitter. They use these platforms to connect with friends, share photos and updates, and follow news and trends. Social media has also become a powerful tool for businesses to promote their products and services.

（2）Topic：Climate change

_____. Rising temperatures, melting glaciers, and more frequent extreme weather events are all consequences of climate change. It is caused by human activities such as the burning of fossil fuels and deforestation. These activities release large amounts of greenhouse gases into the atmosphere, trapping heat and leading to global warming. Moreover, the melting of polar ice caps is contributing to the rise in sea levels, threatening coastal cities and island nations. The increased frequency and intensity of storms, floods, and droughts are disrupting agriculture, causing food shortages and economic instability. Additionally, the disruption of ecosystems due to climate change is endangering many species, leading to a loss of biodiversity.

（3）Topic：Education

_____. A good education can open doors to better job opportunities, higher income, and a more fulfilling career. It not only imparts academic knowledge but also nurtures practical skills like communication, teamwork, and leadership. For instance, a well-educated person is more likely to secure a job that matches his/her skills and interests, leading to greater job satisfaction. It also helps to develop critical thinking, creativity, and problem-solving abilities. These qualities enable individuals to approach challenges with confidence and find innovative solutions. Moreover, education fosters a sense of curiosity and a love for learning, which can lead to personal growth and a broader perspective on the world.

2. 请围绕主题句写一个段落，确保内容紧密围绕主题展开，逻辑清晰，句子间相互关联。

（1）The rise of online shopping has had a significant impact on the retail industry. _____
_____
_____
_____

（2）The importance of learning a foreign language cannot be overstated. _____
_____
_____
_____

（3）Technology has revolutionized the way we communicate. _____
_____
_____
_____

练习5：结尾句写作技巧练习

（1）Building bike lanes in cities has multiple advantages. Firstly, it encourages more people to choose cycling as a mode of transportation. Cycling is an eco-friendly option that reduces carbon emissions and helps combat air pollution. Secondly, bike lanes enhance road safety. They separate cyclists from motor vehicles, reducing the risk of accidents. Additionally, promoting cycling through bike lanes can improve public health. Regular cycling is a great form of exercise that can boost cardiovascular health and reduce the risk of obesity and other chronic diseases. _____
_____
_____
_____

（2）Language learning has numerous benefits. It not only allows us to communicate with people from different countries and cultures, but also opens up new opportunities for travel, work, and education. By learning a new language, we can gain a deeper understanding of another culture and its values, which can enhance our cross-cultural communication skills. Additionally, language learning can improve our cognitive abilities, such as memory, problem-solving, and multitasking. It can also boost our confidence and self-esteem as we overcome the challenges of learning a new language. For example, being able to speak a foreign language can give us an advantage in the job market, as many companies are looking for employees with language skills. It can also enable us to study abroad or engage in international business. Furthermore, language learning can be a fun and rewarding experience, as it allows us to explore new worlds and make connections with people from different backgrounds. _____
_____
_____
_____

3 雅思写作模拟试题

Test 1

WRITING TASK 1

You should spend about 20 minutes on this task.

> *The graph below shows the number of employees with different jobs in the U.S. solar industry from 2010 to 2020.*
>
> *Summarise the information by selecting and reporting the main features, and make comparisons where relevant.*

Write at least 150 words.

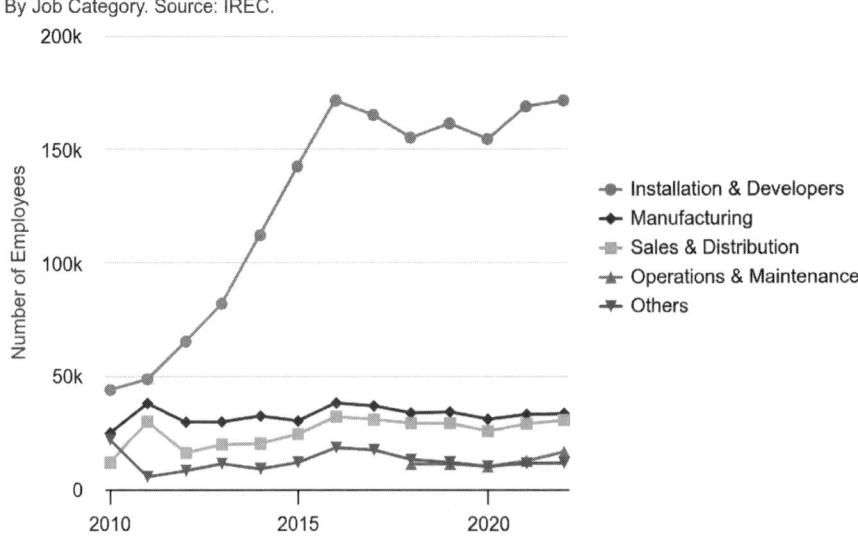

(By Job Category. From IREC: International Renewable Energy Certificate)

WRITING TASK 2

You should spend about 40 minutes on this task.

Write about the following topic:

> *Some people argue that the increasing accessibility of private healthcare is beneficial, while others believe it leads to higher costs.*
>
> *Discuss both views and give your own opinion.*

Give reasons for your answer and include any relevant examples from your own knowledge or experience.

Write at least 250 words.

Test 2

WRITING TASK 1

You should spend about 20 minutes on this task.

> *The graph below shows the historical changes in population numbers (in millions) across different regions of the world in 1990, 2000, and 2021.*
>
> *Summarise the information by selecting and reporting the main features, and make comparisons where relevant.*

Write at least 150 words.

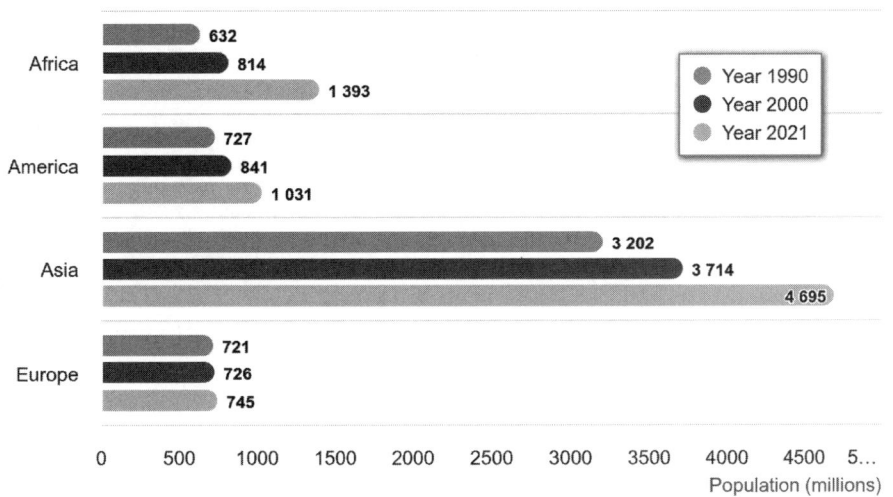

(From Wikipedia.org)

WRITING TASK 2

You should spend about 40 minutes on this task.

Write about the following topic:

> *In today's digital age, people have access to a vast amount of information.*
>
> *Do you think this has more advantages or disadvantages for individuals and society?*

Give reasons for your answer and include any relevant examples from your own knowledge or experience.
Write at least 250 words.

Test 3

WRITING TASK 1

You should spend about 20 minutes on this task.

> *The chart below shows the percentage changes in population sizes among selected European countries in 2013 and 2021. The table presents the absolute population figures for the same period.*
>
> *Summarise the information by selecting and reporting the main features, and make comparisons where relevant.*

Write at least 150 words.

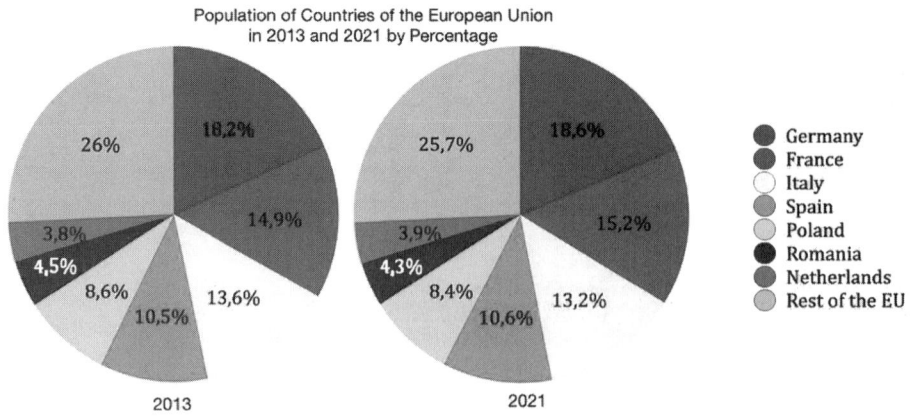

European countries by population (2013 vs. 2021)

Country	2013	2021
Germany	18.247.307	18.615.651
France	14.881.769	15.159.411
Italy	13.628.856	13.226.164
Spain	10.548.501	10.609.575
Poland	8.607.179	8.446.159
Romania	4.521.617	4.278.195
Netherlands	3.802.261	3.923.130
Rest of the EU	25.762.511	25.741.716

(From Writing Support: Pie Charts | Data Literacy | Writing Support)

WRITING TASK 2

You should spend about 40 minutes on this task.

Write about the following topic:

> *Nowadays, the number of people choosing to live alone is increasing.*
>
> *What are the reasons and effects of this trend?*

Give reasons for your answer and include any relevant examples from your own knowledge or experience.

Write at least 250 words.

IELTS
All-in-One Guide
(Basic Edition)

第四部分
雅思口语

1 雅思口语概述

1.1 雅思口语考试构成及流程

雅思口语测试的目的是评估考生用英语进行交际的能力，评估考生是否能自然、流利、自发、准确地使用英语描述自己的学习、工作、生活以及陈述和解释自己的观点。

考试时间总体为 11 ~ 14 分钟，由三个环节构成：

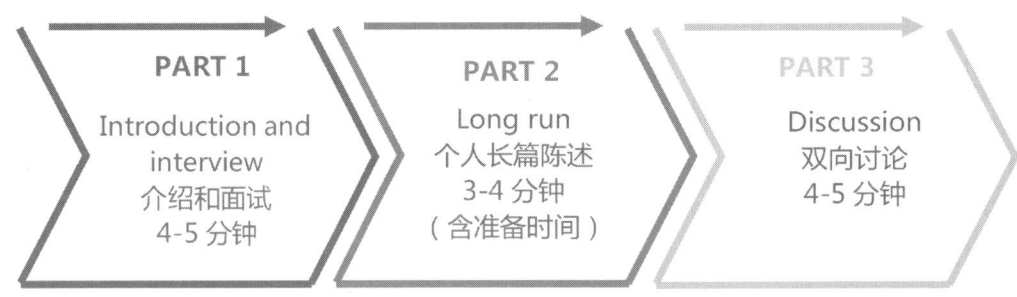

口语部分 1 介绍和面试：考官介绍自己并检查考生的身份，会问考生关于一些熟悉话题的一般性问题，例如家庭、工作、学习或兴趣等。该部分旨在测试考生就日常话题和常见经历等发表观点和提供信息的能力。

The examiner asks the candidate about him/herself, his/her home, work or study and other familiar topics.

EXAMPLE

Food and cooking

- What kinds of food do you like to eat?
- What kind of new food would you like to try? [Why?]
- Do you like cooking? [Why/ why not?]
- What was the last meal you cooked?
- Do you prefer home-cooked food or food from restaurants? [Why?]

（Cambridge ESOL，2005：56）

口语部分 2 长篇发言：考官会给考生一张任务卡，谈论特定的话题。卡片中有主题任务及信息要点的要求。考生有一分钟的准备时间，配有笔纸做简要笔记。考官会在准备时间到后提示考生开始陈述，陈述时间为 1～2 分钟。考官会根据考生的陈述内容再询问 1～2 个相关问题，这样的 follow-up questions 只需简单作答，无须展开陈述。该部分旨在测试考生在给定话题上进行长篇发言的能力，考生需要根据自己的经历，有逻辑地组织恰当的语言进行完整表达。

Describe an interest or hobby that you enjoy.
You should say:
　　how you became interested in it
　　how long you have been doing it
　　why you enjoy it
and explain what benefit you get from this interest or hobby.

You will have to talk about the topic for one to two minutes.
You have one minute to think about what you're going to say.
You can make some notes to help you if you wish.

（Cambridge ESOL，2005：56）

口语部分 3 讨论：考官会就与第二部分相关的问题与考生进行更为深入的讨论。该部分旨在测试考生解释观点的能力，以及对问题进行分析、讨论和推测的能力。

Discussion topics:
The social benefits of hobbies
Example questions:
- Do you think having a hobby is good for people's social life? In what way?
- Are there any negative effects of a person spending too much time on their hobbies? What are they?
- Why do you think people need to have an interest or hobby?

（Cambridge ESOL，2005：56）

简而言之，口语考试的三个环节可以理解为从与个人贴近的各种生活类小话题出发，逐步延伸到对人生经历的描述，再到对抽象性问题的讨论的过程。

1.2 雅思口语考试评分标准

上节中介绍到雅思口语考试分为三个部分，但是评分并不是三个环节分别打分的总和。考生的口语水平会按照"雅思口语考试评分标准"从四个考评维度（见表1），按照 0～9 分的范围打分。虽然在最后的成绩报告中考生只能获知口语的整体得分，不能直接知晓四个分项的小分，但是解读四个维度在不同分数段的具体要求，既可以帮助考生在备考前做好自我诊断，明确短板和长项，制定备考策略,也能锁定目标分段后按要求进行针对性训练,科学有效地提升口语能力。

雅思口语考核的关键评估标准包括流利性与连贯性(Fluency & Coherence)、词汇多样性(Lexical Resource)、语法多样性及准确性(Grammatical Range)、语音(Pronunciation)。

表1 口语评分示例

Criteria	Candidate A	Candidate B	Candidate C
Fluency & Coherence	7	5	4
Lexical Resource	6	5	5
Grammatical Range	6	5	4
Pronunciation	6	6	5
Overall Band	6	5	4.5

1.2.1 流利性与连贯性

主要考查考生是否能以正常的连贯性、语速和表达力进行口语交流,是否能够将思想转化为恰当的语言,形成连贯的言论。

(1)流利性的关键指标。

- 语速:不能太慢(难以将头脑中的词语关联起来)。
- 语言连贯性:应尽量避免错误的开始、不断地回溯、无意义的词语和短语重复以及暂停寻找词语。

(2)连贯性的关键指标。

- 口语句子的逻辑性。
- 清晰地标记(适当运用停顿、口头话语标记和填充词)讨论、叙述或论证中的阶段。
- 口语句子与谈话目的的相关性。
- 口语句子内部和句子之间使用了衔接手段(例如逻辑连接词、代词和连词)。

1.2.2 词汇多样性

考生掌握词汇的多样性会影响其能够讨论的话题范围,以及表达含义和态度的精确程度。词汇多样性包含以下要素。

- 使用词汇的多样化。
- 与以下要求相关的词汇准确性和得体性:指称意义(正确标记事物和概念),语言风格(区分正式和非正式用语),词语搭配(包括习语表达),使用表示说话者态度的词(如认可的、中立的或不认可的)。
- 使用转述(释义表达)的能力(通过使用其他词语来解决词汇缺失问题),并且是否有明显的犹豫。

1.2.3 语法多样性及准确性

主要考查考生是否能准确和恰当地运用语法完成口语测试。语法能力对于表达较为复杂的观点十分重要。

- 语法能力体现在使用语句的长度,是否能恰当使用从句,使用动词短语的复杂程度(含助动词、被动语态等），调整句子结构的能力（如通过调整句子中的某些要素使之成为信息表达的中心）等方法。
- 语法的准确性：错误的密集度，错误对交流的影响程度。

1.2.4 语音

主要考查考生是否能准确和持续地运用一系列语音特征来传达有意义的信息。评估要素包括：
- 是否能把口头表达的句子按照语块进行切分。
- 使用恰当的发音技巧，如节奏、连读、发音省略等。
- 重音的使用以及通过语音语调达到更好的表达效果。
- 单词和音素层面上的发音，是否会造成听者的理解困难。
- 整体的口语是易懂的。

1.3 雅思口语考试评分标准解析

在"雅思口语考试评分标准指导细则"中，四个考评维度都有 0～9 分的详细描述，我们首先提取和解读基础段的要求（4～6 分）以制定该阶段的备考策略。

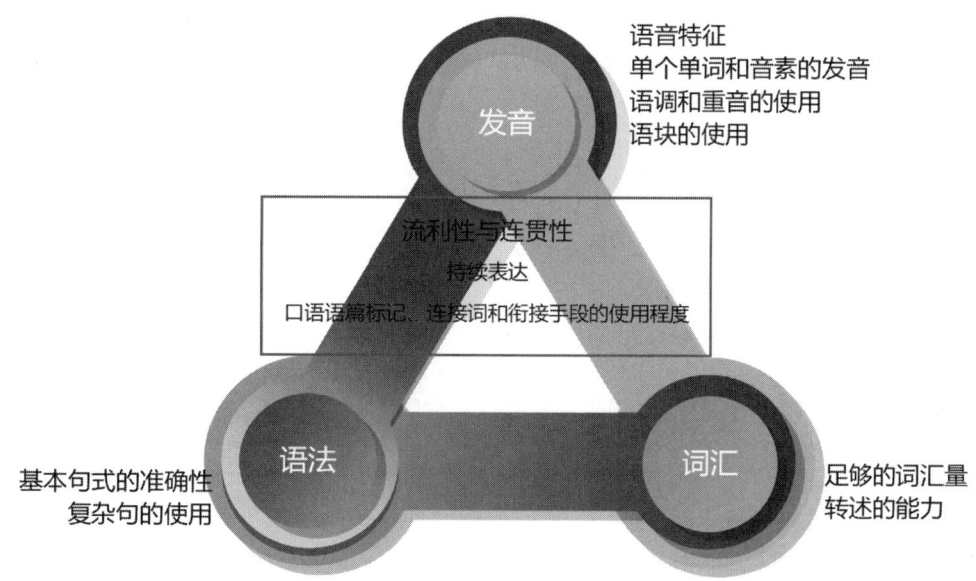

根据评分细则，对英语基础较为薄弱的考生来说，一定要发音、语法、词汇三者有机结合才能达到该阶段流利性与连贯性的要求。鉴于中国考生在英语学习过程中往往输入多于输出，尤其口语输出匮乏的情况，更应该以发音为主线，串起语法和词汇。

1.3.1 发音与词汇：准确发音

英语有 26 个字母，其中 5 个元音字母，21 个辅音字母，可以组成 40 多个元音和辅音音素。每个音素的准确发音是英语口语表达的基础。根据雅思口语考试评分标准，"单词或音素经常发音错误"在语音评分中只能在 4 分段，而 6 分段还能接受"个别单词和音素存在发音错误"。可见，对于一般水平的把英语作为外语使用的学习者来说,雅思口语考试对语音的要求并不是苛刻的、要求完美的。音素正音是语音达到 6 分要求的第一步。

音标表

Short vowels 短元音

/ɪ/	swim building
/e/	red bread friend any said
/æ/	can map
/ʌ/	son sun
/ɒ/	clock hot
/ʊ/	full book
/ə/	about excellent letter doctor sugar Saturday

Long vowels 长元音

/i:/	tree seat field secret kilo
/ɑ:/	can't bar half
/ɔ:/	wall talk saw daughter bought warm more door
/u:/	too group blue
/ɜ:/	bird work turn learn verb

Diphthongs 双元音

/ɪə/	real hear beer here
/eə/	care hair wear where
/eɪ/	came rain say great weight
/aɪ/	time dry high buy
/ɔɪ/	point toy
/əʊ/	cold home slow boat
/aʊ/	now sound

Consonants 辅音

/b/	baby job
/d/	do reading add
/f/	foot café off phone
/g/	go bigger bag
/h/	hand who
/j/	yes yield yawn

/k/	cold talking black
/l/	leave yellow fill
/m/	more summer comb
/n/	now dinner gone know
/p/	pen stopping help
/r/	red sorry write
/s/	sister glass place scissors
/t/	ten better eight washed
/v/	view every five
/w/	well away white
/z/	zero roses scissors jazz
/ʃ/	shop washing cash machine sure national
/ʒ/	television usually
/tʃ/	choose which future
/dʒ/	jeans larger fridge
/ŋ/	thing bank singer
/θ/	thank north
/ð/	then mother with

（马克，2019：110）

1）中文母语者英语发音中常见易混音辨析

中文母语者在学习英语发音时，有以下需要注意的典型易混音素。

/iː/ 和 /ɪ/	leave—live feel—fill field—filled team—Tim
/uː/ 和 /ʊ/	pool—pull fool—full
/æ/ 和 /ɑː/	had—hard match—March pack—park hat—heart
/æ/ 和 /ʌ/	cat—cut cap—cup match—much ran—run
/ɒ/ 和 /ɔː/	shot—short pot—port spot—sport
/e/ 和 /æ/	men—man head—had said—sad pen—pan
/l/ 和 /r/	light—right long—wrong collect—correct leader—reader
/s/ 和 /θ/	sing—thing sort—thought sick—thick mouse—mouth
/v/ 和 /w/	very—well vein—wine
/m/、/n/ 和 /ŋ/	might—night me—knee some—sun some—sung

（马克，2019：113）

2）词尾 -s、-ed 的发音

因为单复数或时态变化，单词增加了不同的词尾会有不同的读音变化，了解其规则有助于准确发音。

名词复数的 -s 和 -es：当词根以清辅音结尾时，复数 -s 发 /s/ 音；当以浊辅音或元音结尾时，

发 /z/ 音；以辅音 /s/ 结尾的词（如 box，bus）会加 -es，且发 /ɪz/ 音。（动词第三人称形式变化时同理）

过去式的 -ed：过去式的 -ed 也有不同的发音。当词根以 /t/ 或 /d/ 结尾时，-ed 发 /ɪd/ 音；当词根以清辅音结尾时，-ed 发 /t/ 音；当词根以浊辅音或元音结尾时，-ed 发 /d/ 音。

请根据基本规则思考以下单词的读音。

	/s/	/z/	/ɪz/
lives			
watches			
beds			
eats			
says			
coughs			
kicks			
bridges			
boys			
dishes			

	/t/	/d/	/ɪd/
wanted			
worked			
pushed			
closed			
kissed			
opened			
climbed			
demanded			
played			
hired			

3）音标中的重音符号以及典型双音节、多音节单词重音

词汇积累是口语准备的基础，然而考生对词义和用法的关注往往多于对发音准确度的关注。考生不仅要注意构成语音的音素，还要注意重音的位置，尤其要注意同源词调整后的重音转移。例如：

economy /ɪˈkɒnəmɪ/　　　　　　　economic /ˌiːkəˈnɒmɪk/
economist /ɪˈkɒnəmɪst/　　　　　　economics /ˌiːkəˈnɒmɪks/
economize /ɪˈkɒnəmaɪz/　　　　　　economical /ˌiːkəˈnɒmɪkl/

练习一

朗读以下句子，注意画线词的音节重音。

1. My dad is a photographer.
2. I'm really into photography.
3. There are loads of photographs of polar area in the exhibition.
4. My hometown is a place with lots of historical sites.
5. My cousin George is a history buff.
6. The highlight of the party was the performance of the magician.
7. Stand-up comedy is quite popular nowadays in China.
8. I want to be a comedian in the future.

有一类双音节词既是名词又是动词，在听力和口语中通过重音的位置变化体现词性的不同。当重音落在第一个音节上，是名词；当重音落在第二个音节上，是动词。例如：

1. What is that object?
2. Do you object to the idea?
3. David broke the world record of skiing.
4. You need to record what they say as evidence.
5. Price continue to increase each year.
6. There was a large increase in divorce rate last year.

练习二

用以下常见的双音节单词口头造句，注意结合语句中词汇的语法功能使用准确的重音。

| protest | transport | survey | subject |
| present | produce | desert | export |

1. 公共交通既省钱又环保。
2. 你在小学最不喜欢的科目是什么？
3. 宠物主人随意抛弃宠物是不负责任的。
4. 茶叶一直以来都是中国最重要的出口产品之一。
5. 你曾经收到过珠宝的礼物吗？
6. 调查表明百分之三十的人都不吃早饭。
7. 有机农产品往往比普通农产品更贵。
8. 当地人民正在抗议这个地区新的核电站的修建。

1.3.2 发音与语法：语块和节奏

1）语法结构与语块

任何语言的自然运用都不是单个词语以不变的音调和节奏机械地连接而实现的，英语更是尤为注意语音语调的有节奏的语言。在口语表达中，说话者按照语块（意群）来进行停顿和节奏调整，既能使表达更为自然，也使听者更容易理解，从而达到沟通的目的。简单来说，说话者要明确语句的核心结构，知道状语、复杂的定语修饰语等附加成分，通过或长或短的停顿来准确表达意图，提高口语的整体流利度。

例如：

I've had this camera/for two years./My parents gave it to me/for my birthday/when I was 18./ I didn't ask for a camera, /so it was a complete surprise,/but it's been really useful.

Since I got the camera,/I've carried it with me/everywhere I've gone on holiday./For example,/in July/I went on holiday to Denmark and Sweden./They're lovely places,/and in summer/it's still light at midnight,/ so I got some great photos there.

练习一

比较以下两种停顿断句方式。哪一个更易于理解？
1. It's a/very modern industrial/city/which is/situated/on the /river Volga.
2. It's a very modern/industrial city/which is situated/on the river Volga.

练习二

按照语块用斜线（/）标记下面段落中应该停顿的地方。

I'd like to talk about a holiday which I took in 2005. It's a holiday that I remember very well because we had such a fantastic time. I went with three other girls, who are all friends of mine, and we still talk about this holiday today.

It was funny, because usually I'm a person who's quite scared of things, and I didn't think I would put a mask on my face or go under the water—but I wanted to see the coral so much.

2）单词中与单词间辅音连缀（不完全爆破）

以下是一些在雅思口语表达中高频出现的单词及其辅音连缀：

interesting (tr-)	comfortable (fr-)	particularly (rt-)
environment (nm-)	probably (bb-)	umbrella (mbr-)
technology (kn-)	experience (sp-)	restaurant (st-)

这些单词中的辅音连缀帮助形成音节，展示了英语中辅音连缀的多样性及其对单词发音的影响。

有时候不需要将每个辅音音素都发得特别清楚，例如：

Se(p)tember	Goo(d)bye	boo(k)shop	brea(k)fast
pi(c)nic	foo(t)ball	pos(t)card	sho(p)keeper

单词间的辅音连缀：

in England	most important	the end	I ate
too often	so amazing	far away	I saw it

当第一个元音是 /aʊ/　/əʊ/ or /uː/ 时，通常会增加一个额外的音 /w/ 来连接两个元音。

有时候不是每一个辅音都能够听清楚，例如：

stop the game	sto(p) the game
last week	las(t) week
and then	an(d) then
put your bag down	pu(t) your ba(g) down

3）常见助动词肯定、否定形式缩略音

缩略式是通常情况下人们讲话的方式，具有口语化（colloquial）特征。

It's	I'm	Let's
I'll	I can't	I've
I'd	There's	They're

1.3.3 基于"发音、词汇、语法"的流畅

1）连读和弱读

（1）单词间的连读是自然发音的典型特征。

（2）前一个单词词尾为辅音音素，后一个单词词首为元音音素，这时要将辅音与元音拼起来连读。例如：

read it	need it	close it	sort it out
work out	fill in the form	run away	wait a moment
me and you	the end	you and me	go outside

（3）前一个单词词尾为元音音素 /ɪ/ 或 /iː/，后一个单词词首为任一元音音素，中间添加 /j/ 进行连读。

（4）前一个单词词尾为元音音素 /uː/ 或 /ʊ/，后一个单词词首为任一元音音素，中间添加 /w/ 进行连读。

（5）大多数的功能词，如代词、连词、介词、冠词等都会在句子中以弱读的形式出现。例如：

tell them	show us	now and then
day and night	a cup of tea	We met at uni.
I've known him for ten years.		
I'm from Chengdu.		
I know I should have enough rest but there's just so much work to do.		

2）填充词

在雅思口语中，填充词（filler words）或短语用来在讲话中暂停思考、引起听众注意或增强语气，是十分常见且实用的，在口语交流中它们还能起到缓冲或衔接语句的作用。

（1）暂停思考：当说话者在思考下一句话或者要表达的内容时，填充词可以帮助他们保持语流，避免尴尬的沉默。

（2）引导注意：填充词或短语可以用来吸引听众的注意力，让他们将注意力集中在即将说出的内容上。

（3）增强语气：某些填充词可以用来增强语句的语气或者表达说话者的感情状态。

例如：

① well 用于引导话题，开始一个句子或者思考下一步。

Well, I think we should consider all the options before making a decision.

② um/uh 用来表示犹豫或者思考下一步内容。

Um, I'm not quite sure about that.

③ you know 用来增强语气或者引起注意。

You know, it's really important to stay focused during the exam.

④ actually 用来表达让步或者提出新信息。

Actually, I have a different perspective on this.

⑤ so 用来引导句子，开始解释或者总结内容。

So, as I was saying, time management is crucial in this situation.

⑥ I mean 用来衔接句子或者强调观点。

I mean, it's not as easy as it sounds.

⑦ like 在描述中用来比喻或者引导例子。

There are many wild animals in China, like bear, elephant, antelope, snow leopard and so on.

这些填充词和短语在口语表达中非常常见，能够帮助说话者更加流畅地表达思想，同时也提高了听众对话语内容的关注度，加深了听众的理解。在雅思口语考试中，适当但不过度单一地使用这些填充词和短语可以使表达整体更加自然和连贯。

3）修饰语

在英语口语中，有一些常用的修饰语（modifiers），它们可以帮助表达情感、程度、观点等。

（1）表示情感或态度的修饰语。

① absolutely：表示完全同意或强调某种状态。

I absolutely love traveling and experiencing new cultures.

② totally：表示完全或彻底。

I totally agree that technology has changed our lives.

③ really：用于强调感受或事实的真实性。

I really enjoyed visiting historical landmarks.

（2）表示程度的修饰语。

① very：表示强烈程度或程度的增强。

I am very interested in environmental issues.

② quite：表示相当程度。

The film was quite entertaining.

③ rather：表示相对程度。

She is rather shy but very friendly once you get to know her.

（3）表示数量的修饰语。

① a lot：表示很多或大量。

I learned a lot from my time volunteering.

② a bit：表示一点点或稍微。

I'm a bit nervous about the speaking test, but I've prepared well.

（4）描述情感或感觉的修饰语。

① incredibly：表示令人难以置信的程度。

She is incredibly talented at playing the piano.

② amazingly：表示令人惊讶的程度。

The exhibition was amazingly well-curated.

在雅思口语考试中，使用这些修饰语可以使回答更具有表现力和细节性。恰当地运用修饰语有助于展示对英语语法的掌握和语言能力。记住，在口语中自然而流畅地使用修饰语，能够增强口语表达效果，但也要注意不要过度使用或使用不当，以免影响语言的自然性。

4）标记语

使用适当的标记语（signposting words）有助于更清晰地组织语言和表达思想，使语言更具连贯性和逻辑性。以下是一些常用的标记语及其示例。

（1）标记顺序：firstly，secondly，lastly。

Firstly, I'd like to talk about the advantages of living in a big city.

Secondly, let's consider the challenges that come with city life.

Lastly, I'll discuss my personal preference regarding this topic.

（2）标记补充信息：furthermore，moreover，in addition。

Furthermore, it's important to consider the environmental impact of our choices.

Moreover, education plays a crucial role in shaping our future.

In addition, we should also take into account the economic factors involved.

（3）标记转折：however，on the other hand，nevertheless。

However, there are certain drawbacks to this approach.

On the other hand, some argue that technology can enhance communication.

Nevertheless, we must weigh the pros and cons before making a decision.

（4）标记总结：in conclusion, to sum up, to conclude。

In conclusion, I believe that education is the key to success.

To sum up, there are both advantages and disadvantages to consider.

To conclude, it's clear that we need to take immediate action.

（5）标记举例：for example, for instance, such as。

For example, many countries have adopted renewable energy sources.

For instance, solar panels are becoming more affordable for households.

Such as, wind turbines are another effective form of clean energy.

（6）标记因果：therefore, consequently, as a result。

Therefore, it's essential to implement stricter environmental policies.

Consequently, air pollution levels have decreased significantly.

As a result, more people are now aware of the importance of conservation.

2 雅思口语答题技巧与策略

2.1 第一部分策略：攻克重点句型

口语第一部分常见话题的回答有以下两个基本要点：

（1）要避免只用很短的句子，甚至只用一个单词。尽管该部分不要求过长的回答，但是也应当围绕主题适当展开。用完整句子进行表达是语法维度的基本要求。

（2）听清楚问题后快速应答（有不明确的可以请求重复一遍问题），尽量根据关键词展开，避免反复重复主题词。在平时的练习中，可围绕第一部分问题的主题词先进行词汇拓展，除了近义词、上下义词的替换外，还要思考构建语句需要的形容词和动词等，这样才是有效的拓展，否则单词背了一大堆，却不能进行语句的表达。

以基础话题 hobby 为例：

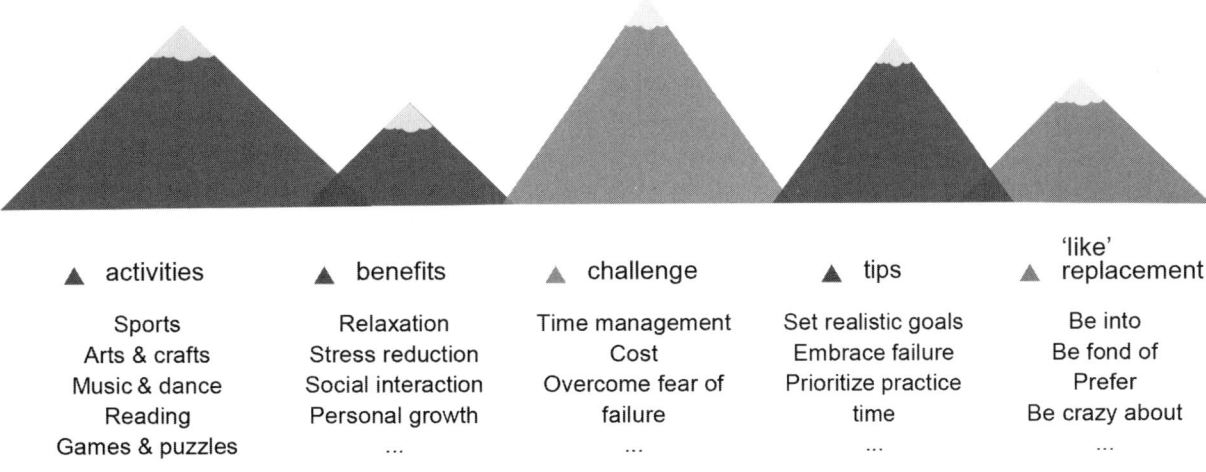

对于雅思口语部分的基础核心话题主题词，如：family, friends, food, health, education, clothing, accommodation, sports, film, music, books, transportation, travelling, culture，可通过思维导图的方式进行词汇拓展。

多样化的词汇和正确的语法是口语表达的基础。

EXAMPLE

Question: What is your favorite hobby?

Answer: I really enjoy painting in my free time. It's a great way for me to relax and express my creativity. I usually paint landscapes or abstract art, and I find it very therapeutic.

Question: Do you live in a house or an apartment?

Answer: I live in an apartment, which is located in the city center. It's quite convenient because there are many amenities nearby, such as supermarkets, restaurants, and public transportation. However, I sometimes miss having a garden or a backyard like in a house. Nonetheless, the apartment suits my current lifestyle, and I enjoy the community atmosphere here.

2.1.1 "主谓宾"句型

"主谓宾"句型是英语中最基本的句型之一，由三个主要部分组成：主语、谓语和宾语。

（1）主语（Subject）：句子中执行动作者或者被描述的对象。主语通常是一个名词、代词或者名词短语，它告诉我们句子中是谁在做什么。

（2）谓语（Verb）：句子中的动作或者状态。谓语通常是一个动词，它说明主语在做什么，并通过词形的变化与对应的助动词配合表达不同的时态。

（3）宾语（Object）：动作的对象或者描述的对象。宾语通常是一个名词、代词或者名词短语，它告诉我们动作的承受者或描述的对象是什么。

雅思口语考试的第一部分有许多关于个人偏好和生活习惯的问题，这类需要快速作答、提供相关信息但无须过于深入阐释的问题都可以从简单的句型着手展开练习。最基础的方法就是先构建句子的核心，再通过添加状语语块的方式使句子更加具体生动。

例如：话题"旅行"。

基本结构：主语 I　谓语 love　宾语 travelling　例句 I love travelling.

添加地点状语：I love travelling to exotic destinations.

添加伴随状语：I love travelling with my friends.

添加原因状语：I love travelling as it can enrich my life.

多个状语作为语块组合起来：I love travelling to exotic destinations with my friends as it can enrich my life.

通过添加这些状语，回答更具信息量，不再只是笼统的低效作答。

注意：当主语是第三人称单数时，动词要配合使用相应形式。

例如：

My mum always gets up earlier than all of us to prepare breakfast.

当问题是关于过去或将来的情况时，要注意对谓语动词的时态做相应的调整。

例如：

When did you start using Internet?

My cousin Jack taught me how to surf online when I was 7.

Will you read more online in the future?

I don't think I will read serious books more online no matter now or future.

鉴于动词的不规则变化是中国考生语法出错较多之处，建议针对高频不规则动词多做一般过去时和现在完成时的造句练习。

练习

相关话题造句。

1. 我偶尔去健身房。
2. 我经常在公园跑步。
3. 我更喜欢在户外锻炼，因为可以呼吸新鲜空气。
4. 我每天练习英语口语。
5. 我想要学习法语，因为我计划去法国旅行。
6. 我从不佩戴任何珠宝。
7. 我买了很多印有可爱图案的 T 恤。
8. 我已经学了十年钢琴了。
9. 我童年时感觉特别孤单。
10. 小时候，我妈不许我吃巧克力。

2.1.2 "主系表"句型

"主系表"句型是一种基本句型，由主语（Subject）、系动词（Linking Verb，也叫作"be 动词"或"系词"）、表语（Predicate）构成。这种句型通常用来描述主语的状态、性质或特征。

（1）系动词：系动词是用来连接主语和表语的一类动词。最常见的系动词是 be，包括 am, is, are, was, were 等。其他的系动词还有 seem, appear, become, look, feel, taste, sound 等。这些动词本身不表达具体的动作，而是起到连接主语和表语的作用。

（2）表语：表语是用来描述主语的状态、性质或特征的词或词组。表语可以是形容词、名词或介词短语，如 happy（形容词），a teacher（名词），in the park（介词短语）。

"主系表"句型是非常重要的英语句型，用于描述主语的状态、性质或特征。在核心句型的基础上进行语块的添加可提升表达的信息载量。

例如：话题"teacher"。

基本结构：主语 Mr. Chen　系动词 is　表语 patient　例句 Mr. Chen is patient.

添加前置定语：My math teacher Mr. Chen is really patient.

添加伴随状语：Mr. Chen is very patient with his students.

　　　　　　　Mr. Chen is particularly patient with naughty boys.

套入典型句型：Mr. Chen is so patient that he never loses his temper.

多个状语作为语块组合起来：My math teacher Mr. Chen is so patient with his students, particularly naughty boys, that he never loses his temper.

注意：根据表达不同时态的需要，主系表结构的系动词要做相应调整。

I was too childish and stubborn.

Bruce Lee was once the most popular Kung Fu star and idol last century.

The environment will be worse in the future if we do not take action to change.

I felt helpless when I lost my key.

练习

相关话题造句。
1. 草莓味是我最喜欢的冰激凌口味。
2. 我家乡的人特别热情好客。
3. 社交媒体似乎越来越受老年人的欢迎。
4. T 恤太好穿了，我夏天就穿不同的 T 恤。
5. 每次数学考试后我都觉得特别挫败。
6. 只要是我妈做的菜都很好吃。

2.1.3 There be 句型

英语中，There be 句型是一种常见的句型，用来表示存在或出现某人、某物或某些事情。这个句型的基本形式是"There + be + 主语"，其中 be 动词需要根据主语的人称和数进行变化。

母语为中文的英语学习者在表达"有"这一概念时往往会直接借助实义动词 have，如：My family has three people. 但是这样的直译往往是典型的中式思维的体现，不符合英语的表达习惯，此时应用 There be 句型。

There be 句型的用法和意义如下所示。

（1）表示存在：用来表示某个地方存在某人、某物。

There is a cat under the table.

（2）引起注意：用来引起听者对某事物的注意。

There are two points I want to discuss.

（3）描述现象或事件：用来描述某地发生的现象或事件。

There was an accident on the highway.

> **练习**
>
> There be 句型造句。
> 1. 桌子上有一本书。
> 2. 我家有四口人。
> 3. 音乐会上有很多人。
> 4. 未来会有新的机遇。

2.1.4 It 开头的典型句型

英语中以 It 开头的句型有很多种，它们在表达天气、时间、距离、强调结构、形式主语和形式宾语等方面具有重要作用。以下是一些常见的以 It 开头的句型。

（1）表示天气的句型：It is + 形容词（形容天气状况）。

例子：It's sunny today.

　　　It's raining now.

（2）表示时间的句型：It is + 时间。

例子：It's five o'clock.

　　　It's late.

（3）表示距离的句型：It is + 距离 + to 地点。

例子：It's two miles to the nearest gas station.

　　　It's a long way from here to the airport.

（4）强调结构：It is/was + 被强调部分 + that/who + 句子剩余部分。

例子：It was John who broke the vase.

　　　It is in the garden that we will have the party.

（5）形式主语句型：It is + 形容词 + to do something。

①当句子的真正主语是从句、动名词或不定式时，用 it 作为形式主语，真正的主语放在后面。

例子：It is important to study hard.

　　　It is difficult to solve this problem.

②It is + 形容词 + that 从句。

例子：It is essential that you be there on time.

　　　It is surprising that he didn't come.

（6）形式宾语句型：主语 + 动词 + it + 形容词 + to do something。

类似于形式主语句型，当动词的宾语是一个从句或不定式时，用 it 作为形式宾语，将真正的宾语放在后面。虽然这个句型并不以 It 开头，但因有相关性，故放在此处一并介绍。

例子：I find it easy to talk to her.

　　　She made it clear that she disagreed.

（7）特殊结构。

① It takes + 时间 + to do something。

例子：It takes an hour to get there.

　　　It took me two weeks to finish the project.

② It seems/appears + that 从句。

例子：It seems that nobody knows the answer.

　　　It appears that they have left.

（8）It 开头的固定短语和表达。

① It looks like…

例子：It looks like it's going to rain.

② It sounds like…

例子：It sounds like a good idea.

练习

It 句型造句。

1. 我记得那是阳光明媚的一天。
2. 我们到酒店的时候已经很晚了。
3. 离最近的加油站还有两公里。
4. 是小猫打破了花瓶。
5. 我觉得和她交谈很容易。
6. 我花了一个月才学会游泳。

2.1.5 被动语态的使用

与写作相比，被动语态在口语中的使用频率不是特别高，但在一些典型的话题中适当地使用被动语态可以展示考生对语法的掌握，并使回答更加丰富和多样化。

（1）关于工作或学习。

Question: What do you do?

Answer: I am employed by a multinational company as a software developer.

Question: Where did you go to school?

Answer: I was educated at the University of Beijing, where I studied economics.

Question: Do you enjoy your job?

Answer: Yes, I enjoy it a lot because my skills are constantly being utilized and appreciated.

（2）关于居住地。

Question: Can you describe the place where you live?

Answer: I live in an apartment that was built two years ago. It is located in a quiet neighborhood.

Question: Are there any changes happening in your area?
Answer: Yes, several new parks are being constructed to improve the community's green spaces.

（3）关于兴趣爱好。

Question: What do you do in your free time?
Answer: In my free time, I enjoy reading books. Recently, a lot of interesting novels have been recommended to me by friends.
Question: Do you like to watch movies?
Answer: Yes, I love watching movies. A good variety of films are shown in the local cinema.

（4）关于旅行。

Question: Have you travelled to other countries?
Answer: Yes, I have travelled to several countries. Last year, I was invited to a conference in Germany.
Question: Do you plan to travel soon?
Answer: Yes, a trip to Japan has been planned for next summer with my family.

练习

根据提示信息完成句子。

1. 关于工作或学习

What is your job role? 提示信息：职位 / 职责 / 部门

I am _____ as a _____ in the _____ department.

Where did you receive your higher education? 提示信息：学校 / 城市 / 专业

I was _____ at _____ University in _____, where I majored in _____.

2. 关于居住地

Can you describe the neighborhood where you live? 提示信息：社区 / 设施 / 特点

My neighborhood is well-known for its _____. Recently, several new amenities have been _____.

Are any renovations happening in your building? 提示信息：建筑 / 翻新 / 目的

Yes, the building where I live is currently being _____ to _____.

3. 关于兴趣爱好

What hobbies are you interested in? 提示信息：爱好 / 参与 / 时间

I am particularly interested in _____. Recently, I have been _____ in various activities related to it.

Do you enjoy sports? 提示信息：运动 / 活动 / 俱乐部

Yes, I really enjoy playing sports. I am currently _____ by a local sports club.

4. 关于旅行

Have you ever been on a business trip? 提示信息：商务旅行 / 城市 / 任务

Yes, I have been _____ on business trips to _____, where I was responsible for _____.

Are there any upcoming vacations you are excited about? 提示信息：假期 / 计划 / 家庭成员

Yes, a vacation to _____ has been _____ for next month with my _____.

2.2 第二部分策略：攻克典型主题

雅思口语考试第二部分是个人陈述的环节，通常称为"个人陈述"或"长篇演讲"。在这一部分，考生需要根据考官给出的话题卡进行1~2分钟的陈述。

（1）理解题目：首先，仔细阅读题卡，准确理解任务，尤其是对于时空的要求。题目可能是关于个人经历、喜好、观点或者理想的话题。

（2）结构清晰：陈述开头，先简单明确地提出观点或者主题，例如，I'd like to talk about…。

（3）使用举例和细节：使用具体的例子、经历或细节支撑观点或描述，这样既可以使讲述更加生动和有说服力，也有助于填充时间。

（4）表达流利：尽量使用多样化的词汇和句型来表达自己的想法，展示语言能力，避免使用重复的词汇或句式。

（5）积极回应考官：如果考官在考生陈述之后有任何的追问或者需要更多细节，应积极地回应但无须过度展开陈述。

万丈高楼平地起，完整的长篇讲述建立在句子表达的基础上，考生要按照题卡要点组织语言，有条理、完整地表达，在熟练掌握上一节句型的基础上，进一步掌握叙事几大关键要素（时间、地点、人物、经历、过程等）的表达技巧。

2.2.1 描述时间

描述时间时，可以使用一些常见的句型和表达，这些句型和表达有助于更清晰地传达时间的概念和顺序。

（1）过去的经历。

When I was younger, I used to…

A few years ago, I…

In my childhood, I often…

Back in high school, I…

（2）现在的情况。

Currently, I am…

These days, I…

At the moment, I…

Nowadays, I often…

（3）将来的计划。

In the near future, I plan to…

Next year, I hope to…

In a few months' time, I am looking forward to…

By this time next year, I aim to…

（4）频率和习惯。

Every weekend, I…

On a daily basis, I…

Twice a week, I usually…

Once a month, I like to…

（5）时间顺序。

Firstly, I…

Subsequently, I…

Following that, I…

Finally, I…

（6）时间的相对关系。

Before that, I…

Afterwards, I…

Prior to that, I…

Subsequent to that, I…

（7）时期和阶段。

During my university years, I…

Throughout my career, I have…

Over the past decade, I have noticed…

In the early stages of my life, I…

Example:

Describe a time when you helped someone.

Introduction: The experience I'm going to talk about is when I helped a neighbor with her computer problems.

Details: It was a Sunday afternoon, and I heard a knock on my door. My neighbor, Mrs. Smith, was standing there, looking rather frustrated. She explained that her computer had suddenly stopped working, and she didn't know what to do. I offered to take a look at it, and after a few minutes of troubleshooting, I discovered that it was a simple software issue. I fixed it quickly, and Mrs. Smith was relieved and grateful.

Conclusion: Helping Mrs. Smith with her computer not only made her day better, but it also made me feel good about myself. It's always rewarding to be able to lend a helping hand to someone in need.

2.2.2 描述地点

（1）具体描述地点。

One of my favorite places is…

I often visit _____, which is…

In _____[city/country]_____, there is a place called…

At _____[specific location]_____, you can find…

（2）地点特征。

It's located in the heart of…

The atmosphere there is…

It's known for its…

The most striking feature of _____ is…

（3）去过的地方。

I have been to _____ several times.

During my travels, I visited…

Last summer, I explored…

（4）喜欢的地点。

One place I really enjoy is…

I feel most relaxed when I'm at…

My ideal getaway spot is…

（5）时间和地点结合。

During _____[season/time of year]_____, _____[place]_____ is…

In the evenings, _____ becomes…

During weekends, _____ is bustling with…

（6）与地点相关的活动。

People often gather at _____ to…

It's a popular spot for…

You can often see people _____[activity]_____ at _____.

（7）个人经历的地点。

I have a lot of memories associated with _____.

The first time I visited _____, I…

Whenever I go to _____, I always…

Example:

Describe a place you like very much.

Introduction: I am going to talk about a beautiful beach that I have been to frequently for its soft sand, crystal-clear sea water and sea breeze.

Setting: The beach I like is located on the southwestern coast of China. It's close to my hometown and just beside the mountains, where it can receive sufficient sunlight. It has beautiful landscapes, from lush forests and cliffs on both sides of the beach, down to clear water below and all-day-sunny sky above.

Description: There is no industry nearby this beach. Hence it's still largely untouched by development, offering me the wonderful opportunity to enjoy its natural beauty. The beach is about 2 kilometers long and covered with soft white sand. When you walk on it, it feels like walking on a cloud. The sea water here is crystal-clear and you can see all kinds of sea creatures underwater clearly. Besides, there are also many beautiful shells on the beach that you can collect.

Conclusion: In short, this beach is my favorite place because it is so beautiful and serene. It reminds me of my childhood memories and provides me with a relaxing environment for my body and soul.

2.2.3 描述人物

（1）外貌和特征。

One person I admire is _____. He/She has _____ [appearance characteristic], such as _____ [specific feature].

I know a person named _____, who has _____ [attribute], like _____ [specific detail].

A person I find interesting is _____. He/She is _____ [adjective] and has _____ [specific feature].

（2）性格和个性。

He/She is known for being _____, such as _____ [example of behavior or trait].

One thing I really like about _____ is his/her _____ [positive trait], which is evident in _____ [example of behavior or trait].

I admire _____'s _____ [trait], which makes him/her _____ [positive attribute].

（3）对你的影响。

This person has had a significant impact on my life because _____ [specific reason].

I've learned a lot from _____, especially _____ [specific lesson or quality].

Meeting _____ has influenced my perspective on _____ [topic or aspect of life].

（4）个人经历或故事。

I first met _____ [name] when _____ [describe when you met them].

An interesting story about _____ [name] is _____ [share an anecdote or experience involving them].

I remember _____ [name] once _____ [describe a memorable event involving them].

（5）总结或结论。

Overall, _____ [name] is someone I greatly admire because of _____ [specific reasons].

In conclusion, _____ [name]'s impact on my life has been _____ [positive/negative/inspirational], shaping my views on _____ [related topic or aspect].

这些句型和表达可以帮助考生在口语考试中描述人物时更加清晰和有条理。记住要展示你对这个人的态度和感受，并用具体的例子来支撑你的描述。

Example:

（1）Describe a teacher who has influenced you.

Introduction: I'd like to talk about a teacher who has had a significant influence on me, Mr. Smith.
Body Paragraphs:
- *Topic sentence 1:* One of the key traits that made Mr. Smith an exceptional teacher was his passion for the subject matter.
- *Support with examples:* He would often share interesting facts and stories related to the topic, making every lesson engaging and fun.
- *Topic sentence 2:* Another important aspect of his teaching style was his ability to create a supportive and inclusive classroom environment.
- *Support with examples:* He encouraged participation from all students and made sure everyone felt valued and respected.
Conclusion: In conclusion, Mr. Smith's passion, patience, and dedication have not only enriched my knowledge but also inspired me to pursue my own interests with enthusiasm.

（2）Describe a person who has significant impact on you.

The individual I'd like to talk about is my best friend, John. He's someone who's always been there for me, through thick and thin. John is known for his attitude towards life. No matter what challenges he faces, he always finds a silver lining.

For instance, when he lost his job last year, instead of getting discouraged, he saw it as an opportunity to pursue his passion for photography full-time. His positive mindset is something that has rubbed off on me, and I've learned to be more optimistic in my own life.

Apart from his positive attitude, John is also extremely reliable. He's always punctual and ready to lend a helping hand whenever needed. I remember once when I was going through a tough time, he was there, offering support and advice.

In conclusion, John is not just my best friend but also a great role model. His positive attitude and reliability are qualities that I admire and strive to emulate. He's someone who has had a significant impact on my life, and I'm grateful to have him as a friend.

2.2.4 描述经历

（1）描述经历的起因。

One memorable experience I had was when…

I'll never forget the time when…

An interesting experience I had was…

（2）时间和地点的说明。

It happened several years ago, in _____ [place].

During _____ [specific event or period], I…

（3）具体的经历。

What happened was that…

I found myself in a situation where…

The most striking part of the experience was…

（4）你的感受和反应。

At that moment, I felt _____ [emotion], because…

I was surprised by _____ [aspect of the experience].

It made me realize _____ [lesson learned or insight gained].

（5）对你的影响或你的教训。

This experience taught me that…

I learned a valuable lesson from this, which is…

It changed my perspective on _____ [related topic or issue].

（6）总结或结论。

Looking back, I now understand that…

Overall, this experience was significant because…

In conclusion, I believe that this experience helped me grow as a person by…

Example:

Describe a memorable social event you attended.

Introduction: I'd like to talk about a memorable social event that I attended, a friend's birthday party.
Body Paragraphs:
- *Topic sentence 1:* One of the highlights of the event was the unique venue.
- *Support with details:* It was held at a local art gallery, creating a stylish and sophisticated atmosphere.
- *Topic sentence 2:* Another memorable aspect of the event was the creative entertainment.
- *Support with details:* The host had organized interactive art workshops, allowing guests to create their own pieces of art, which was both fun and relaxing.
- *Topic sentence 3:* In addition, the food and drinks were exceptional.
- *Support with details:* There was a wide variety of delicious dishes, catering to different dietary

preferences, and a selection of refreshing beverages.

Conclusion: In conclusion, this birthday party was a unique and memorable social event that I thoroughly enjoyed, thanks to its creative venue, engaging entertainment, and delicious food.

2.2.5 描述过程

（1）开始。

The process began when…

It all started with…

Initially, I…

（2）进行中的描述。

During the process, I encountered…

One step in the process involved…

（3）具体的步骤或细节。

Firstly, I had to…

Next, I…

After that, the next step was to…

（4）面对的挑战或困难。

One challenge I faced during the process was…

I found it difficult when…

Dealing with _____ [specific issue] was tough because…

（5）解决问题或应对的策略。

To overcome this challenge, I…

I managed to solve the problem by…

I learned to handle _____ [issue] by…

（6）完成和总结。

Finally, after _____ [time frame], I successfully…

In the end, I achieved…

Reflecting on the process, I realized…

（7）学到的经验或教训。

This process taught me the importance of…

I learned a valuable lesson about…

Going through this process helped me understand…

（8）对未来的影响或应用。

Moving forward, I plan to apply what I learned from this process by…

This experience will definitely help me in _____ [related context].

I believe this process has prepared me for…

2.3 第三部分策略：攻克问题模式，按需作答

第二部分和第三部分之间有着密切的内在联系，第二部分（个人陈述）通常由一个特定的话题引导，如描述一个人、地方、经历或事件等。这些描述和观点提供了第三部分讨论的基础，在第三部分中进一步展开。

第三部分的问题要求考生从多个角度加以分析和讨论。考生需要提供更多的观点和例子来支持自己的意见。该部分尤其考查考生在复杂语境下的语言表达能力和运用能力，包括使用恰当的词汇和时态，正确应用语法来准确表达自己的意见；考查考生是否具有良好的逻辑思维能力，是否能够清晰、有条理地组织自己的观点和论据，使回答内容连贯且具有说服力。

例如：

Part 2 Topic Card

Describe a place in your country that you would like to visit.

You should say:

　　where it is

　　what you know about this place

　　what you would do there

and explain why you would like to visit this place.

在第三部分中考官会问到与旅行或旅游业相关的问题，如：Do you think tourism has a positive or negative impact on local communities? 考生的回答应涉及旅游业带来的经济利益、文化交流等积极方面，以及给环境和社会带来的负面影响。

答题贴士

明确问题的类型：听清楚考官提问，明确是需要提供事实性的陈述分析，还是需要给出观点，或是进行比较等。借助典型的句型能使回答既准确又不会冗长。

2.3.1 表达观点

在雅思口语第三部分，表达观点是非常重要的考查方面。考官通常会要求考生就某个话题或问题发表看法，并进一步探讨和解释。

（1）表达强烈赞同或不赞同。

I completely agree that technology has greatly improved our lives.

I absolutely think that social media has both positive and negative impacts on society.

There's no doubt in my mind that climate change is a pressing issue that needs immediate attention.

（2）表达部分赞同或不赞同。

I tend to agree/disagree with the idea that education should focus more on practical skills.

While I agree with some aspects of globalization, **I believe that** it also poses challenges for local cultures.

I see your point, but personally, I feel that stricter gun control laws are necessary to reduce violence.

（3）表达中立或保留意见。

I see both sides of the argument. On the one hand, technology has made communication easier, **but on the other hand,** it has reduced face-to-face interaction.

I'm not entirely sure, but I think that the government should play a role in promoting renewable energy sources.

I haven't really thought about it in depth, but my initial feeling is that stricter regulations are needed to protect endangered species.

（4）引出观点并进行解释。

From my perspective, cultural diversity enriches societies and fosters understanding among different groups.

In my opinion/view, the benefits of studying abroad outweigh the challenges.

I believe that learning a second language is important **because** it opens up new career opportunities and enhances cultural understanding.

（5）提出建议或提议。

I think it would be a good idea to introduce more recycling programs in schools to raise environmental awareness.

Perhaps we could consider implementing flexible working hours to improve work-life balance.

It might be worth considering stricter penalties for littering to keep our environment clean.

示例

Question:	Do you think the education system should prioritize academic subjects over practical skills? Why or why not?
Answer:	I believe that the education system should strike a balance between academic subjects and practical skills. While academic subjects are important for developing critical thinking and analytical abilities, practical skills are essential for preparing students for the demands of the workforce. For example, in my own experience, I found that learning how to code and use software programs in school gave me a valuable skillset that I now use in my career. At the same time, the academic subjects I studied helped me develop a strong foundation of knowledge that I continue to build upon. Therefore, I think it's important for schools to provide opportunities for students to develop both academic and practical skills.
Question:	Do you think technology has made our lives easier or more complicated?
Answer:	(Opinion) I believe technology has both simplified and complicated our lives in different ways. (Explanation) On one hand, it has made tasks like communication and accessing information much easier. We can stay connected with people across the globe and find answers to questions instantly. (Complex Language) However, on the other hand, the overuse of technology can lead to addiction and isolation, complicating our social interactions. (Discuss Both Sides) Additionally, the constant updates and advancements

in technology require us to keep up with the latest trends, which can be overwhelming. (Conclusion) Overall, I think it's about finding a balance and using technology as a tool to enhance our lives rather than being enslaved by it.

Question: Do you think technology has had a positive or negative impact on our lives?
Answer: (Starting with an opinion) I believe technology has had a predominantly positive impact on our lives. (Giving examples) For instance, it has made communication much easier and faster. We can now connect with people from anywhere in the world instantly through platforms like social media and video calls. Additionally, technology has also improved our efficiency in various aspects of life, such as work and education. (Discussing both sides) However, it's also true that excessive use of technology can lead to issues like addiction and a lack of social interaction. (Concluding) Overall, I think the benefits outweigh the drawbacks, and we should strive to use technology in a balanced way.

2.3.2 解释及给出理由

在雅思口语第三部分，解释及给出理由是非常重要的方面，考生不仅应就提问表达观点，还要能够清晰地解释并提供论据支撑。简洁明了地解释每一个观点背后的原因，结合具体例子或数据，能够使回答更具深度，更有说服力。

（1）解释观点。

I think online shopping is more convenient **because** you can shop anytime and anywhere.

The reason for this is that exercise helps to reduce stress and improve overall health.

It's mainly because of the Internet that information is now easily accessible to everyone.

One of the main reasons people choose to live in cities **is** that there are more job opportunities.

（2）给出理由。

Firstly, studying abroad exposes you to different cultures. **Secondly**, it enhances your language skills. **Thirdly**, it broadens your career prospects.

Another reason people prefer public transportation **is that** it helps reduce traffic congestion.

Moreover, social media allows us to stay connected with friends and family regardless of geographical distance.

Furthermore, renewable energy sources are crucial because they reduce our dependence on fossil fuels.

（3）强调重要性。

It's crucial /vital/important to protect endangered species **because** they contribute to the biodiversity of ecosystems.

It's essential to invest in education **because** it empowers individuals and drives economic growth.

It's significant to address climate change **because** it threatens our planet's future.

（4）提供实际例子或证据支持观点。

For example, in countries where recycling is mandatory, the amount of waste going to landfills has significantly decreased.

Studies/researches have shown that regular exercise not only improves physical health but also enhances mental well-being.

Statistics indicate that unemployment rates have dropped since the government implemented new job creation initiatives.

（5）引导进一步讨论或总结观点。

Therefore/Thus/In conclusion, I believe that stricter laws should be enforced to protect endangered wildlife.

In summary, the benefits of traveling outweigh the challenges.

To sum up, technology has revolutionized the way we communicate and conduct business.

示例

Question: What are the benefits of team sports for children?

Answer: Team sports offer several benefits for children. Firstly, they foster teamwork and collaboration, as children learn to work together towards a common goal. This is crucial in developing social skills and learning to value the contributions of others. Secondly, team sports promote physical activity, which is essential for maintaining a healthy lifestyle. Regular exercise through sports can help reduce the risk of chronic diseases later in life. Finally, participation in team sports can also boost children's self-confidence and resilience, as they learn to handle wins and losses gracefully.

2.3.3 比较

雅思口语第三部分经常会涉及比较不同事物或观点的问题，考生需要有效比较并给出合理解释。

（1）表达不同之处。

Living in a rural area **is different from** living in a city **in that** rural areas offer more tranquility and less pollution.

Public transportation and private cars **differ in terms of** convenience and environmental impact.

While studying abroad enhances language skills, studying in one's home country provides familiarity and support.

（2）表达相似之处。

Learning a musical instrument **is similar to** learning a new language **in that** both require practice and patience.

Both traditional **and** online education **share** the goal of providing knowledge and skills to students.

Like traditional classrooms, online courses **also** require students to participate actively and complete assignments.

（3）强调优缺点。

While living in a big city **has its advantages** such as better job opportunities, it **also has drawbacks** like higher living costs.

Living in a suburban area **is preferable to** living in a city in terms of affordability and space.

On the other hand, working in a startup **offers** more opportunities for innovation compared to working in a large corporation.

（4）提供例子或数据支持比较。

For example, in terms of environmental impact, hybrid cars emit less carbon dioxide compared to traditional gasoline-powered cars.

Statistics show that in terms of academic achievement, students in private schools perform better on standardized tests compared to students in public schools.

Studies indicate that in terms of job satisfaction, employees in flexible work environments are happier compared to those in traditional offices.

（5）引导进一步讨论或总结。

In conclusion, although both traveling solo and traveling with a group have their merits, I believe traveling solo allows for greater personal growth.

To sum up, while technology has improved communication globally, face-to-face interactions still play a crucial role in building relationships.

Therefore/Thus, although studying abroad can be expensive, the cultural exposure and language proficiency gained justify the investment.

示例

Question: What are the benefits and drawbacks of online shopping compared to traditional shopping?

Answer: Online shopping offers several benefits, such as convenience and accessibility. You can shop from home at any time, and the selection is often wider. However, there are drawbacks. For instance, you cannot try on clothes or see products in person, which can lead to dissatisfaction. Additionally, online shopping may pose security risks if personal information is not properly protected. In contrast, traditional shopping allows customers to touch and feel products before purchasing, but it can be time-consuming and limited by store opening hours.

Question: What are the advantages and disadvantages of living in a big city?

Answer: I believe that living in a big city has both its pros and cons. On the one hand, the main advantage is the convenience it offers. Big cities have a wide range of facilities, from top-notch healthcare to diverse cultural activities. There are also more job opportunities, which is especially appealing to young professionals. However, there are also disadvantages. The cost of living in big cities is often much higher, and the competition for resources like housing and education can be intense. Additionally, the fast-paced lifestyle and high levels of stress can be overwhelming for some people. So, while living in a big city can be exciting and rewarding, it's important to carefully consider the pros and cons before making a decision.

Question: What are the advantages and disadvantages of using technology in education?

Answer: Well, one advantage of using technology in education is that it makes learning more engaging and interactive. For example, students can use multimedia tools to create presentations or videos, which can help them to better understand and remember the material. Additionally, online learning platforms can provide personalized learning experiences tailored to each student's needs.

On the other hand, one disadvantage of relying too heavily on technology in education is that it can lead to a lack of face-to-face interaction between students and teachers. This can make it difficult for students to ask questions or get clarifications when they need them. Furthermore, not all students have access to the necessary technology, which can create a digital divide and limit their educational opportunities.

2.3.4 谈论过去与现在

在雅思口语第三部分经常会遇到需要比较过去和现在的题目，例如过去与现在的生活方式、工作环境、教育方式等。

（1）表达过去和现在的不同之处。

In the past, people used to rely more on letters and telegrams for communication, whereas today we use instant messaging and social media.

Back then, lifestyles were simpler and more family-oriented compared to today's fast-paced and individualistic lifestyles.

Historically, education was more focused on rote learning and memorization, whereas today it emphasizes critical thinking and creativity.

（2）强调过去和现在的变化。

Over the years, there has been a shift towards digitalization in almost every aspect of life, from banking to entertainment.

Today, compared to the past, there is more emphasis on work-life balance and mental well-being in the workplace.

With advancements in technology, information **has become more accessible than it was in the past**, thanks to the Internet and smartphones.

（3）提供例子或数据。

For example, statistics show that life expectancy has significantly increased over the past century due to advancements in healthcare.

Today, unlike in the past, people are more likely to change careers multiple times throughout their lives to pursue personal growth and fulfillment.

Compared to previous generations, today's students have access to a wider range of educational resources and learning tools.

（4）表达趋势和影响。

The trend towards urbanization **is evident in** the increasing migration of people from rural areas to cities.

This shift towards remote work **has had a profound impact on** commuting patterns and the demand for flexible work arrangements.

As society evolves, attitudes towards gender roles **have changed significantly**, with more emphasis on equality and diversity.

（5）引导进一步讨论或总结。

In conclusion, while the past had its own charm, the conveniences and opportunities of modern life make it preferable in many aspects.

Overall, the changes from the past to the present highlight the rapid pace of technological advancement and its impact on everyday life.

To sum up, the differences between then and now reflect not just technological progress but also shifts in societal values and priorities.

示例

Question: Do you think people in your country are less healthy than they used to be?

Answer: Yes, definitely. I would argue that the invention of TV has led to people being much too sedentary. I know some people who refuse to have a television because they think that without one they are much more likely to keep active—it's all too easy to become a couch potato. Also, most people work in offices so they just sit in a chair all day long and only move to go to the photocopier. That's very unhealthy. People used to work the land and so be on the go from morning till night. Obesity was unknown then, except among the super rich, I imagine.

2.3.5 表达赞同或反对

雅思口语第三部分经常会涉及需要表达赞同或反对的话题，比如某种观点、政策、社会现象等。

（1）表达赞同。

I completely agree with the idea that education should be accessible to all regardless of their financial background.

I couldn't agree more that governments should invest more in renewable energy sources to combat climate change.

I'm in favor of stricter laws to protect endangered species from extinction.

I support the view that cultural diversity enriches societies and promotes understanding among different communities.

（2）表达部分赞同。

While I agree with some aspects of globalization, **I believe that** it's important to preserve local traditions and cultures.

I see your point about the benefits of social media, **but I think** it also has negative effects on personal relationships.

I agree to a certain extent that technology has made our lives more convenient, **but** it has also led to increased social isolation.

（3）表达反对。

I disagree with the idea that standardized tests are the best way to evaluate students' knowledge and abilities.

I don't think that's necessarily true because not all forms of entertainment are harmful to society.

I'm opposed to the policy of increasing taxes on basic necessities as it disproportionately affects low-income families.

I'm not convinced by the argument that banning fast food advertisements will solve the problem of obesity.

（4）提供理由和支持。

The reason I think is that education is the key to breaking the cycle of poverty.

One example that supports this is the success of countries that have invested heavily in renewable energy.

Studies have shown that diverse teams are more innovative and productive in the workplace.

（5）引导进一步讨论或总结。

In conclusion, I believe that governments should prioritize environmental protection to ensure a sustainable future.

Overall, while there are valid arguments on both sides, I tend to lean towards the idea that stricter gun control laws are necessary to reduce violence.

To sum up, my view is that social media can be both a blessing and a curse depending on how it is used.

2.3.6 推测未来

（1）表达可能性。

I think that in the future, technology will continue to advance rapidly.

It's likely/probable (that) climate change will have serious consequences for global agriculture.

There's a good chance that renewable energy sources will become the dominant source of power in the next decade.

It's possible that artificial intelligence will revolutionize healthcare in the coming years.

（2）表达预测。

I predict that autonomous vehicles will become common on our roads within the next five years.

I foresee a shift towards sustainable living becoming more mainstream in the near future.

It's expected that the population of urban areas will continue to grow rapidly.

Experts forecast that advancements in biotechnology will lead to significant medical breakthroughs.

（3）提供理由和支持。

One possible scenario is that renewable energy prices will drop dramatically, making them more accessible globally.

Evidence suggests that climate change will continue to affect weather patterns around the world.

（4）引导进一步讨论或总结。

In conclusion, I believe that advancements in technology will lead to a more interconnected world.

Overall, while there are uncertainties, I think that environmental awareness will bring significant changes to our lifestyles.

To sum up, my view is that artificial intelligence will play a crucial role in shaping industries in the coming decades.

示例

Question:	What technological developments do you think will have the greatest impact on our lives in the next 10 years?
Answer:	I think that artificial intelligence will have the greatest impact on our lives in the next decade. It's probable that AI will become more integrated into everyday devices, making them smarter and more intuitive. I predict that autonomous vehicles will be commonplace, revolutionizing transportation. Evidence suggests that AI will also transform industries like healthcare and education, improving efficiency and accessibility. In conclusion, I believe that AI will significantly alter how we live and work in the near future.
Question:	What are the challenges facing the younger generation?
Answer:	Well, I think one of the biggest challenges facing the younger generation is adapting to a fast-paced, technology-driven world. With so many new technology advancements such as social media and digital communication, young people have to learn how to adapt quickly and efficiently to keep up with the pace of change. In addition, they also have to deal with the pressure of finding a job in a highly competitive job market, which can be challenging for many young people.

3 雅思口语模拟试题

3.1 考场实战小贴士

（1）放松心情：考试前尽量保持放松，深呼吸，保持自信。考官希望看到考生的自然表现，不要过于紧张。

（2）注意时间：考试通常分为三部分，每部分有固定时间。掌握时间安排，确保每部分的回答都能全面、简洁地完成。

（3）发音清晰：说话时注意发音清晰、语调自然。不要说得太快，也不要过于拖延。

（4）回答充分：对于每个问题，尽量提供详细的回答，给出例子和理由。展现语言能力和思维深度。

（5）真实表达：诚实地表达自己的观点和感受。考官更关心考生能否用英语表达自己的真实想法。

（6）积极互动：如果没有听清楚问题，礼貌地请求重复或澄清。不要害怕提出问题或表达你的疑虑。

（7）结构清晰：回答问题时，尝试使用清晰的结构，比如"首先……其次……最后……"，这有助于你的回答条理分明。

（8）扩展回答：尽量避免回答简单的"是"或"不是"。扩展回答，解释为什么、如何，提供更多细节。

（9）练习常见话题：在考试前，练习一些常见话题，如旅行、兴趣爱好、家庭等，这样可以帮助考生在考试时更快适应。

（10）保持自然：不要刻意使用复杂的词汇或句子结构。自然流畅的表达是最重要的。

没听清楚问题，请求重复，可用以下句型：

Could you say that again?

Could you please repeat the question?

Would you mind repeating the question?

I'm sorry, I didn't catch that. Could you say it again?

I'm sorry, I'm not sure I understand the question.

I didn't hear that clearly. Could you repeat it?

Could you go over that question once more?

3.2 雅思口语模拟试题

PART 1 Introduction and interview (4-5 minutes)

Do you work or are you a student?
Why did you choose that course or job?
What is the most difficult thing about your studies or job?

Let's talk about keeping fit.
What do you do to keep fit?
Are you good at sport?

What's your mother tongue?
What other languages do you speak?

What do you think is the best way to keep in touch with friends?
Do people keep in touch differently now compared to fifty years ago?

PART 2 Individual long turn (3-4 minutes)

> **Describe an interest or hobby that you enjoy.**
> **You should say:**
>   how long you have been doing it
>   how often you do it
>   what benefits you get from it
> **and explain why you enjoy it.**

You will have to talk about the topic for one to two minutes.
You have one minute to think about what you're going to say.
You can make some notes to help you if you wish.

PART 3 Two-way discussion (4-5 minutes)

Hobbies

Do you think men and women tend to have different types of hobbies?
Why do some people get obsessed with their hobby?
Do you think hobbies that keep you fit are better than hobbies that you can do sitting down?

Free time

Do you think it can be a disadvantage to have too much free time?
Should people feel a duty to do something constructive in their free time?
Do people have more free time now than in the past?

参考文献

CAMBRIDGE ESOL, 2005. Cambridge IELTS 4 Student's book with answers: examination papers from university of Cambridge ESOL examinations[M]. Cambridge: Cambridge University Press.

CAMBRIDGE ESOL, 2007. Cambridge IELTS 6 Student's book with answers: examination papers from university of Cambridge ESOL examinations [M]. Cambridge: Cambridge University Press.

CAMBRIDGE ESOL, 2009. Cambridge IELTS 7 Student's book with answers: examination papers from university of Cambridge ESOL examinations [M]. Cambridge: Cambridge University Press.

CAMBRIDGE ESOL, 2013. Cambridge IELTS 9 Student's book with answers: examination papers from university of Cambridge ESOL examinations [M]. Cambridge: Cambridge University Press.

CAMBRIDGE ESOL, 2015. Cambridge IELTS 10 Student's book with answers: examination papers from university of Cambridge ESOL examinations [M]. Cambridge: Cambridge University Press.

CAMBRIDGE ESOL，2016. Cambridge IELTS 11 Student's book with answers: examination papers from university of Cambridge ESOL examinations [M]. Cambridge: Cambridge University Press.

CAMBRIDGE ESOL，2017. Cambridge IELTS 12 Student's book with answers: examination papers from university of Cambridge ESOL examinations [M]. Cambridge: Cambridge University Press.

CAMBRIDGE ESOL, 2018. Cambridge IELTS 13 Student's book with answers: examination papers from university of Cambridge ESOL examinations [M]. Cambridge: Cambridge University Press.

CAMBRIDGE ESOL, 2019. Cambridge IELTS 14 Student's book with answers: examination papers from university of Cambridge ESOL examinations [M]. Cambridge: Cambridge University Press.

CAMBRIDGE ESOL，2020. Cambridge IELTS 15 Student's book with answers: examination papers from university of Cambridge ESOL examinations [M]. Cambridge: Cambridge University Press.

参考文献

CAMBRIDGE ESOL, 2021. Cambridge IELTS 16 Student's book with answers: examination papers from university of Cambridge ESOL examinations [M]. Cambridge: Cambridge University Press.

Cambridge IELTS, test types[EB/OL].[2024-06-01]. https://ielts.org/take-a-test/test-types/ielts-academic-test.

KOVACS K, 2011. Speaking for IELTS[M]. New York: HarperCollins Publishers.

汉考克，2019. 剑桥国际英语语音在用·中级[M]. 修订版. 姚虹，徐一洲，译. 北京：北京语言大学出版社.

马克斯，2019. 剑桥国际英语语音在用·初级[M]. 修订版. 姚虹，张丽，译. 北京：北京语言大学出版社.

IELTS
All-in-One Guide
(Basic Edition)

听力文本

2.3.1

1. Black bears live throughout most of North America, including northern Mexico.
2. In fact the animal may travel 50 miles a day to find food.
3. When you arrive at the turtle bay, you could see some wildlife.
4. These rabbits often live on the edges of fields, farms, and other open spaces far from highly populated areas.
5. Your assignment should create a favorable first impression to the examiner, this implies that your work should be orderly, utilize standard writing style and ensure that your points are clearly spelt out and use correct referencing style.

2.3.2

1. If you fail a course in the first attempt, you may be permitted to opt for a resit.
2. The price includes a reef education presentation, a hot and cold buffet lunch, and snorkelling, diving activity.
3. Clear assignment instructions which were emailed to students will help them understand the assignment objectives, the steps students will need to take to successfully complete it, and what the grading criteria is.
4. There are some materials but not enough to support the purpose of your presentation. And part of the materials provided in your presentation are inaccurate.
5. We were interested in knowing how blind people use sounds to learn about moving objects. We found that people who became blind during early childhood were better at following sounds than sighted people.

2.3.3

In recent years, there has been a significant increase in awareness regarding environmental conservation. While governments worldwide have implemented stricter regulations to control carbon emissions, industries have been forced to adopt greener technologies. Moreover, consumers are now more inclined towards sustainable products, which has encouraged companies to emphasize eco-friendly practices. Therefore, there has been a gradual shift towards renewable energy sources such as solar and wind power. This change not only benefits the environment but also ensures long-term energy security. Later, the global energy landscape is evolving towards sustainability, contrasting sharply with past dependency on fossil fuels.

2.3.4

Today, we will dive into the fascinating world of artificial intelligence, or AI. Artificial intelligence refers to the simulation of human intelligence in machines that are programmed to think like humans and mimic their actions. It's a field that's rapidly evolving, with applications ranging from virtual assistants like Siri and Alexa to more complex uses in healthcare and finance.

One of the key components of AI is machine learning, where computers use algorithms to analyse data, learn from it, and then make decisions or predictions based on what they've learned. This ability to learn from data is what allows AI systems to improve over time without being explicitly programmed for every task.

In healthcare, AI is revolutionizing diagnostics with its ability to analyse medical images and detect patterns that might not be visible to the human eye. Similarly, in finance, AI algorithms are used to analyse vast amounts of data to predict market trends or detect fraudulent transactions.

However, AI also raises ethical concerns, particularly around issues like privacy and job displacement. As AI systems become more advanced, questions arise about who owns the data they collect and how it's used. Moreover, there's ongoing debate about the impact of AI on the job market, with some fearing that automation will lead to widespread unemployment.

Despite these challenges, AI continues to be a driving force in technological innovation, promising to reshape industries and improve our lives in ways we never imagined.

2.3.5

Step 1: Harvesting the Coffee Beans

Coffee fruit is removed from the trees using one of two processes: strip picking or selective picking. However, selective picking which is generally done by hand, is more labor intensive than the strip picking.

Step 2: Separation

Whatever the harvesting method, green and overripe coffee cherries inevitably end up mixed together with the perfectly ripe coffee cherries. There are two main methods of separation: wet and dry. In the wet method, overripe and underdeveloped coffee cherries, sticks, and leaves float in water, while ripe coffee beans and green coffee cherries sink. In dry processing, harvested cherries are separated by hand but can also be done mechanically.

Step 3: Processing and Drying the Cherries

There are three main methods used to process and dry coffee cherries: the dry process, the wet process, and the semi-dry process.

Step 4: Hulling and Polishing

Hullers are used to remove the outer covering of the bean. Polishing is an optional method that removes any remaining silver skin from the beans following hulling. It is done to improve the appearance of the green beans.

Step 5: Cleaning, Sorting, and Grading

Fine coffee is sorted and cleaned through a multi-step process. Air sorters, sieve shakers, and gravity separators are used to separate based on density and size. Color sorting is performed using machines or by hand. Final grading is based on size, growing location and taste, etc.

Step 6: Roasting

Beans are commonly roasted in large commercial roasters, placing beans in large metal cylinders and blowing hot air on them. Roasting gradually raises the temperature of the beans to between 180°C and 230°C. This triggers the release of steam, causing the beans to swell as well as darken in color and develop roasted flavors.

And now you can brew and enjoy your coffee.

2.3.6

How to encourage early language development in children

The best way to encourage your child's language development is to do a lot of talking together about things that interest your child. It's all about following your child's lead as they show you what they're interested in by waving, babbling or using words.

Talking with your child

From birth, talk with your child and treat them as a talker. The key is to use many different words in different contexts. For example, you can talk to your child about an orange ball and about cutting up an orange for lunch. This helps your child learn what words mean and how words work.

When you finish talking, pause and give your child a turn to respond.

As your child starts to coo, gurgle, blow raspberries, wave and point, you can respond to your child's attempts to communicate. For example, if your baby coos and gurgles, you can coo back to them. Or if your toddler points to a toy, respond as if your child is saying, 'Can I have that?' For example, you could say 'Do you want the block?'

When your child starts using words, you can repeat and build on what your child says. For example, if your child says, 'apple,' you can say, 'You want a red apple?'

And it's the same when your child starts making sentences. You can respond and encourage your child to expand his/her sentences. For example, your toddler might say 'I go shop'. You might respond, 'And what did you do at the shop?'

When you pay attention and respond to your child in these ways, it encourages him/her to keep communicating and developing his/her language skills.

Reading with your child

Reading and sharing books about plenty of different topics lets your child hear words used in many different ways.

Linking what's in the book to what's happening in your child's life is a good way to get your child talking.

For example, you could say, 'We went to the playground today, just like the boy in this book. What do you like to do at the playground?' You can also encourage talking by chatting about interesting pictures in the books you read with your child.

When you read aloud with your child, you can point to words as you say them. This shows your child the link between spoken and written words, and it helps your child learn that words are distinct parts of language. These are important concepts for developing literacy.

Your local library or mobile library is a great source of books.

2.4.1

Hello everyone! Today I'm going to introduce five different tourist destinations and tell you which tourist groups they are most suitable for.

Let's start with Destination One. It's a place full of historical charm. You can walk along the ancient streets paved with stone slabs and admire the centuries-old buildings. There's also a wonderful history museum that showcases precious relics. This destination is perfect for those travelers who have a passion for history and culture.

Now, Destination Two. It's a coastal area with a long and beautiful sandy beach. The sun shines brightly here. It offers a wide range of water sports like surfing and sailing. Besides, there are many seafood restaurants where you can taste delicious seafood. Couples who are looking for romantic places will surely enjoy this destination.

Destination Three is a peaceful mountain retreat. It has vast forests and numerous hiking trails. The air is incredibly fresh. There are several viewpoints on the mountains that offer breathtaking panoramas. And don't forget the natural hot springs that can help you relax. It's an ideal place for retired elders seeking quietness.

Destination Four is a modern and bustling city. It's filled with skyscrapers, shopping malls, and a variety of international cuisine restaurants. There are also famous art exhibition centers and theaters. Young people who love shopping and urban art will have a great time here.

Finally, Destination Five. It's a rural area surrounded by vast farmlands and pastures. You can have the chance to feed livestock and pick fresh crops. There are cozy rural inns for you to stay in. This destination is just right for tourists desiring rural life and pleasures.

So, that's all about the five destinations. Hope this helps you plan your perfect trip!

2.4.2

Hello everyone! Let's talk about some important projects. First, let's look at Project One. This project is centered around improving the local transportation system. We'll be building new roads and upgrading the public transportation facilities. You know what? This project is being handled solely by Tom. Tom, if you have a problem, you can check with Mary. She was responsible for that last year. Now, moving on to Project Two. It's all about setting up a new community center that will offer a wide range of activities and services for the residents. Well, last year, this was not in the working list, but this year we added them to the list to give you more experience. We would like to give this chance to Mary. She's been working hard to make it happen. And then there's Project Three. This one focuses on protecting the environment by promoting recycling and reducing waste. It is a challenging task, so concerning the work load, both Mary and Tom are involved in this project. They're collaborating to make a positive impact. Finally, Project Four. The aim is to enhance the educational resources in the area, including building new schools and providing better teaching equipment. Since Tom and Mary have already taken care of too much work, we'll have other students handle this work. So, that's the overview of these four projects and their responsible persons.

2.5.2

Hello everyone! Today I'm going to give you some useful travel tips for your upcoming journey.

First, let's talk about the clothing you need to bring. The weather in the destination can be quite unpredictable and chilly at times, especially in the evenings. So, it's highly recommended that you pack some warm clothes to keep you comfortable.

Now, when it comes to exploring the local area, the best way to truly immerse yourself in the local culture and get a close-up view of the surroundings is by walking. You can discover hidden gems and soak in the unique atmosphere at your own pace.

As for the local cuisine, the place is renowned for its delicious and fresh seafood. You'll have the chance to taste a wide variety of mouthwatering seafood dishes.

When it comes to the most popular tourist attraction in the city, an ancient palace stands out. It attracts countless visitors every year with its magnificent architecture and rich history.

Finally, the peak tourist season in this place is during the summer months. The pleasant weather and various events and activities make it the most crowded and lively time.

Hope these tips and information are helpful for your travel plans!

2.6.2

Hello everyone. Let me share with you the details of my recent unforgettable trip. I had the pleasure of staying at a truly remarkable hotel named 'Sunshine Hotel'. The moment I stepped into the lobby, I was greeted with warm smiles and a sense of welcoming hospitality. The rooms were spacious and beautifully decorated, providing a cozy and comfortable atmosphere. The amenities were top-notch and the service was simply outstanding. Every staff member went above and beyond to ensure my stay was nothing short of perfect.

Now, let me tell you about the tour I embarked on. It was an absolutely amazing and enriching experience that lasted for a full five days. Each day was filled with new adventures and discoveries. We explored magnificent landscapes, from breathtaking mountains to serene lakes and ancient ruins. We also had the opportunity to immerse ourselves in the local culture, visiting traditional villages and interacting with the friendly locals. The guided tours were informative and engaging, making the entire journey both educational and enjoyable.

This time around, I wasn't alone on this wonderful adventure. I had the company of my dear family. We laughed, we shared precious moments together, and created memories that will last a lifetime. The kids were full of excitement and curiosity, making the trip even more lively and fun. It was truly a bonding experience for all of us and strengthened the ties that bind us as a family.

I sincerely hope that you too will have the chance to embark on such wonderful trips and create your own cherished memories.

Test 1

Part 1

Interviewer:	Hello, Miss Stevens. My name is John Phillips. I'm the personnel director.
Applicant:	Pleased to meet you.
Interviewer:	Have a seat, please.
Applicant:	Thank you.
Interviewer:	According to your resume, you have several years of office experience.
Applicant:	Yes. I've had over 10 years' experience.
Interviewer:	Tell me about your qualifications.
Applicant:	I can type 100 words per minute. I'm proficient in many computer programs. I have excellent interpersonal skills, I am well organized, and I'm a very fast learner.
Interviewer:	I see that you have excellent references. Do you have any questions about the position?
Applicant:	Yes. What are the responsibilities in this position?
Interviewer:	We're looking for someone to supervise two office clerks, handle all the correspondence, arrange meetings and manage the front office. Have you had any supervisory experience?
Applicant:	Yes. I supervised three typists in my last position. What are the office hours, Miss Phillips?
Interviewer:	8.30 to 4.30, with an hour off for lunch. What are your salary expectations, Miss Stevens?
Applicant:	I expect to be paid the going rate for this type of position. Can you tell me about the benefits you offer?
Interviewer:	Yes. We provide full medical and dental coverage, a pension plan and a three-week holiday

	per year.
Applicant:	That's very generous. When is the position available?
Interviewer:	We're hoping the successful applicant can start at the beginning of next month. We'll finish our interviews tomorrow and make a decision by the weekend. We'll contact you next week.
Applicant:	Thank you very much. It's been a pleasure meeting you. I hope to hear from you soon.
Interviewer:	Thank you for coming in to see us, Miss Stevens.

Part 2

Welcome, members of Global Travel Agency. I'm Stephanie, your guide for this trip, and I'll now introduce the itinerary for our journey in Redang Island.

Redang Island is recognized as one of the most beautiful islands in Malaysia. It is located in the Redang Island Marine Park, where the movie *Summer Tea* was filmed. There are many resorts on the island for tourists to stay. The white sandy beaches here are delicate and beautiful, and diving courses are also available. Visitors can enjoy the unique scenery of the Southeast Asian coast from the bottom of the sea. The heart-shaped bay in the north of Redang Island is a 250-meter-long sandy beach. The sand here is fine, soft, pure and white. Known as *Crystal Beach*, the white sandy beach is extraordinarily pure and contrasts against the clear blue-green water. Every time the sun sets in the west, it complements the gorgeous sunset on the coastline. It makes for a beautiful postcard when you take a photo. The waters near the diving resort of Redang Island are extremely clear. The transparency of the sea water of Redang Island under the sunlight can reach nearly 35 feet deep, which is an ideal place for diving enthusiasts. The waters here are very rich in marine life, including brightly colored coral groups, peculiarly shaped tropical fish and lazy swaying turtles, etc., which can be enjoyed while diving.

We have arranged a variety of island activities for you. After a night of rest, on the first morning, you can take a leisurely walk along Redang's beach or gear up to swim in the ocean. In the Afternoon, when time permits, we'll visit Langzhong Island which is a small island located between Perhentian Island and Redang Island, meaning the island where the eagle lives. This is a well-known diving destination in Malaysia for its colorful and magnificent underwater world. The scenery is beautiful and it is a good place for leisure and vacation. The place has no entrance fee, but there is a requirement to pay $10 for round-trip boat fare and $10 for meals.

The morning of the second day, we will be going to another beautiful island Pinang island. The place is a paradise for tropical fish. There are more than 500 species of coral reefs and more than 1,300 species of tropical fish distributed on the seabed, making it a paradise for divers. We have arranged a one-hour diving session for you. For those of you who can't swim, we also provide enjoyable activities. Standing in the beautiful crystal waters, a group of curious fish will be attracted by this strange behemoth and circle around, and even try to launch harmless attacks. If you carry bread with you, you can quickly become their favorite friends. The flat fee for this trip is 30 dollars, but with the membership discount, you now just need to pay 25 dollars.

In the afternoon, we have arranged to pay a visit to the More More Tea Inn, a place famous because of a movie. The colorful house built for the filming of the film later became a popular attraction and photo spot on Redang Island. We have left you enough time for taking photos. There is a heart-shaped wreath concave with flowers on the side of the hut, which is very suitable for couples to take pictures here. After taking photos, you will enjoy delicious afternoon tea at the bar on the second floor. Sitting by the window with a view of the beautiful scenery, enjoying delicious food while admiring the sea view, will provide you with a wonderful experience. The fee is included in the price of the package.

For the last day you stay in Redang, we will go to the last island of the trip, Pulau Kapas. Kapas Island is famous for its crystal clear emerald green waters and white sandy beaches with dancing palm trees. Here is another dazzling underwater world and coral reef area. The waters here are completely uncontaminated and ideal for diving. Here, we offer you a range of water activities: diving, surfing, canoeing and boating, you name it. Lying on a beach lounger and enjoying the swaying shadows of the trees and the happy people is a wonderful experience. As a member benefit, this trip will only cost you $40. The cost includes boat fare and three meals. Normally, the regular price for this journey is $80.

I hope our three-day itinerary brings you wonderful memories.

Part 3

Sam:	Hi Mohit, how are you?
Mohit:	Long time, Sam! I am great, how about you?
Sam:	I am also good. All my mental energy has been exhausted after the board exams. Plus, the Economics exam. What was that even!
Mohit:	Same here. The papers were slightly trickier than before. Thank goodness there wasn't anything difficult in the re-exam. Last year's exams were really difficult to pass.
Sam:	Indeed! So what are your plans now? You had Physics, Chemistry, Biology, right?
Mohit:	Oh yes! And you, I guess, were in the Physics, Chemistry, Medical stream? I think I will choose the medical exams. Both my parents are doctors and I guess it is only natural that I also become one.
Sam:	Haha! I think you should go for a career in medicine only if you are really interested, no?
Mohit:	You are right. Though medicine will be my major focus, if I'm unable to pass the competitive exams, I will enroll in a B.Sc course and prepare for the Civil Services. What about you? Planning for engineering?
Sam:	Hmm, I am confused. Most of my classmates plan to appear for JEE Mains and JEE Advanced which are usually chosen by students opting for engineering, but I don't really know whether engineering is my calling. You know Gary? Our senior in school?

Mohit:	Oh Gary? Yes, I do. He passed JEE, right?
Sam:	Yes, he did. But he didn't find it interesting. Do you know what he is doing these days?
Mohit:	No, what?
Sam:	He is a wildlife photographer!
Mohit:	Whoa! That's crazy!
Sam:	My future plan is to get a master degree in Business administration so I really wonder if engineering will be appropriate for graduation. I think Business, Economics or even Law would be better.
Mohit:	Do whatever interests you, man! Don't just follow other people's choices. Most people just follow their peers and get into engineering. Then they regret it because they are simply not cut out for it.
Sam:	Yes, I think I will apply to a good college. Really hope that the board results are good. Fingers crossed!
Mohit:	Indeed. By the way, why didn't you opt for commerce after Class 10? Wouldn't it have been better than science, given your future course of action?
Sam:	Hah! If I had taken commerce, my parents would have gone into a state of perennial depression, thinking my life has been ruined.
Mohit:	Haha! So sorry for you, man. That's the case with most parents today. I am pretty sure that even if I crack the Civil Services, there would be a tinge of disappointment in my parents for not becoming a doctor.
Sam:	Same case everywhere! By the way, did you hear that Pep education is conducting a career counselling workshop online soon?
Mohit:	Oh no, I didn't. Are registrations still open?
Sam:	Yes, they are. I will give you the link. I heard there's a student discount of 20%.
Mohit:	Oh, I thought it was free.
Sam:	You can't expect free workshop to provide you with high-quality counselling, right?
Mohit:	You are right! See you at the workshop!
Sam:	See you!

Part 4

In this section, we begin talking about schools of psychology and the major players that made psychology what it is today. The first group that we shall start talking about is the Structuralists.

There are a couple of major players in this group. The first individual was Wundt, who is considered to be the first psychologist, and a true psychologist. Titchener was one of his students and he's considered to be the first United States psychologist.

The Structuralists were the first real school or group of psychologists. These individuals were impressed by what was going on in the physical sciences, such as chemistry and biology. Especially chemistry, where people were breaking down complex things into simple things. The Structuralists thought that they could do the same kind of thing with mental thoughts.

Well, next, what we have to do is kind of sit down and think and use what they called introspection. Basically what you would do is train an observer to reflect on and analyze a particular mental experience. It requires someone who is very highly trained. This individual would sit down and basically think of a concept. The classic example would be a table, and as we see in slide four, that person would take the table and break it down into its basic elements.

Now for the Structuralists, there were some things that were extremely important. Number one, experience was an extremely important concept.

Number two, the mind is passive. That is, when one thought comes in, it is followed by another thought, and on and on and on.

Number three, the structuralists believed that you could break down complex thoughts into very simple thoughts and study these. In essence, each thought was the sum of other thoughts. That is, all the other thoughts that you had in your system. Finally they were empiricists. That is, they gathered information by observation and recording.

Now what was the problem with the Structuralist school? Let's take the concept of love as an example. What I'd like you to do is to break down the concept of love. Well, a lot of people put down lots of different things for love. For example, they might put down intimacy, and lots and lots of other things such as caring, compassion and all these kinds of things.

Ok, so which of those groups is right? People would say, well, my concepts are better than your concepts and so on. So the first problem with the Structuralist's model is that it had no reliability. As a consequence, it really couldn't test what it was supposed to be testing, so it had no validity as well.

The first major group that criticized the Structuralists was the second school of psychology and is called the Gestalt School. The three major players in the Gestalt School were Kohler, Werner, and Kofka. For them, the saying developed, "The whole is greater than the sum of the parts."

Now a third school also developed around this time is the Functionalism School or the Functionalists. There are several major players. They include people like James, Hall, Cattell, and Angel. They also developed as a reaction to the Structuralists.

The Functionalists weren't really concerned with the elementary elements of consciousness. They were more concerned with how the mind works. And they examined both humans and animals to try to determine what the function of some particular thing was.

The next major model is the Behaviorist School. There are many players that will be involved in this school. Watson, Hull and many others. They believe science really can't study the mind. You can't study consciousness, images, or whatever because they cannot be observed. So the goal for them was to discover particular laws that could predict the behavior. Ultimately if we can predict it, we can control behavior.

As a result, we can use animals to discover the basic laws. Based on the concepts of evolution, if the same laws hold in animals or we discover a law in animals, it should hold in humans. That's exactly what we have found.

So the next time when we get together, we'll continue to talk about other schools of psychology. So until that time, you have yourself a good day.

Test 2

Part 1

Customer: Hello, is this the Youth Art Center?

Centre staff: Yes, Sir. How may I help you?

Customer: I've heard a lot about your Children's Music Workshops and I'm really keen to find out more. Can you fill me in?

Centre staff: Sure thing! We have the workshops every Sunday, and it's a must for adults to accompany kids under 8.

Customer: Got it. So, how much does it cost to join?

Centre staff: It's just £3.00 per child. Pretty affordable, right?

Customer: Yeah, that's great. Where exactly do these workshops take place?

Centre staff: They're held in Spring Hall, which is on Main Street. It's a nice and spacious place.

Customer: I see. What about the security? How do we get in?

Centre staff: Well, you need to enter the password on the security device to open the door. That way, we can keep the kids safe.

Customer: Okay, that makes sense. Where should I park my car when I come for the workshops?

Centre staff: You can park it in front of the library. There are plenty of parking spots there.

Customer: Thanks for the info. And how do I go about booking the workshops?

Centre staff: Just give us a call on 555678. Our team will be more than happy to help you with the booking.

Customer: Thanks! Who should I call? I mean, who's responsible for the booking?

Centre staff: Oh, that will be Mrs. Waddell. I'll spell that for you. W-A double D E-L-L. Waddell.

Customer: Awesome. Now, I'm also curious about the next two workshops. What are they going to be like?

Centre staff: On December 18th, we'll have a workshop called 'Playing Drums'. We suggest that the kids wear comfortable clothes for this one, and if they can, it would be great if they bring

	sticks along.
Customer:	That sounds like a lot of fun. And what about the workshop on 25th of December?
Centre staff:	On that day, the focus will be on 'Singing'. There's no particular dress code for this workshop, but if it's easy for the kids, they can bring song sheets.
Customer:	I think these workshops will be really fantastic for the children. Thanks so much for your help.
Centre staff:	No problem at all. We're looking forward to having your kids join us and have a great time at the workshops!

Part 2

Hello everyone! Welcome to our company. I'm David Brown, manager of the human resource department. I'm truly delighted to guide you through our company today.

As we proceed, I'll elaborate on some of the crucial aspects of our company's operations and functions. Now, talking about the task of preparing the financial reports, it is typically taken care of by the department specializing in finance. When it comes to organizing a product launch event, this responsibility often lies with the team dedicated to marketing. And for conducting employee training sessions, it used to be the domain of the human resources department. However, this year they already have other work arrangements. Now, we delegated the task of employee training to the customer service department.

Now, let's focus on the detailed schedule for the day. At 8.30 am, we have John Miller presenting. He'll furnish you with comprehensive information regarding benefits and will distribute the employee benefit cards. Come 9.00 am, Mary Smith will step up. She'll elaborate on the office layout and provide explanations about the arrangements for the lighting setups and air conditioning. If you have any questions, you can call her. I'll give you her mobile number later. At 9.30 am, it's the much-needed tea break. You can unwind and relax in the Staff Lounge located on the second floor. Believe me, you'll definitely need that. And you can also take the time to get to know each other. Then, at 10.00 am, a presentation awaits. You are required to make your way to the conference room. The title of the presentation is 'Prospects and Strategies for Our Company'. The CEO of our company will give you a great presentation to help you understand where you will be working, and also give you valuable advice on your career planning. At 11.00 am, a group discussion will take place in the meeting hall. And finally, at 12.00, it's time to enjoy the buffet lunch. We'll head to the rooftop garden area to savor the meal and have an enjoyable conversation.

Alright, let's keep moving and uncover more fascinating aspects of our company.

Part 3

Professor:	Hi, Olivia. Come on in.
Olivia:	Hi, Professor. Thanks for providing me with this tutoring. I'm really struggling with this project on Ancient Literature. It feels like there's an overwhelming amount of material to cover.

Professor: I recommend you to read Professor Smith's book. I'm sure his literary history books will give you a clear framework.

Olivia: The Professor Smith of our department?

Professor: Yes. His literary history is always on my recommended list. Well, let's break it down. So, apart from the reference books, what specific aspects are causing you the most trouble?

Olivia: Well, first of all, I'm finding it hard to manage my time. Between classes, assignments, and other commitments, there just aren't enough hours in the day.

Professor: I understand that. Have you thought about creating a detailed schedule to help you organize your tasks more effectively?

Olivia: I did consider that, but it's been difficult to stick to it. Also, some of the research materials I need are quite hard to find.

Professor: I see. Have you considered doing some of your research in the library? They have some excellent resources and librarians who can assist you.

Olivia: I thought about using the online database, but I think I'll give the library a try.

Professor: Good idea. Now, when would be a good time for you to come for feedback? Monday morning is usually busy for me.

Olivia: How about Wednesday afternoon?

Professor: I think I have plans on that day. Wait a minute. Sorry, that's the plan for last month. Wednesday afternoon? Yes, that works for me. Now, let's talk about your tasks. How's the preparation of the presentation slides coming along?

Olivia: It's half done. I still need to add more images and make sure the content is clear and concise.

Professor: Great. And what about the summary?

Olivia: I haven't started that yet. I'm a bit intimidated by the amount of information I need to condense.

Professor: Well, don't worry. Start by outlining the main points and then gradually fill in the details. Make sure you finish it by next week. What about revising the essay?

Olivia: It's in progress. I'm working on improving the structure and flow of my arguments.

Professor: Good. Once you're done, be sure to check for grammar errors and also ensure your citations are accurate.

Olivia: Professor, I was also thinking about studying in a group for the next assignment. Do you think that's a good idea?

Professor: Well, it has some benefits. For example, you can share ideas and improve your communication skills. Group discussions often lead to new perspectives and insights that you might not have thought of on your own.

Olivia: Oh, that sounds great. But I'm also worried about potential conflicts or differences in work styles among group members.

Professor:	That's a valid concern. It's important to establish clear roles and expectations from the beginning. Make sure everyone is committed and willing to contribute equally. Also, set up regular check-ins to monitor progress and address any issues promptly.
Olivia:	Right, I'll keep that in mind. So, do you think group study can also save time compared to working alone?
Professor:	It can sometimes speed up the process, but it doesn't always guarantee saving time. It depends on how well the group functions and coordinates. However, it can definitely benefit your communication skills because you obviously can't avoid talking to different people in a group.
Olivia:	That makes sense. Thank you for your advice, Professor.
Professor:	You're welcome. Keep up the good work and don't hesitate to reach out if you have any more questions.

Part 4

Hello everyone! Welcome to today's lecture on nutrition.

Now, let's start by discussing what we need to know when preparing for a meaningful discussion on healthy eating. One of the key elements is understanding nutrients. You must realize that a truly healthy diet is made up of various components such as delicious fruits, vegetables, and grains.

Looking back in time, we find that our earliest understanding of healthy eating centered primarily around calorie intake. But as we delve deeper, we encounter several puzzling questions. For example, why is it that some people are so resistant to making changes to their diet? Is it because of habits, taste preferences, or something else? Then there's the question of why certain diets are not suitable for everyone. We all have our unique bodies and metabolisms, and what works for one person might not work for another. And finally, we wonder why it's so difficult to stick to a healthy diet. Is it the temptations of junk food, a lack of time, or perhaps a lack of knowledge about proper nutrition?

Moving forward to the present day, we see that the more modern and effective approach is to emphasize personalized nutrition plans. This means taking into account an individual's specific needs, goals, and genetic makeup to create a diet that is tailored just for them.

Now, let's turn to some important findings. A new study has come out that clearly shows how diet can have a profound and significant impact on our well-being. It's not just about looking good or fitting into a certain size of clothes. It's about feeling good, having energy, and reducing the risk of various diseases. For people with certain health conditions, being careful about their diet choices is of utmost importance. Those with diabetes, for instance, need to watch their sugar intake. Those with heart problems might need to limit their saturated fat consumption. And when we overindulge in processed foods, we open ourselves up to a whole host of health issues. These can range from weight gain and high blood pressure to more serious conditions like diabetes and heart disease. That's why it's so crucial that we include more fiber in our diet. Fiber helps with digestion, keeps us feeling full longer, and can even lower cholesterol levels.

In conclusion, maintaining a balanced diet holds significant importance. It is not just a nice idea. It's essential for our overall health. A combination of a healthy diet with moderate training and rest can make our bodies healthier. Let's all make an effort to eat right and take care of our bodies.

Test 3

Part 1

Landlord: Hi there! So, you're looking for a place to rent, right? What's your name?

Sarah: I'm Sarah Taylor.

Landlord: Nice to meet you, Sarah. Now, how many bedrooms are you looking for?

Sarah: I'm thinking two bedrooms. One bedroom would be a bit cramped. Sometimes, my mum comes to visit me, and it will be more convenient if she has her room.

Landlord: Got it. And what's the purpose of renting?

Sarah: I'm here for an internship.

Landlord: Oh, that's great. What area would you prefer?

Sarah: I'd like to be near the university. Or maybe somewhere close to the city centre if the price is right.

Landlord: Understood. And what's your maximum monthly rent?

Sarah: Ideally, £800. But I might be able to stretch it to 850 if the place is really amazing.

Landlord: Alright. How long do you need the place for?

Sarah: Nine months. Although if the situation changes, I might need it for a bit longer or shorter.

Landlord: When are you planning to start?

Sarah: August 15th. I thought about a few days earlier but I have to finish up some things. 15th would be more suitable.

Landlord: And what kind of proof of identity can you provide?

Sarah: I can give you my driving license. Or maybe my passport if that's better.

Landlord: Your driving license will do. Now let me tell you about some of the properties I have. There's one on Oak Lane. It has a living room and a separate kitchen. The rent is £580. But it has no parking space. Some people say it's not a big deal as there's street parking nearby, but it can be troublesome.

Sarah: Hmm, that could be a problem. What about others?

Landlord: Well, there's a place on Willow Street. I can spell the word for you. It's W- 'i', double 'l', 'o', and 'w' Street. It has a large living room and kitchen. The rent is £720. But the kitchen is a bit old. Some tenants don't mind it as it still functions fine.

Sarah: That's not ideal.

Landlord: Then there's one on Cedar Road. It has a bathroom and a storage room. The rent is £650.

	But it's too far from public transport. Although there's a bike path that some people use to get around.
Sarah:	That's not so good either.
Landlord:	And finally, there's a place on Rose Square. It has a living room, kitchen-diner, and a small garden. The rent is £700. But it's next to a busy main road. Some say the noise isn't too bad once you get used to it.
Sarah:	I'll have to think about these options, and I'll get it back to you soon. Thanks for your time.

Part 2

Hello there! As your landlord, I want to show you how to use the coffee machine in your rental unit first. Afterwards, I will give you some suggestions for traveling in the neighborhood.

Now, pay attention to the on/off switch. This is what you use to turn the appliance on and off. But be aware, even after you switch it off, the machine can still be live. So always remember to unplug it from the socket to make it completely voltage-free for safety.

The start and stop button on the control panel is very useful. You can use it to start or interrupt the coffee making process at any time. Maybe you need to pause for a moment or stop it for some reason, this button comes in handy. It's extremely important to know that this machine is only for making coffee and/or tea and warming water. Do not use it for any other purposes as it can be dangerous.

Let me point out the other parts of this coffee machine. We have a basket filter with a leak stop device and a basket filter paper. The machine comes with 2 jugs or coffee pots which are obviously used to hold the coffee. Careful, it can be very hot. I once had a tenant burned by hot coffee. So make sure you use the handle on the side. This appliance is fitted with a jug detector that operates the leak stop under the filter. This jug detector also ensures that the appliance only makes coffee if there is a jug or pot under the filter. If the jug is removed during the coffee brewing process, the process will be interrupted and the leak stop in the filter will prevent coffee dripping on the hot plate. The control panel is crucial. It has a display, a descale indicator light, a brewing process indicator light, a selection button, and of course, the start/stop button we just talked about. There's also the top hot plate which can be used to make sure the coffee is always warm. You simply remove the jug or pot from the bottom hot plate and put it on the top plate. You can have the hot coffee for hours.

There are other functions of the machine, but I don't think you will be using them. Anyway, call me if you are interested in the other functions. I hope you enjoy using this coffee machine.

Now, I'm so excited to introduce to you some truly remarkable tourist attractions and activities in our area.

First of all, the local beach is an absolute gem. I strongly suggest you head there in the morning. You see, during this time, it's not packed with people like it is in the afternoon or evening. The tranquility and serenity of the beach in the early hours allow you to truly soak in the beauty of the ocean and the soft sand beneath your feet.

If you have a passion for history, the local museum is an absolute must-visit. It houses an extensive and fascinating collection that offers profound insights into our area's rich and diverse past. From ancient artefacts to detailed chronicles of significant events, it's a journey through time that will leave you enlightened and captivated. There is a castle near the museum. You can also go and have a look if you have time.

For those of you who are enthusiasts of outdoor activities, hiking in the mountains is a better choice than cycling. You see, the town is built on side of the mountain, so the roads are quite steep. As you make your way up the trails, you'll be treated to breathtaking panoramic views of the surrounding landscapes. The lush greenery, the chirping of birds, and the fresh mountain air all combine to create an unforgettable experience. Not only will you enjoy the spectacular natural scenery but also get a great workout and a sense of rejuvenation.

The local park is another wonderful spot, but try not to visit there in the afternoon. It's best explored early in the morning. At this time, the park is bathed in the gentle rays of the rising sun, and the air is filled with the sweet fragrance of blooming flowers. The peace and quiet allow you to unwind and connect with nature on a deeper level.

To truly immerse yourself in the essence of the local culture, attending a local festival which is held near a traditional village is highly recommended. These festivals are a vibrant celebration of our traditions, customs, and community spirit. You'll have the opportunity to savor mouthwatering local delicacies, be entranced by the rhythmic beats of traditional music, and be swept away by the energetic performances of local dancers. It's a chance to become a part of the local fabric and create memories that will last a lifetime.

Well, hope you have a pleasant stay here, and call me if you need anything.

Part 3

Mary:	Hey, Sam. Do you know the exam is approaching soon? I'm starting to feel the pressure.
Sam:	Hi, Mary. I've been so caught up with other things. I'm not exactly sure when it is. Do you have a clearer sense of the timeline?
Mary:	I think it's coming in about three weeks. We really need to kick our preparations into high gear. Time is slipping away quickly.
Sam:	Right. And for the presentation we have to do, what kind of materials do we need to prepare? I'm a bit confused about that.
Mary:	Well, I think we need to come up with something that really engages the audience and makes our points stand out. You know, arrange some activities that can involve them actively.
Sam:	Oh, that sounds quite challenging. I'm worried about pulling that off effectively. So,

	what's the main topic of our project again? Is it Animal conservation? Sorry, I get lost in all the details.
Mary:	Actually, it's focused on environmental protection. We need to explore various ways to promote sustainable living and find practical solutions to the current ecological issues.
Sam:	Great. But where do you think is the best place for us to conduct the necessary research? I'm thinking the city museum?
Mary:	I believe the school library is our best bet. They have a wealth of resources related to environmental studies and we can access them easily.
Sam:	That makes sense. But when do you think is a good time for us to actually sit down and work on the project together? Are you free on weekends? Or after class?
Mary:	How about in the evenings? We might have a few quiet hours then to focus without too many distractions.
Sam:	Okay, that would work. Let's talk about the study methods. Making notes seems like a useful way to keep track of important points, don't you think?
Mary:	Yes, definitely. It helps us remember the key elements and organize our thoughts. And group discussion is also crucial as it allows us to exchange and build on different viewpoints.
Sam:	And reading textbooks provides us with in-depth knowledge and a solid foundation for our research.
Mary:	Exactly. But we also have some significant difficulties with this project.
Sam:	Like what? I feel like we've been so focused on moving forward that we haven't really stopped to assess the challenges.
Mary:	Well, for one, there's a huge amount of pressure because of the limited time we have. Luckily, we've found enough resources. And the instructions given by the professor aren't as clear as they could be. It makes it hard to know exactly what's expected.
Sam:	Yeah, we need to figure it all out and do our absolute best. I'm so glad to cooperate with you. Let's stay positive and keep pushing forward.

Part 4

Hello everyone! Welcome back. Before we start today's lecture on education innovation, let's quickly remember what we talked about in our last class. We talked about how education is always changing and how important it is to be open to new ideas. And this class we'll move on to the new changes of education: education innovations.

Education innovation means more than just using new technologies in the classroom. It involves rethinking teaching methods and curriculums. For example, project-based learning allows students to actively engage in real-world problems, developing critical thinking and problem-solving skills. Activities like building a Solar-Powered Car, creating a school garden or running a business are designed for students to develop skills and knowledge for the real world. Instead of simply memorizing facts, they learn to apply knowledge and collaborate with others.

Moreover, personalized learning is an important aspect of education innovation. Every student has unique learning styles, strengths, and weaknesses. With the development of technology, a new data analytical tool: Artificial intelligence (AI) has emerged. AI can analyze a student's performance data, such as test scores, homework assignments, and class participation, to create a personalized learning plan. This plan can be tailored to the student's specific needs and learning style, helping them to achieve better results. Apart from that, it also helps students reach their full potential and build their confidence.

Another area of innovation is the integration of STEAM (Science, Technology, Engineering, Arts, and Mathematics) education. By combining these disciplines, students gain a more comprehensive understanding and are better equipped to handle the complex issues of the modern world. They develop creativity, innovation, and the ability to think across different fields. The benefits of STEAM education are numerous. It prepares students for careers in a rapidly changing job market that requires skills in multiple disciplines. It also promotes creativity, innovation, and collaboration, which are essential for success in the 21st century.

However, implementing education innovation also faces challenges. Teachers need proper training and support to adapt to new teaching methods and technologies. There may also be resistance from traditional educational systems and mindsets. Many educators and institutions are accustomed to traditional teaching methods and may be reluctant to adopt new approaches. This resistance can be due to a lack of understanding of the benefits of education innovation or fear of the unknown. Overcoming this resistance requires extensive training and professional development for educators to understand the importance and effectiveness of innovative teaching methods.

Another challenge is the availability of resources. Education innovation often requires access to technology, such as computers, tablets, and software. However, not all schools and educational institutions have the necessary resources to implement these technologies. Additionally, there may be a lack of funding for educational innovation initiatives, making it difficult to sustain and expand these efforts.

Assessing the effectiveness of education innovation is also a challenge. It can be difficult to determine whether new teaching methods and technologies are actually improving student learning outcomes. This requires the development of appropriate assessment tools and metrics to measure the impact of education innovation on student achievement.

In conclusion, education innovation is essential for the future of our society. It empowers students with the skills and knowledge they need to succeed in a constantly evolving world. By embracing new ideas and approaches, we can create a more engaging, effective, and inclusive educational experience for all.

IELTS
All-in-One Guide
(Basic Edition)

参考答案

听力答案

1.4.1

1.4.1.2

(1) ① bird　　　　　fir　　　　　　sir　　　　　　shirt　　　　　flirt
　　② worse　　　　worst　　　　　worm　　　　　worker
　　③ turkey　　　　turn　　　　　turtle　　　　　purple
(2) ① tower　　　　clown　　　　　howl　　　　　brown
　　② snow　　　　throw　　　　　show　　　　　know　　　　　window
(3) ① wait　　　　　pain　　　　　gain　　　　　paid　　　　　trait　　　snail　　　tail
　　② say　　　　　play　　　　　hay　　　　　Jay　　　　　ray　　　　clay　　　way
　　③ sleigh　　　　neighbour
(4) draw　　　　　　lawyer　　　　strawberry　　yawn　　　　　awful　　　paw
(5) high　　　　　　might　　　　　bright　　　　height

1.4.2

(1) The sun sets in the west.

This rock art was like a school book.

Many of the engravings show footprints of animals.

Books can also offer us a wide range of experience.

Carriage is running at a speed of 8 to 9 miles an hour.

Almost everything we use in our everyday life comes from nature.

The widespread water shortage is an example in point.

Wildlife species are disappearing from the country at an alarming rate.

Home is often referred to as the place that we live in with our families.

In the early times when human beings hunted and gathered food, they were not in control of their environment.

参考答案

It is possible to feel "tired" physically and still be unable to fall asleep, because while your body may be exhausted, you do not feel sleepy.

Today people have far more free time to use, more choices to make, and more problems to solve. "How to" books help people to deal with modern life.

（2）Professional sports are not only very popular in the United States, but also a big business. The most popular sports are baseball, football and basketball. Each sport has its own season and individual teams have millions of supporters. Professional teams are named for the cities where they are located. The N.B.A is gaining new fans and supporters around the world. Basketball has been called the "national pastime".

We are in the computer age today. The computers are working all kinds of wonders now. They are very useful in automatic control and data processing. At the same time, computers are finding their way into the home. They seem to be so clever and can solve complicated problems that some people think sooner or later they will replace us. But I do not think that there is such a possibility. My reason is very simple: computers are machines, not humans. And our tasks are far too varied and complicated for any one single kind of machine to perform.

2.3.1

1. bears   northern
2. 50 find food
3. turtle   wildlife
4. edges   open spaces   populated
5. first impression   standard writing style   correct

2.3.2

1. resit
2. hot and cold
3. (clear) assignment instructions   grading criteria
4. presentation   inaccurate
5. sounds   early childhood

2.3.3

递进	Moreover, not only…but also…
对比	While, contrasting with
原因/结果	Therefore
表示顺序	Later

2.3.4

1. actions
2. healthcare
3. decisions
4. human eye
5. unemployment

2.3.5

1. selective
2. hand
3. (remaining silver) skin
4. fine
5. flavors / flavours

2.3.6

1. different words 2. respond 3. repeat 4. child's life 5. local

2.4.1

1. E 2. F 3. B 4. A 5. D

2.4.2

1. B 2. A 3. C 4. D

2.5.2

1. A 2. B 3. C 4. A 5. B

2.6.2

Question 1   Sunshine Hotel.
Question 2   five/5 days.
Question 3   (her) family/ families.

Test 1

Part 1

1. 10 years
2. (many) computer programs
3. interpersonal
4. fast learner
5. supervise
6. meeting(s)
7. 4.30
8. dental
9. 3-week/3 weeks'/three-week/three weeks'
10. beginning

Part 2

11. C
12-14. A E G (in any order)
15. $20/20 dollars
16. diving
17. $25
18. Taking photos
19. Surfing
20. $40/40 dollars

Part 3

21. C
22. B
23. A
24. C
25-27. ACF
28. commerce
29. career counselling
30. 20%

Part 4

31. students
32. chemistry
33. mental experience
34. passive
35. recording
36. caring
37. whole
38. mind
39. observed
40. evolution

Test 2

Part 1
1. the age of 8/8/eight
2. Main
3. password
4. library
5. 555678
6. Waddell
7. Drums
8. sticks
9. singing
10. song sheets

Part 2
11. A
12. B
13. F
14. employee benefit
15. lighting
16. second
17. conference
18. Strategies
19. meeting
20. (rooftop) garden

Part 3
21. Ancient Literature
22. (Professor) Smith
23. A
24. A
25. B
26. images
27. started
28. grammar errors
29-30. AD (in any order)

Part 4
31. nutrients
32. Vegetables
33. calorie intake
34. taste
35. nutrition plans
36. well-being
37. diet choices
38. health issues
39. fiber
40. rest

Test 3

Part 1
1. two (bedrooms)
2. university
3. £850
4. August 15th
5. driving license
6. parking (space)
7. Willow
8. (a bit) old
9. £650
10. (small) garden

Part 2
11. C
12. D
13. E
14. F
15. A
16. A
17. B
18. A
19. C
20. A

Part 3
21. B
22. B
23. A
24. A
25. B
26. C
27. E
28. A
29-30. CE（in any order）

Part 4
31. (new)technologies
32. school garden
33. learning styles
34. learning plan
35. comprehensive
36. careers
37. resistance
38. fear
39. funding
40. assessing

阅读答案

Test 1

Reading Passage 1, Questions 1–13

1 TRUE
2 NOT GIVEN
3 NOT GIVEN
4 FALSE
5 FALSE
6 TRUE
7 NOT GIVEN
8 moonlight
9 light sources
10 traffic noise
11 glare
12 parks
13 high-efficiency light sources

Reading Passage 2, Questions 14–26

14 nutrients
15 micronutrient
16 grey matter
17 eating habits
18 C
19 E
20 B
21 D
22 F
23&24 *IN EITHER ORDER*
 A
 B
25&26 *IN EITHER ORDER*
 B
 E

Reading Passage 3, Questions 27–40

27 C
28 A
29 F
30 D
31 C
32 D
33 F
34 B
35 A
36 C
37 FALSE
38 NOT GIVEN

39 TRUE

40 TRUE

If you score ...

1–17	18–26	27–40
You are unlikely to get an acceptable score under examination conditions and we recommend that you spend a lot of time improving your English before you take IELTS.	You may get an acceptable score under examination conditions but we recommend that you think about having more practice or lessons before you take IELTS.	You are likely to get an acceptable score under examination conditions but remember that different institutions will find different scores acceptable.

Test 2

Reading Passage 1, Questions 1–13

1. FALSE
2. TRUE
3. FALSE
4. TRUE
5. FALSE
6. NOT GIVEN
7. TRUE
8. apprentice
9. algae
10. animalcules
11. plaque
12. diaphragm
13. family

Reading Passage 2, Questions 14–26

14. E
15. A
16. F
17. E
18. B
19. productivity
20. youth
21. frustration
22. genes
23. B
24. E
25. A
26. C

Reading Passage 3, Questions 27–40

27. C
28. A
29. C
30. C
31. F
32. A
33. H
34. D
35. E
36. G
37. YES
38. NO
39. NOT GIVEN
40. YES

If you score ...

1–17	18–26	27–40
You are unlikely to get an acceptable score under examination conditions and we recommend that you spend a lot of time improving your English before you take IELTS.	You may get an acceptable score under examination conditions but we recommend that you think about having more practice or lessons before you take IELTS.	You are likely to get an acceptable score under examination conditions but remember that different institutions will find different scores acceptable.

Test 3

Reading Passage 1, Questions 1–13

1 vi
2 iii
3 i
4 ii
5 v
6 viii
7 iv
8 commercial
9 environment
10 crops
11 bushmeat
12 medicinal
13 jewelry

Reading Passage 2, Questions 14–26

14 D
15 F
16 E
17 B
18 C
19 farming
20 carbon dioxide
21 (cool) breezes
22 kite
23 NOT GIVEN
24 FALSE
25 TRUE
26 NOT GIVEN

Reading Passage 3, Questions 27–40

27 D
28 B
29 A
30 B
31 C
32 E
33 B
34 A
35 NOT GIVEN
36 NO
37 YES
38 NOT GIVEN
39 NO
40 YES

If you score...

1–17	18–26	27–40
You are unlikely to get an acceptable score under examination conditions and we recommend that you spend a lot of time improving your English before you take IELTS.	You may get an acceptable score under examination conditions but we recommend that you think about having more practice or lessons before you take IELTS.	You are likely to get an acceptable score under examination conditions but remember that different institutions will find different scores acceptable.

写作答案

2.1.1

语态练习题

1. 互联网极大地改变了人们获取信息的方式。

主动语态：The Internet has greatly changed the way people obtain information.

被动语态：The way people obtain information is greatly changed by the Internet.

2. 环境污染对我们的健康造成威胁。

主动语态：Environmental pollution poses a threat to our health.

被动语态：Our health is posed a threat by environmental pollution.

3. 应该鼓励人们采取可持续的生活方式，以减少对环境的负面影响。

主动语态：We should encourage people to adopt sustainable lifestyles to reduce the negative impact on the environment.（添加主语）.

被动语态：Sustainable lifestyles should be encouraged to be adopted by people to reduce the negative impact on the environment.

4. 人们强烈要求采取行动来解决城市交通拥堵问题。

主动语态：People strongly demand taking actions to solve the problem of urban traffic congestion.

被动语态：Actions are strongly demanded by people to solve the problem of urban traffic congestion.

5. 科学家们一直在努力探索新能源，以应对日益严峻的能源危机。

主动语态：Scientists have been making great efforts to explore new energy sources to cope with the increasingly severe energy crisis.

被动语态：Great efforts have been made by scientists to explore new energy sources to cope with the increasingly severe energy crisis.

6. 有效的教育政策可以提高国民素质，促进国家的发展和进步。

主动语态：Effective educational policies can improve the quality of the nation and promote the development and progress of the country.

被动语态：The quality of the nation can be improved and the development and progress of the country can be promoted by effective educational policies.

7. 许多人认为，家庭教育对于孩子的成长起着至关重要的作用。

主动语态：Many people believe that family education plays a crucial role in children's growth.

被动语态：A crucial role is played by family education in children's growth, which is believed by many people.

8. 学校应该提供更多的课外活动，以帮助学生培养兴趣爱好和社交能力。

主动语态：Schools should offer more extracurricular activities to help students develop their interests and social skills.

被动语态：More extracurricular activities should be offered by schools to help students develop their interests and social skills.

改错练习题

1. In the city center, there are many buildings and streets.

2. During the summer vacation, people usually do a lot of activities and have fun.

3. The government should take measures to improve the economy, because it is crucial for the country's development.

4. We need to protect the environment, since it is our responsibility to ensure a sustainable future.

5. The situation changes quickly, which affects our plans.

6. The number of tourists continues to increase.

7. Reading books is a great way to expand your knowledge.

8. Going to the gym to do exercise helps to keep fit.

9. We should reduce waste and protect the environment.

10. People need to be more aware of climate change and take action.

11. The family of five has moved to a new city.

12. The class of students is excited about the field trip.

13. Someone in the audience wants to ask a question.

14. Everyone in the room has his/her own agenda.

15. The teacher and the student are discussing the assignment.

16. The singer and the dancer have their own talents.

17. What we need to do is to take action immediately.

18. How many people are involved in this project is unknown.

19. Reading is an important skill for personal growth.

20. We should respect human rights.

21. The importance of education cannot be overstated.

22. History is a fascinating subject.

23. She is a university student.

24. The students who are the best in the top class have the right to choose which universities to go.

25. The class has many students, and each of them has his/her own unique ideas.

26. The company is facing some challenges that are causing operational difficulties, but it is not clear which departments will be most affected by these challenges.

27. We need to buy some supplies, but it's not clear which store has them in stock.

28. The development of technology has brought many benefits, but some people argue that it has also caused some negative impacts on society.

29. Some people believe that money can buy happiness, but I think there are more important things in life than money.

30. Traveling can bring us a lot of pleasure and inspiration; it allows us to experience different cultures and landscapes. Yet, many people don't have enough time or money to travel.

2.1.2

词汇翻译练习题

气候变化 climate change	全球变暖 global warming
环境污染 environmental pollution	空气污染 air pollution
噪声污染 noise pollution	环境退化 environmental degradation
荒漠化 desertification	森林砍伐 deforestation
水资源短缺 water resources shortage	生态平衡 ecological balance
自然资源 natural resources	生物多样性 biodiversity
环保意识 environmental awareness	塑料污染 plastic pollution
回收和再利用 recycling and reuse	减少碳排放 reduce carbon emissions
保护野生动物及其栖息地 protect wild animals and their habitats	节约能源和资源 save energy and resources
可持续发展 sustainable development	建立自然保护区 establish nature reserves

词汇搭配练习题

1. None can negative the importance of money.（形容词 negative 被误用为动词。正确的动词应该是 deny）

2. Pollution effects the citizens' living standards negatively.（名词 effect 被误用为动词。正确的动词应该是 affects）

3. The forests are destroyed, but few people concern about it.（concern 应改为 are concerned）

4. On the one hand, technology brings convenient; on the other hand, it also causes some problems. （convenient 改成 convenience）

5. The government plays a crucial role in promote economic development.（promote 改成 promoting）

6. Scientists make great contributions in the progress of society.（in 改成 to）

7. Succeed is often associated with hard work and determination.（succeed 改成 success）

8. The government should give prior to the development of education.（prior 改成 priority）

9. The government should make effective measures to reduce crime.（make 改成 take）

10. The lacking of exercise contributes to the increase in obesity rates.（lacking 改成 lack，或者

The lacking of 改成 Lacking）

2.1.3

句子结构练习题

1. 简单句1：气候变化是一个严峻的问题。

    翻译：Climate change is a serious issue.

    简单句2：气候变化问题急需全球关注和一致努力。

    翻译：Climate change demands urgent attention and concerted efforts of the whole world.

    合并：Climate change is a serious issue that demands urgent attention and concerted global efforts.

2. 简单句1：教育对个人成长至关重要。

    翻译：Education is crucial for personal growth.

    简单句2：教育帮助人们开发潜能和实现梦想。

    翻译：Education can help individuals develop their potential and achieve their dreams.

    合并：Education is crucial for personal growth as it can help individuals develop their potential and achieve their dreams.

3. 简单句1：环保是每个人的责任。

    翻译：Environmental protection is everyone's responsibility.

    简单句2：我们应该减少废物排放和能源消耗。

    翻译：We should reduce waste emissions and energy consumption.

    合并：We should reduce waste emissions and energy consumption because environmental protection is everyone's responsibility.

4. 简单句1：全球化促进了国际贸易。

    翻译：Globalization has facilitated international trade.

    简单句2：全球化使各国能够共享资源和知识。

    翻译：Globalization enables countries to share resources and knowledge.

    合并：Globalization has facilitated international trade, which enables countries to share resources and knowledge.

5. 简单句1：全球变暖问题不容忽视。

    翻译：The issue of global warming should not be overlooked.

    简单句2：全球变暖对生态系统产生了严重的影响。

    翻译：Global warming has severely influenced ecosystems.

    合并：Global warming, an issue that should not be overlooked, has severely influenced ecosystems.

6. 简单句1：学生需要掌握多门语言。

    翻译：Students need to master multiple languages.

    简单句2：掌握多门语言可以帮助他们在国际舞台上取得成功。

    翻译：Mastering multiple languages can help them succeed on the international stage.

合并：Students need to master multiple languages, which can help them succeed on the international stage.

7. 简单句 1：健康越来越受到人们的关注。

   翻译：Health have received increasing attention from the public.

   简单句 2：饮食和运动习惯对人们的健康有很大影响。

   翻译：Diet and exercise habits have a significant impact on people's health.

   合并：Diet and exercise habits have a significant impact on people's health which have received increasing attention from the public.

2.1.4

逻辑连贯性练习题

1. 句子 1：Education is essential for personal development.

   句子 2：It provides individuals with the knowledge and skills they need to succeed.

   重组后：Education is essential for personal development, as it provides individuals with the knowledge and skills they need to succeed.

2. 句子 1：The Internet has revolutionized the way we access information.

   句子 2：It has also led to the spread of misinformation.

   重组后：The Internet has revolutionized the way we access information. However, it has also led to the spread of misinformation.

3. 句子 1：Many cities are facing serious traffic congestion.

   句子 2：Public transport should be improved.

   重组后：Many cities are facing serious traffic congestion, so public transport should be improved.

4. 句子 1：The demand for renewable energy is increasing.

   句子 2：Fossil fuels are becoming scarce and polluting.

   句子 3：Solar energy and wind energy are viable alternatives.

   重组后：The demand for renewable energy is increasing, owing to the fact that fossil fuels are becoming scarce and polluting. As a result, solar energy and wind energy are viable alternatives.

5. 句子 1：Poverty is a major challenge in many developing countries.

   句子 2：Education can be a powerful tool in the fight against poverty.

   句子 3：Education helps individuals gain skills and knowledge that lead to better job opportunities.

   重组后：Education can be a powerful tool in the fight against poverty which is a major challenge in many developing countries. Specifically, education helps individuals gain skills and knowledge that lead to better job opportunities.

2.2.4

Task 1 写作技巧练习

1. 基本情况：表格展示了2020年东京奥运会金牌榜前六名国家的奖牌情况，包括各国的金牌、银牌、铜牌和总奖牌数。

关键信息和数据点：①总体排名。②金牌分布：美国金牌最多，为39枚，中国38枚次之等。③奖牌类型差异：美国银牌数41枚，排名第一，俄罗斯奥委会银牌数28枚，也较多；铜牌数方面，美国33枚最多，英国和澳大利亚均为22枚，日本最少；英国三种奖牌数基本相等。

写作框架：

①开头段：简要介绍表格内容。

②概述段：总结主要趋势，如美国和中国在金牌数和总奖牌数上的领先地位，以及日本作为东道主的表现。

③描述段1：详细描述美国和中国的奖牌分布，并进行对比。

④描述段2：描述其他国家的奖牌分布，并注重关键信息和数据的提取和比较。

2. 写出开头段（一句话改写题目）

The table illustrates the number of medals won by the top six countries in the 2020 Tokyo Olympic Games, presenting information on gold, silver, and bronze medals as well as the total number of medals for each nation.

3. 写出概述段

It is notable that there were differences in the distribution of medal types among these 6 countries. Overall, the United States dominated the medal table with the highest total number of medals, followed closely by China. The remaining four countries, namely Japan, Great Britain, the Russian Olympic Committee, and Australia, had fewer medals.

4. 写出描述段

描述段1：

The United States and China were the top performers in the 2020 Tokyo Olympics. The US amassed a total of 113 medals, comprising 39 gold, 41 silver, and 33 bronze medals. It ranked first among countries in terms of the numbers of three types of medals. While, China followed closely with 88 medals, including 38 gold, 32 silver, and 18 bronze medals. Notably, while the US had a higher number of silver and bronze medals, China was only one gold medal behind the US.

描述段2：

Japan, hosting the Games, secured 58 medals in total, with 27 gold medals, ranked the third. Great Britain and the Russian Olympic Committee also had strong showings, with 65 and 71 medals respectively. Great Britain had a relatively balanced distribution of medals, between 21 and 22. The Russian Olympic Committee, on the other hand, had a larger number of silver and bronze medals, with 28 and 23 respectively. For Australia, the number of bronze is the same as that of Great Britain, and its silver medal count was the lowest among the group, only 7, making its medal distribution different from that of the other countries.

2.3.5

练习1

（1）题目一

主题词：education（教育）、job market（就业市场）、personal development（个人发展）

关键词：main purpose（主要目的）、prepare individuals（培养个人）

题目类型：双边讨论并给出个人观点类（Discuss both views and give your opinion）

涉及的观点和角度：

观点一：教育的主要目的是为个人进入就业市场做准备。角度包括教育如何传授职业技能、满足市场需求、提高就业竞争力等。

观点二：教育应该专注于个人发展。角度包括培养个人的兴趣爱好、道德品质、综合素质、自我认知等方面。

写作方向和重点：写作方向是分别阐述两种观点的合理性，即教育为就业市场做准备的好处以及专注个人发展的益处。重点在于对两种观点进行深入分析，比较它们的差异和互补性，最后清晰地给出自己的观点，并对观点进行合理的论证，说明为什么支持其中一方或认为两者需要平衡。

（2）题目二

主题词：government（政府）、affordable housing（经济适用房）、transportation system（交通系统）

关键词：spend more money（投入更多资金）、providing（提供）、improving（改善）

题目类型：同意与否类

涉及的观点和角度：

• 支持政府花更多钱提供经济适用房的观点及角度：

①社会公平角度：为低收入群体提供基本居住保障，减少贫富差距带来的居住不平等问题，促进社会稳定和谐。

②民生需求角度：住房是人们的基本生活需求，解决住房问题能提高民众的生活质量和幸福感。

• 支持政府花更多钱改善交通系统的观点及角度：

①经济发展角度：良好的交通系统有利于人员和物资的流动，能促进商业活动和区域经济发展。

环保角度：高效的公共交通系统可以减少私家车使用，降低尾气排放，有利于环境保护。

②生活便利性角度：改善交通能缩短人们的通勤时间，提高出行效率，方便人们的日常生活。

写作方向和重点：

①写作方向：明确表明自己是同意还是不同意题目中的观点。如果同意，则阐述为什么政府应该把更多资金投入经济适用房建设；如果不同意，则要说明为什么政府应在交通系统改善上投入更多资金。或者，也可以采取折中的观点，即认为政府应该在两者之间合理分配资金，并说明理由。

②重点：重点在于对自己观点的论证，要详细阐述支持自己观点的理由和依据，可以结合实际例子或数据来增强说服力。

练习3

（1）参考答案：Social media has exerted a positive influence on individual lives. Firstly, it serves as a platform for individuals to express themselves and share their thoughts. Many bloggers, for instance, by sharing their life reflections and professional expertise on social media, have not only garnered the support of fans but also found like-minded friends, enriching their mental lives. Secondly, social media has fortified interpersonal bonds. During the pandemic, numerous families maintained their connections through video call applications, feeling each other's presence and support despite residing in diverse cities or even countries, underscoring its significance in preserving familial and social ties.

（2）参考答案：Telecommuting has undoubtedly enhanced work efficiency in several aspects. Employees can schedule their working hours according to their habits and peak performance, eliminating the time wasted on commuting and thus dedicating more time to the tasks at hand. However, some argue that telecommuting hinders team collaboration. Face-to-face communication, crucial in team projects, is often surpassed by the limitations of remote exchanges, leading to inaccurate information transfer or misunderstandings. Although telecommuting introduces flexibility and efficiency, the weakening of team collaboration cannot be overlooked. Consequently, I believe that while embracing the conveniences telecommuting offers, measures should be taken to strengthen communication and collaboration among team members.

练习4

1.（1）Social media is an integral part of modern life and has a profound impact on people's daily activities and business operations.

（2）Climate change, caused by human activities, is having a wide range of negative impacts on the environment.

（3）Education plays a crucial and multi-faceted role in an individual's personal and professional development.

练习5

（1）The construction of bike lanes in cities is a win-win strategy that not only contributes to environmental protection, road safety, and public health but also paves the way for a more sustainable and healthy urban lifestyle.

（2）To conclude, language learning is a valuable and enriching pursuit that can broaden our horizons, enhance our personal and professional development, and foster cross-cultural understanding.

Test 1

WRITING TASK 1

The line graph illustrates the number of employees in different job categories within the U.S. solar industry between 2010 and 2020.

It is notable that the U.S. solar industry witnessed a significant expansion in the Installation & Developers sector, while other job categories remained relatively static or had modest growth. This indicates a clear shift in the employment structure within the industry over the ten-year period.

Starting at around 45,000 in 2010, the number of employees in the Installation and Developers sector skyrocketed to approximately 175,000 by 2015, before it kept fluctuating around 150,000-175,000 until 2020. Before 2017, there were no individuals engaged in Operations & Maintenance in the U.S. solar industry. It was only from 2017 that full-time staff emerged, numbering just 5,000, and this figure gradually increased to around 15,000 by 2020.

In contrast, the number of employees in Manufacturing remained relatively stable throughout the period, staying between 20,000 and 30,000. Sales & Distribution also shared a similar steady pattern, with the employee count fluctuating around 20,000. In addition to this, other jobs had fewer than 10,000 employees throughout the entire decade.

WRITING TASK 2

In recent years, the growing accessibility of private healthcare has sparked a significant debate. Some individuals advocate that it brings numerous advantages, while others express concerns about the associated high costs. This essay will delve into both perspectives before presenting my own stance.

Those in favor of the increasing accessibility of private healthcare highlight several benefits. First and foremost, it offers patients more choices. In private healthcare facilities, patients can select from a wider range of medical services, specialists, and treatment options. For example, they may choose to receive cutting-edge treatments that are not readily available in public hospitals due to budget constraints. Moreover, private healthcare often provides a higher level of comfort and personalized care. Patients can enjoy private rooms, shorter waiting times for appointments and surgeries, and more individualized attention from medical staff. This can greatly enhance the patient experience and potentially lead to better recovery outcomes.

On the other hand, the claim that private healthcare raises costs is well-founded. Since private providers aim for profit, they must cover expenses and earn, leading to much higher medical service costs than in public facilities. For example, a private specialist consultation can cost several times more than a public doctor visit. Additionally, the increasing accessibility of private healthcare may divert resources, including skilled professionals, away from public systems. Private providers offer better pay, conditions, and equipment, enticing experienced and skilled medical staff from public hospitals. This leaves the public system under-staffed, with fewer experts for complex cases. As a result, public healthcare patients face longer waits and inferior treatment, widening the service-quality gap between the rich and the poor.

In conclusion, while the increasing accessibility of private healthcare can enhance choice and quality of care, it also risks driving up costs and exacerbating the problem of medical resource allocation. From my perspective, we should not simply embrace or reject the increasing accessibility of private healthcare. Instead, a balanced approach is needed to make the most of its advantages while mitigating its negative impacts. To address the concerns, governments should play a more active role, such as regulating the pricing of private healthcare services to prevent excessive charges.

Test 2

WRITING TASK 1

The bar chart illustrates the historical changes in population numbers (in millions) across four major world regions—Africa, America, Asia, and Europe—in the years 1990, 2000, and 2021.

It is notable that Asia has been the most populous region throughout the period. Overall, there have been significant growth trends in Africa and America, while Europe has shown relatively mild population changes.

In 1990, Asia's population stood at 3,202 million, a figure far surpassing the others. By 2000, it had grown to 3,714 million, and by 2021, it soared to 4,695 million, firmly maintaining its leading position in global demographics. Europe, on the other hand, had a population of 721 million in 1990, which increased marginally to 726 million in 2000 and then to 745 million in 2021, showing a rather stable and slow-growth pattern.

Africa and America, conversely, witnessed more vigorous growth. Starting with a population of 632 million in 1990, Africa experienced a dramatic upsurge, reaching an impressive 1,393 million in 2021, more than doubling its initial size. America, too, showed a significant increase, growing from 727 million in 1990 to 1,031 million in 2021, a rise of approximately 304 million.

WRITING TASK 2

In the contemporary digital era, the accessibility of a vast amount of information has become a defining characteristic. While some individuals may argue that this situation brings about numerous disadvantages, I firmly believe that the advantages it offers to both individuals and society far outweigh the drawbacks.

On the positive side, the digital age has significantly broadened access to information, empowering individuals and societies in numerous ways. For individuals, they can now access online courses, academic journals, and educational resources from anywhere in the world, which enables them to expand their knowledge beyond the limitations of traditional classrooms. Take platforms like Coursera as an example. It allows learners to acquire new skills and knowledge from top universities at their own pace. Socially, the abundance of information contributes to the progress of research and innovation. Scientists and researchers can easily share their findings, collaborate with colleagues globally, and stay updated on the latest developments in their fields. This accelerates the pace of scientific discovery and technological advancement. For instance, in the fight against diseases like COVID-19, researchers were able to quickly share data and research results, which significantly contributed to the development of vaccines and treatment methods.

However, it is undeniable that the vast amount of digital information also presents some challenges. Firstly, the spread of misinformation. With anyone being able to publish content online, false or misleading information can easily go viral, causing confusion and panic. Another problem is the potential for information overload. People may find it difficult to filter through the vast amount of data, which can be time-consuming and overwhelming. Yet, these challenges are solvable. With media literacy education and advanced filtering tools, we can better identify misinformation and manage the data flood.

In conclusion, although the easy access to digital information has some demerits such as the spread of misinformation and information overload, I do hold that its benefits in terms of promoting learning, personal growth, research, and innovation are more substantial. By addressing the drawbacks through education and technology, individuals and societies are expected to be able to harness the full potential of the digital age for a brighter future.

Test 3

WRITING TASK 1

The two pie charts present the percentage changes in the population sizes of European Union countries from 2013 to 2021, and the table illustrates their absolute population figures.

Notably, Germany consistently held the position as the most populous country among EU countries throughout the period. Overall, while the population percentage shares of most countries underwent minor fluctuations, there were diverging trends in the absolute population numbers, with some countries experiencing growth and others declining.

Germany saw its population share rising from 18.2% to 18.6%, corresponding to an increase from 18.25 million to 18.62 million residents. France and Spain similarly experienced upward momentum. France's population share climbed from 14.9% to 15.2% (14.88 million to 15.16 million), and Spain's share rose by 0.1%. In contrast, Italy's population share decreased marginally from 13.6% to 13.2%, yet its actual figures fell sharply by 40,200.

Turning to other nations, Poland and Romania exhibited diverging trends. Poland's population decreased by 161,000 (8.6 million to 8.45 million), yet its share dropped only slightly from 8.6% to 8.4%. Romania faced a steeper decline, losing 243,000 residents (4.52 million to 4.28 million). Conversely, the Netherlands bucked the trend with both a rising population (3.80 million to 3.92 million) and an increased share (3.8% to 3.9%).

WRITING TASK 2

In modern society, an increasing number of individuals are opting to live alone. This trend can be attributed to various factors, and it has significant implications for individuals and society. This essay tends to explore the reasons behind it and discuss its effects.

There are multiple factors contributing to the rise in the number of people living alone. Firstly, economic independence plays a crucial role. Now, more and more people have stable jobs and sufficient income to afford their own living spaces. They no longer need to rely on others for financial support and can enjoy the freedom of living independently. Secondly, changing social attitudes also encourages this trend. Traditional values that emphasized living in large families are gradually being replaced by a focus on personal space and self-fulfillment. People now prioritize their own well-being and are more willing to live alone to pursue their interests and goals without interference.

The effects of this trend are multifaceted. On an individual level, living alone can foster personal growth and self-reliance. It provides opportunities for people to develop life skills, manage their time effectively, and explore their interests without external influences. However, it can also lead to feelings of loneliness and social isolation; even worse, it may give rise to mental health problems such as depression and anxiety. On a societal level, the rise in solo living has economic and environmental implications. Economically, it drives demand for housing, benefiting industries such as real estate, construction, and home furnishings. However, it also places pressure on urban infrastructure, as cities must accommodate a growing number of smaller households. Environmentally, solo living tends to increase resource consumption and waste generation. Smaller households often use more energy and produce higher carbon emissions per person compared to shared living arrangements, contributing to environmental challenges.

In conclusion, the rise in solo living, driven by economic independence and changing social values, offers personal freedom but also brings challenges like loneliness and environmental strain. To address these issues, governments should promote mental health support and sustainable urban planning. Balancing the benefits and drawbacks of this trend is crucial for a harmonious and sustainable future.

口语答案

1.3.1

练习二

1. Public transport is inexpensive and green.

2. Which is your least favorite subject in primary school?

3. It's irresponsible that some pet owners desert their pets.

4. Tea has always been one of the most important exports in China.

5. Have you ever received any jewellery as present?

6. The survey showed that 30% people do not have breakfast.

7. Organic produce is usually more expensive than ordinary one.

8. Local people are protesting against the construction of a nuclear power plant in this region.

1.3.2

练习二

I'd like to talk about a holiday/which I took in 2005./It's a holiday that I remember very well/because we had such a fantastic time./I went with three other girls,/who are all friends of mine,/and we still talk about this holiday today.

It was funny,/because usually I'm a person/who's quite scared of things,/and I didn't think/I would put a mask on my face/or go under the water/—but I wanted to see the coral/so much.

2.1.1

1. I go to the gym occasionally.

2. I usually go jogging in the park.

3. I prefer outdoor sports for the fresh air.

4. I practise English speaking every day.

5. I want to learn some French as I'm planning a trip to France some time in the future.

6. I never wear any jewelry.

7. I've bought many T-shirts with adorable patterns.

8. I have learned to play piano for ten years.

9. I felt very lonely in my childhood.

10. My mum didn't allow me to eat chocolate when I was little.

2.1.2

1. Strawberry is my favorite flavor in ice cream.

2. People in my hometown are friendly and hospitable.

3. Social media seems to be more and more popular with the elderly.

4. T-shirt is so adaptable that I wear different T-shirts all the time in summer.

5. I feel extremely frustrated after every math test.

6. Anything my mum cooked tastes delicious.

2.1.3

1. There is a book on the table.

2. There are four people in my family.

3. There were many people at the concert.

4. There will be new opportunities in the future.

2.1.4

1. I remember it was a sunny day.

2. It was really late when we arrived at the hotel.

3. It was two kilometers to the nearest petrol station.

4. It was the cat who broke the vase.

5. I find it easy to talk to her.

6. It took me one month to learn how to swim.

2.1.5

1. assigned / project manager / IT 或 appointed / sales representative / marketing

enrolled / Tsinghua / Beijing / computer science 或 admitted / Fudan / Shanghai / business administration

2. safety and cleanliness / added 或 vibrant atmosphere / introduced

renovated / improve energy efficiency 或 refurbished / modernize the facilities

3. painting / involved 或 gardening / participating

coached 或 trained

4. sent / New York / negotiating contracts 或 assigned / Tokyo / attending conferences

Thailand / booked / family 或 Australia / arranged / friends

3.2

Sample answers

Part 1

Examiner:	Do you work or are you a student?
Candidate:	I've just finished secondary school. I got the best results in my year so I'm hoping to get a scholarship to study English Literature.
Examiner:	Why did you choose that course?
Candidate:	Because I love literature. I love getting lost in a book; I mean, it's a form of escapism for me. But I also enjoy learning about the historical and cultural contexts that influenced a work and I'll have ample opportunity to learn about these things at university.
Examiner:	What was the most difficult thing about your studies?
Candidate:	At secondary school, the most difficult subject for me was Chemistry. I can't stand Science, and I would dread every lesson! I struggled in Chemistry lessons, and I had to work really hard to pass my exam. For some reason, I just couldn't remember all those chemical symbols and equations no matter how long I spent revising.
Examiner:	Let's talk about keeping fit. What do you do to keep fit?
Candidate:	I go to the gym twice a week. I don't really enjoy it, to be honest, but it's an easy way to keep fit. I mainly do cardiovascular exercises, rather than muscle building.
Examiner:	Are you good at sport?
Candidate:	Not really, but I try my best. I prefer individual sports to team sports because if I do badly in a team game I always feel I'm letting everyone down.
Examiner:	What's your mother tongue?
Candidate:	My mother tongue is Portuguese. It's predominantly spoken in Brazil but also in other parts of the world, such as Portugal and Africa.
Examiner:	What other languages do you speak?
Candidate:	Although I grew up in Brazil, I can also speak Italian because my mother and one set of grandparents are Italian and I grew up hearing the language all around me. I'm really proud to be bilingual and I'd like my children to be bilingual too.
Examiner:	What do you think is the best way to keep in touch with friends?
Candidate:	It depends on how far you are from your friends. If you are geographically close, you should meet up face-to-face. Long-distance communication can cause misunderstandings and resentments to build up. When you write, you only have the words on the page, not

	body language or tone of voice.
Examiner:	Do people keep in touch differently now compared to fifty years ago?
Candidate:	Well, of course, people use the Internet now and mobile phones. I'm quite young but even when I was a teenager nobody in my friendship circle had a mobile. Now it's seen as indispensable and you would feel left out if you didn't have one. But as I said before, I think it's better to meet up with friends than to communicate using technology. There's much to be said for communicating in so-called old-fashioned ways.

Part 2

Candidate:	One of my favourite hobbies is going shopping. I've always loved it. I think I get it from my mum, who used to take me to the nearest town every weekend to visit shops and boutiques. She taught me about buying a few quality items that you may pay a premium for but that last a long time so are a good investment. She also taught me about how to check for the quality of a garment by looking at the way it's sewn together and also creasing the fabric to see if it stays creased or not. If it stays creased then it's a poor quality fabric. Another thing I learnt from her is how to find a bargain. You need to shop around and not be afraid of trying the smaller boutiques where you're more likely to find a shop owner who's happy to offer a discount. I've been shopping on my own since I was a student. Then, I could not afford to buy many things but stuck to what my mum taught me and kept my eyes open for a quality bargain. The rest of the time, I would window shop. Nowadays I can afford designer clothes but I still love the sales, when I hunt for a bargain and the odd top-designer item. One thing I hate, however, is trying things on because there are always long queues and it means you have less time for shopping. It's not a problem, not trying things on, because if something is not the right size I can take it back to the shop as long as I've kept the receipt. I go shopping every week. I find it therapeutic. It always makes me feel good to get hands on a nice quality piece at a bargain price, and if I'm feeling a bit down there's nothing like a bit of retail therapy. I find shopping exciting as well. You spend time in the poshest part of town where you can mix with fashionable people. There's a buzz and it's busy and noisy and colourful. Shopping lets you keep up to the latest trends. So all in all, I think it has a lot of benefits and I love it.
Examiner:	What's the best bargain you've ever got?
Candidate:	I once bought a designer coat, 100% cashmere, absolutely beautiful, for 25% of the full price. It was in a closing-down sale.

Part 3

Hobbies

Examiner:	Do you think men and women tend to have different types of hobbies?

Candidate:	Yes, I do. The men I know have sports as hobbies. The women usually enjoy more sedentary and peaceful hobbies, like reading or crafts. Having said that, there are of course women who love exhilarating hobbies or are fanatical about cycling or something. And there are men who take up pottery or sewing. There are always exceptions to every rule.
Examiner:	Why do some people get obsessed with their hobby?
Candidate:	I think everybody finds at least one thing absolutely fascinating. It can be anything—subjects like history of art, or a sport like basketball, or a craft like card-making. Everyone is different and one person's interest can appear strange to other people. However, not everyone has time to indulge themselves with their hobby. Mothers of young children, for example, get little free time and so they appear less 'obsessed' than a single man who spends every weekend, all weekend playing computer games.
Examiner:	Do you think hobbies that keep you fit are better than hobbies that you can do sitting down?
Candidate:	No, I think hobbies that open you up to new things are the best, ones that enrich you and give you a new skill. That can be anything, but it is important always to grow as a person and not become boring by never trying anything new.

Free time

Examiner:	Do you think it can be a disadvantage to have too much free time?
Candidate:	Well, they say that the devil makes work for idle hands and I think it's true that the less you have to do the less active you become and the more time you waste. People who have too much time to spare tend to become lazy and lethargic. People who are always on the go, on the other hand, think nothing of fitting one more thing into their busy schedules.
Examiner:	Should people feel a duty to do something constructive in their free time?
Candidate:	No, not necessarily. Everyone deserves some downtime. Modern life is stressful and hectic and so we need times when we let go of our responsibilities and just do something fun. We can still draw benefits from hobbies that are not generally considered constructive. For example, we can develop our abilities to work in teams by doing team sports, and we can increase our attention spans by reading a novel with long chapters.
Examiner:	Do people have more free time now than in the past?
Candidate:	It's a strange irony that although we now have so many labour-saving devices such as washing machines and dishwashers, we feel we have less free time. Many of my acquaintances are always complaining that they are too busy. But actually I think our ancestors had less free time than us. The average worker hardly ever got any time off and worked six or seven days a week.